FROM THE OUTHOUSE
TO THE PENTHOUSE

INDIGORIVER
PUBLISHING

FROM THE OUTHOUSE TO THE PENTHOUSE

The Football Journey of Hall of Famer Larry Little

JOE ZAGORSKI

From the Outhouse to the Penthouse: The Football Journey of Hall of Famer Larry Little

© 2025 by Joe Zagorski

Library of Congress Control Number: 2025909362
ISBN: 978-1-964686-61-5 (paperback) 978-1-964686-62-2 (ebook)
978-1-964686-64-6 (hardcover)

This is a work of nonfiction. While every effort has been made to ensure accuracy, some names, dates, and details may have been altered or reconstructed based on research, interviews, and interview subjects' recollections. Any errors or omissions are unintentional.

Editors: Austin Hatch, John Irvin
Cover Design: Bobby Mallozzi
Cover Image: Tom DiPace
Interior Design: Emma Elzinga

Printed in the United States of America

First Edition

3 West Garden Street, Ste. 718
Pensacola, FL 32502
www.indigoriverpublishing.com

Ordering Information:

Quantity sales: Special discounts are available on quantity purchases by corporations, associations, and others. For details, contact the publisher at the address above.

Orders by US trade bookstores and wholesalers: Please contact the publisher at the address above.

With Indigo River Publishing, you can always expect great books, strong voices, and meaningful messages. Most importantly, you'll always find . . . *words worth reading.*

This book is dedicated to everyone who does not give up.

CONTENTS

ACKNOWLEDGMENTS

Writing a former National Football League player's biography can be one of the most rewarding experiences that any sportswriter could ever ask for. Such was the case for me when I was offered the opportunity to write Larry Little's biography. Anyone who is familiar with the history of the NFL, or the Miami Dolphins, or the Pro Football Hall of Fame, can easily recall the accomplishments of a warrior like Larry Little. This attempt of mine to shine a new spotlight onto his fame has as its hope a simple one. I would love to see the game's younger fans take notice of some of the greatest players of the 1970s, and Larry Little certainly fits that description. It was an era where the sport of football really started to become the nation's new national pastime. Thanks to men like Little and his contemporaries, millions of fans began to take notice of pro football, then in a short amount of time, those fans would not be able to get enough of the sport. They were effectively bitten and smitten by the NFL bug, and it would stay in their system for the rest of their lives.

I am one such fan. I started watching the pro game back in the 1970s, and I never stopped watching it, studying it, writing about it, and enjoying it. Football was always there for me, and it was always an important part of my life. The same is true for Larry Little. He knew as a youngster that playing football was something that he wanted to strive for more than virtually anything else. When I started interviewing him, I came to a quick realization that his love for the sport was equal to mine. So, the starting point for my thanks in helping me out with this book simply must go to Larry Little, a gentleman who was always willing to discuss all the memories of his life. It was indeed my honor and privilege to interview him and to discover all the great and unique events and stories of his extraordinary life.

One of the main reasons why this book has been written is due to the efforts of Dave Burch, who I met on Facebook, and who was the first person to discuss with me the opportunity to write a book about his good friend, Larry Little. Dave hit all the right notes, because he knew that I loved to write about different aspects and players of the NFL during the 1970s. Furthermore, Dave had great timing, because he suggested this idea at a time when I was in between projects, which is always the perfect time. So, a big thank you goes out to my friend, Dave Burch!

Another person worthy of my thanks is Jon Kendle, who serves as the official research historian at the Ralph C. Wilson Research Library at the Pro Football Hall of Fame in Canton, Ohio. Jon has helped me out with all my previous books and my numerous articles. His knowledge of pro football microfilmed data is virtually unmatched by most living members of the NFL's media circles today.

Still another friend of mine who once again deserves my thanks is Chris Willis of NFL Films. Like Jon Kendle, Chris Willis has been a regular contributor to all my previous books and articles. Chris has provided me with numerous interview transcripts over the years, and important raw films as well.

Yet another friend of mine who needs to be listed on these pages is T.J. Troup, whom I (and many other people) fondly call "Coach." Nobody that I know of has explored and researched more pro football films over the years than Coach Troup, who prior to his retirement was an actual high school and college football coach. If the subject is football strategy or football history, chances are very good that Coach Troup knows more about it than virtually anyone else.

Bobby Kinsey of Biloxi, Mississippi, helped me out by sending me timely information on a particular chapter in Larry Little's life that I needed background information.

I would also like to extend my thanks to Bobby Mallozzi for designing the book's front and back cover, and to Tom DiPace for contributing his photographs on the front and back cover.

Most important of all, I would like to thank Larry and Rosie Little for devoting their precious time and efforts to this project. Mr. Little's input on the narrative, and his answers to my hundreds of questions, were indeed inspiring to me. His story will hopefully inspire you, the readers of this book, as well.

FOREWORD

No quarterback in the sport of football can succeed without a strong and sturdy offensive line protecting him. That was true many years ago, and it will always be true as long as the game is played. I was fortunate to call the signals for the Miami Dolphins behind one of the greatest offensive lines in the history of pro football from 1967 to 1980. One of the men who was an outstanding blocker for our team on that offensive line is the subject of this book in your hands, written by the exemplary NFL writer, Joe Zagorski.

Larry Little came to Miami back in 1969 with little fanfare, if any. No one at that time really knew what to expect from him. We all knew that he was a big guy. We all figured that for his size, which was six-foot-one and 270 pounds in 1969, the chances were good that he was also a very strong guy. Summer training camp annually weeds out those that are lacking in strength, and there are plenty of drills and exercises available for the coaches to measure the physical strength of every player. Larry would show us all an abundance of his tangible strength. But one thing that nobody can measure or determine when you look at a player—when you look at any player—is the size of his heart. Well, let me tell you. . . I can readily attest that Larry Little has a great big heart, and it was his heart for the game that we all acknowledged in a very short amount of time. Larry Little was as dedicated to his sport and to his position of offensive guard as anyone that those involved with pro football has ever seen.

Larry had a strong desire to be a member of a winning team. He knew that he had to have the mindset of a winning player, which he did, because we were on the road toward improvement in Miami at that time. Thanks largely to his efforts, we all followed his examples of dedication and diligence in working hard in every practice and in every game. The obvious result was that he and all of our players went on to become members of a winning team. . . of a championship team. Larry Little did everything that Coach Shula and the rest of the coaches asked of him, and then even more, to help to make the Dolphins a consistently better team, year after year.

Winning became a habit for us in the early 1970s, and we all enjoyed winning very much. Yet there was always a chance that we could as individuals fail at one time or another, at one aspect of the game or another. But failure was difficult to see when you looked at Larry Little. He was simply not going to allow the slightest bit of failure to seep into the way that he played the game. He knew that if he played as hard as he could on every play, whether it was in a game or in practice, he was indeed giving his all to his teammates, all for an effort to make us all successful. With a guy like Larry Little on our roster, it would be virtually impossible for us not to improve and become winners, mostly because he himself was a winner.

Over fifty years have passed since our perfect, undefeated season of 1972. Everyone seems to remember that season after all of these years. That season is a big part of NFL history. But that season would not have been accomplished without a guy like Larry Little on our team. Perhaps no other group of men in the history of pro football has ever had a roster of players who sacrificed as much for each other than our Dolphins team did in 1972. And Larry was a big part of that team, thanks to the sacrifices that he made. He was also a big part of us winning two Super Bowls in a row in 1972 and 1973. He was a team leader, and he let his actions do his talking. We all could see it, and we all were inspired by it, and by him.

There is a proper place for a player like Larry Little, and that place is the Pro Football Hall of Fame in Canton, Ohio. I am one of several of our former teammates who is honored to share the tribute of enshrinement with him there. I hope that you enjoy reading about the legacy of greatness and success that Larry Little gave to the game and to his team within the pages of this outstanding and long overdue book.

Bob Griese

March 9, 2022

PREFACE

Former offensive guard Larry Little had boundless desire on
the gridiron that helped him reach the top of his profession.
Only a few men ever achieve membership in the Pro Football
Hall of Fame in Canton, Ohio. Larry Little, the former undrafted
rookie who signed on as a free agent with the San Diego Chargers,
and who eventually became a Miami Dolphins All-Pro and team
leader, acclaimed the pinnacle of the NFL. He is a Hall of Famer.

Little's journey to that mountaintop began with the struggle to
survive. From the earliest days of his youth, Larry Little witnessed
a line of people—coaches and even some fellow players—who
tried to get the younger players on the football team to give up
and walk away from the sport. Little's resolute determination
to stay the course, however, separated him from many of his
peers. He was a born survivor. Regardless of what challenges or
problems presented themselves in his life, Little dealt with them
by making his own decisions.

Little, now in his late seventies, recalled first trying out for
football in ninth grade as a thirteen-year-old. The other players
didn't make it easy for him. "I was called all kind of names, but
I did not quit."[1]

Everyone else who tried out for the Booker T. Washington
Senior High School football team decided to quit, rather than

enduring the physical duress and mental abuse that every freshman was subjected to. But there was something at work inside the chubby kid who was slated to play along the line of scrimmage as an offensive and defensive lineman. He had that inner desire to see what would happen if he stayed on the team.

At its most refined level, the decision not to quit is a basic choice made by everyone who has a job, starts a business, or applies to college. It's a fundamental, down to earth choice. Tenacity yields positive results. It stems from a sense of purpose. It gives one an income and the ability to put food on the table and a roof overhead.

From the Outhouse to the Penthouse explores how a common man like Larry Little can become an uncommon success story. Because Larry Little is an inspiring man, his story will inspire you. He had a desire to make a name for himself, and football provided him with a vehicle to do so. In football, Little discovered his best opportunity to accomplish great things. The 100-yard landscape he called home would test his body and his mind in ways that no other activity could. The game gave him a sense of belonging and an identity, going all the way back to his childhood. Like all youngsters, Little yearned to participate in one kind of activity or another. Football served as his favorite activity. It gave him a dual purpose, as it broke up the boredom monotony of his daily regimen of life. But perhaps most importantly, it gave him something to look forward to each day. It added to his happiness.

Some people contend that a common man like Little can seldom—if ever—make his mark in any walk of life. But Little defied them. He took whatever disappointments or failures that came along, such as being forced to sit on the bench for several years, as he waited for any kind of opportunity to get on the field to play in a game. Little used those disappointments as his springboard to visualize and focus in on what he would do whenever his chance to play would finally come about. His tenacity was a moral compass of sorts, and it has served him well throughout his life.

It seemed that every time that I interviewed Larry, he offered new insights about football. He was a treasure-trove of knowledge. Personal stories from his years at Bethune-Cookman University, in San Diego with the Chargers, and in Miami with the Dolphins, make this book unique. Many of his quotes that are throughout this biography, which shares the experiences and memories of his life and career, were shared in interviews that were held from 2022 to 2024, to faithfully and honorably depict his perspective and thoughts on his life that are being adapted to this biography.

Offensive linemen rarely get any media attention. They generally operate in the trenches, behind the scenes, and they don't stack up glamorous statistics. Fans of the sport are usually following the ball carriers, not the blockers. The nuances of line play are complex, with its own set of signals and intricate movements along the line of scrimmage. As a result, line play is often less understood and less appreciated by many football fans. Larry Little's comments throughout this book will attempt to correct that oversight.

A common stereotype suggests football players are nothing but a bunch of "dumb jocks." Nothing could be further from the truth. Having athletic ability alone is not enough to keep a player from being cut from a team. Take members of the typical offensive line, for example. Every offensive lineman must possess a wealth of brain power to coincide with his strong athletic abilities to be successful.

An offensive guard like Larry Little has to be quick thinking. Within a split second, just before the ball is snapped by the team's center, the offensive guard has to call out and receive blocking assignments amid the various changing defensive alignments.

At the same time, they must listen to the quarterback in case the play changes at the line of scrimmage. Finally, the offensive guard must be ready to break out of his three-point stance on the correct signal, barked out by his quarterback, in order to avoid getting a penalty for illegal motion or offsides.

Indeed, the duties and assignments for an offensive lineman are numerous and challenging. Only a few truly bright individuals serve their teams well in those positions.

An offensive lineman's intelligence must coexist with the brutal strength required by everyone who plays along the line of scrimmage. A man's muscular strength is the most common denominator of all linemen. He must have the force and the power to be able to move an equally strong opponent out of the way of his intended path. Intense practice leads to the hitting and blocking that appears on the gameday field. Regular weightlifting sessions are a critical part of the practice regimen for everyone who plays on the line, whether offense or defense.

There was no doubt that Larry Little had that strength in his repertoire of talents, and as his pro career continued, his foes understood they would have their work cut out for them whenever they lined up against Little.

But possibly the most important element of an offensive lineman's duties and/or talents involves the poise that he must have to regulate what is going on at the line of scrimmage. A savvy offensive lineman who can maintain his blocks, open holes for the running backs, keep defensive linemen and linebackers off his quarterback, and yet still be able to make split-second decisions that will enhance his offense's chances for success is yearned for by every team's coaching staff. If he can successfully perform those duties well on a regular basis, then an offensive lineman can become great at his job.

Finally, adding to the physical strength, agility, and poise of a great offensive lineman, one can revert to that simple word again: desire. How bad do you want to succeed? How much do you want to be a great player at your position? Larry Little continually asked himself those questions during his football career. Even though he may not have recognized it at the time, Little was actually responding in a step-by-step way regarding his desire to shut up his critics. He wanted to prove to the people who said that he could not accomplish several great feats were indeed wrong. Little wanted everyone to see that a man with an abundance of inner desire to succeed could succeed, despite what others might say about him.

Nobody can excel on a football field unless the offensive linemen are first able to do their jobs. Nothing else can happen beforehand. All the gained yardage, all the fluid runs downfield, all the graceful catches across a zone defense, all the quarterback's pinpoint passes—none of those things can take place unless the offensive linemen are able to initially ply their trade. Larry Little recognized the importance of his position. He knew that he was vital to the success of his team, and that fact was important to him.

Today, as a member of the Pro Football Hall of Fame, Larry Little has earned the respect and honor that such a distinction provides. His accomplishments in the sport have run the gamut from being named to numerous All-Pro teams over the years, to being a member of a team that went to three straight Super Bowls and won two of them. But perhaps the most defining moment of his greatness was his participation in the season of 1972. It was the perfect season for the Miami Dolphins, a team that became the only team in pro football history to finish the year with an unblemished 17-0 record. Some teams since then have flirted with that mark, but none of them besides the 1972 Dolphins ended the year with a zero in the loss category.

When I first began researching Larry Little's pro football career, I came to the realization that there was a lot more to him than what was written about him. He has a past that is intriguing to say the least. Many success stories of professional athletes begin within the realm of unpredictability. Little's story also begins there, but it does not end there. His character and his inner drive to make something of himself and to achieve success is a demanding part of his persona. It all speaks to a basic and foundational determination that seems to be at the core of anyone who refuses to accept the status quo. . . who refuses to accept the norms of what society feels is his worth. Knowing this, I was equally determined to find out more about Larry Little. The more that we discussed his career and his life, the more that I wanted to discover more facts and stories about him. Most importantly, however, was the fact that the more that I got to know him, the more that I wanted to write his biography.

I began interviewing Mr. Little back in January of 2022. Since then, I began to observe several connections that I have to him, even though we grew up in a different time and in different family situations. The basic backbone of my similarities with the subject of this book can best be described as both of our willingness to not give up. . . to not quit. The exact examples are different, but the core idea is the same. You only lose if you allow yourself to lose. . . if you allow yourself to quit. That is the theme of Larry Little's life. Never quitting turned out to be everything to Little, and it served as a springboard to any future good thing that has ever happened to him. It can become the same for us today.

Larry Little was just as eager for his story to be written as I was to write it. He knew that there were some lessons for younger people to take account of within these pages, and anything positive that can be passed on for the benefit of future generations is a good thing. But I also think that he wanted to leave a mark in this world to prove to everyone that he was here. . . to prove that he was a part of this world, and he was able to succeed in this world. That commendable fact is worth proclaiming, if only to state that he was able to accomplish a variety of endeavors and to prosper in his chosen field of life. If you took a close look at the beginning of his life, you might not believe that such a result was possible. But perhaps the most important fact about his story is that he did not believe that he was destined to fail, like so many others that he knew of did. Rather, he always felt that he was going to make it in this world. That self-confidence is what this book is all about. That self-confidence is what Larry Little is all about.

Many people will have debates on the greatness in a man, and on how an average man can become a great man. Some say that a man's greatness is measured by how many friends he has. Some say that a man's greatness is determined by how successful he is in life and in his profession, while others define a man's greatness by the character that he displays throughout his life. Larry Little has ownership of all three of these reasons to aptly illustrate his greatness, but it is his character which shows itself. . . more than anything else.

CHAPTER 1

AN OUTHOUSE
POINT OF VIEW

Horatio Alger's "rags to riches" tales would probably be regarded as an appropriate fit for the story of Larry Little. The future All-Pro and Hall of Fame offensive guard for pro football's Miami Dolphins was born on November 2, 1945, in Groveland, Georgia. It was a location where luxuries were rare for a family as big as theirs, which in time would consist of two parents, three boys, and four girls. In fact, the Little household had to rely on an outhouse to relieve themselves while living in Georgia. The youngster did not spend much time in the Peach Tree State, however. In fact, he spent just three weeks there before George C. and Ida Mae Little would move their family to Florida. It would be in that beautiful Sunshine State where he would grow up and make a name for himself, and where he would eventually become famous.

During his childhood, however, Little would spend his early years in nondescript ways that are seen in the lives of most kids of that era. Indeed, there were not many cultural opportunities like visiting art or history museums for the Little children to participate. And just like the rest of the youngsters all throughout his neighborhood in the city of Miami, he would face his formative years hovering close to the forlorn borders of poverty. Most blue-collar jobs in Miami would not offer particularly high wages during the 1950s and 1960s. Larry was the third-oldest child in his family, and he and his two brothers and four sisters were stuck in a world where they would watch their parents live paycheck to paycheck, where used clothes were passed on to the next youngest sibling, and where the future appeared to be no more promising than the previous day. It seemed to be a despondent existence, where the hopes for a better life and a better way of living in the future would seldom enter the minds of the members of the Little family. They were all too busy living one day at a time.

But to his credit, Larry in the beginning did not think too much about what few things he had, and what numerous things others did. He was more concerned with his day-to-day life, and the basic world in which he found himself. As he transferred from Dunbar Elementary School to Phyllis Wheatley Elementary School, his imagination and his thoughts just did not seem to find any focus on the lives of others. Instead, he spent his time thinking about the lives of his family members and of the local kids in his neighborhood.

"I didn't realize that there were some people who had more money than us growing up," admitted Little. "It was something that I didn't even think about. Most of us in that neighborhood in Miami had two-parent homes. We were all poor, but I didn't realize how poor we were."[1]

Feeding a large and struggling family was as difficult in the 1950s and 1960s as it still seems to be today, perhaps even more so. Snacking during the day was a rarity if it was ever experienced by the kids in the Little household. So, when dinner time came around each evening, Larry Little sat down and ate. And ate. And then ate some more. He was darn good at it. Perhaps one of the best food eaters who ever came out of his Miami neighborhood.

"Back home in Miami, I would often go back for second and third helpings," recalled Little, "and then would wipe clean anything my brothers and sisters left on their plates. I ate more than anyone else in the family. We were poor, but somehow we never went hungry. My mother would cook for everybody, but if they were having something that I didn't like, she'd cook for me separately. My mother provided for us, but not for herself. She went quite a few years without buying a dress to care for us.[2] She worked very hard, and everything she made went on our backs."[3]

Mrs. Little's selfless example to her children was certainly not lost on any of them. They knew that the patriarchal and matriarchal governance of the family, as evidenced by how their parents addressed child rearing, was always going to be the main focus for guidance, structure, and strength in the Little abode. In addressing if he had to suddenly become a stay-at-home leader in their family, Larry Little was quick to confirm that such was not the case.

"I never got that feeling," admitted Little. "My mom, and my father too. . . neither one of them graduated from high school. So, they were a stickler on us kids getting an education. We were the kind of family that if it rained, you still had to go to school. If it came to it, my mom would call a cab to take us to school."[4]

Once there in the classroom, learning took over. And to a point so too did reality. Over time, Little eventually did become acutely aware of the distinction between the haves and the have-nots in American society, especially in the day-to-day world that he experienced in the slummy areas of Miami. He noticed that some kids had more clothes and more toys than he did. He did not let it affect him, however, except for the fact that it did give him a reason to become motivated. He used that lack of an advantage like a chip on his shoulder, and eventually, it grew to be just the impetus that he needed to excel at the sport of football.

"What I had to prove. . . what I wanted to prove to people, was that I could be a good football player," affirmed Little. "You know when you're in school, you would go to see a counselor, and they would ask you the question, 'What do you want to be in your life?' I always said that I wanted to be a professional football player or a lawyer. I don't know why I said lawyer. I guess that it was just to put something [else] down. But I always put down professional football player. That was my lifetime goal, even as a young kid."[5]

But even as a young kid, Larry Little had to see up close how a deck of cards was being stacked against him in the 1950s and 1960s in Florida, and all because he had a different skin color than some other people. The inherent unfairness of how one group gets treated differently than another group, all because of something that they had absolutely no control over, was enough to get any youngster disheartened at the possibilities for success in America. Looking back on those days, Larry Little was sagacious enough in his older years to observe the arc of success in society. He has witnessed and lived through how African Americans were forced to live when he was a child, and he can compare those days to how the social fabric of the races has developed in this current day and age.

"We've come a long way in America, as far as civil rights go," Little contends. "But it's still not where it should be, I don't think. I was a product of being required to ride on the back of the bus. I was a product of going to the store in downtown Miami called W.T. Grant, and they had the colored water fountain right next to the white-water fountain. And I would sneak when no whites were looking and drink the white folk's water, to see if the white folk's water was any different. And it was! The white folk's water was cold, and the colored folk's water was warm. And in another place in downtown Miami called McCrory's, which was a department store. . . they had the best hotdogs. You could buy a hot dog there, but you couldn't sit at the counter there unless you were white. I remember all of that stuff as if it were yesterday."[6]

Sometimes, it takes something bad to learn about things. . . about society. The society that Larry Little observed as a youth while growing up in the hard-scrabble sections of Miami was both unfair and unfortunate. But it at least gave him a taste of right and wrong. It gave him a taste of knowledge as to the ways of the world. Treating one set of people differently than others was a practice that he knew was wrong. It just took a few decades longer for more folks in America to realize what he already realized, judging by what he saw with his own eyes.

Like most young kids, Little tried to imitate the actions and mannerisms of the people around him. Consequently, he also at times imitated the other kids that he grew up with. Many of the stories, Larry Little would later find, came with important morals and lessons. The end results of those tales and events would ultimately fall under the "nobody is perfect" category, as evidenced by the mistakes that he would eventually make.

"I was suspended from school in both the fifth and sixth grade at Phyllis Wheatley Elementary School," admitted Little. "I had a lisp when I spoke, way back in the third grade, and my mom got me a speech therapist to help me. I had to keep working on my speech. . . using Ss and Cs and stuff like that. It was called being tongue-tied. . . that's what they called it back then. People thought that I was kind of dumb or stupid because of the way I spoke. I eventually grew out of it, but my suspensions. . . I don't know if I was acting out because of my lisp or what. I may have done that to keep from being bullied. I was a chubby kid growing up."[7]

Regardless of his appearance or his tone of voice and diction, being a kid came with its share of hardships and opportunities. Some of the opportunities were good, such as playing sports and hanging out with his friends in the neighborhood. But some were not so good. Most youngsters make a bad choice or two during their sprightly lives, especially when they are faced with a possible bad outcome. Such a choice often occurs in a split second, where the person in question must weigh the potential rewards versus penalties, results, and consequences. One of those decisions would lead to an unfortunate event in Little's life, one that he would remember for many years.

"When I was suspended in sixth grade, I probably got the worst beating that I ever got," said Little. "In fact, I know it was. I was in the Boy Scouts, and when I got suspended, it was not only me, it was a friend of mine also. But we plotted whether we would go to school or not go to school. During the time that I was a kid, I tried to make a little money, and I got some greeting cards to sell. When I got the suspension letter from the school to take to my parents, I put that letter in with my greeting cards. So, I never told my parents that I was being suspended. And so, we were walking along Biscayne Boulevard here in Miami, and one of my mom's fellow church members was on a bus going to work, and she saw me. We were walking down the street, and I heard her holler 'Larry!' And I took off running."[8]

Little thought that he could run away from this problem, but it had presented itself as a very worrisome situation. An unexpected entity in the form of his mother's church-going friend had integrated herself into his ruse, and he was now stuck in a spot that was filled with panic. His initial choice to not inform his parents of his suspension had led to more problems and presented him with more questions that he had to be thinking about at this time. What if his mom's friend informed her of his truancy? That was probably a certainty. What would happen to him when his parents found out that he was skipping school, and that he was suspended? Those questions were indeed worrisome at this moment to Larry Little.

Unfortunately for Little, he was not done making mistakes and making more bad choices in this episode. His next actions would further compound his problems at home, and just like a snowball gains more snow to its mass as it rolls down a snowy hill, so too did Larry Little's troubles multiply with seemingly every move that he made. In retrospect, he should have quit while he was seemingly already in enough trouble in this affair. But he did not.

"We didn't have any cellphones back then," explained Little, "but there was a phone booth in between the houses where we stayed at. So, my mom was cooking, and she got a phone call. So my mom sent me down to see who was calling her, and it was the lady who knew my mom from church and who saw me earlier on Biscayne Boulevard. Her name was Inez Cheeks. But I went to take the phone call before my mom got to the phone booth. Well, Mrs. Cheeks said, 'Larry, let me speak to your momma.' I said, 'She's not home.' And then I hung up. But my mom was home.

"So, on her way to a meeting at church later that night, Mrs. Cheeks came by our house, and she told my momma that she saw me playing hooky, because she didn't know that I had been suspended. Later that day, I was at a Boy Scout meeting, and my older brother came out and got me, and said to me, 'Oh Larry, mother wants you to come home right now.' So, I rode my bicycle home, and my momma said, 'Why were you playing hooky from school?'"[9]

Practically every young boy who ever had disciplinarians for parents can relate to what was happening to Larry Little at this moment in his young life. His mind would think of two separate things at once. One of these things involved trying to come up with a quick statement that he could use to get out of a mess that he was now in. That assertion did not necessarily have to be truthful, it just had to be effective. But Larry realized he had to face the scenario as it was. .. the time for honesty had long since passed. Such excuses to his disciplinary parents would only compound his difficulties.

Little simply feared the inevitable. He would await whatever mean-spirited punishment was headed his way. There was no optimism going through his brainwaves at this moment. No, by the time he realized the severity of what was happening, he knew there was typically bad, worse, and worst. How bad? How worse? According to Little, as bad and as worse as it ever got.

"So, my mom started beating me," Little recalled. "And I had a cousin who lived next door to us. . . an elderly cousin. And she had a barber shop strap. So, my mom gave my cousin a turn at beating me with her barber shop strap. They were trying to get through with it before my father got home. Well, my dad got home, and he was wondering why they were beating me. And so, I told him that I got suspended from school. And this man attacked me, because my father was abusive. He was a strict disciplinarian. And he beat me, and he beat me, and he beat me some more. Man, that was rough.[10] My dad was only five-foot-eight, but none of us kids ever argued with him.[11] I feared him, but I also respected him."[12]

There were probably many places which may have seemed like a favorable alternative to where Little currently found himself at this specific moment in his life. Only those young kids who have ever gotten a solemn beating by one (or both) of their parents can truly commiserate with what Larry Little was going through when his mom, then his cousin, and finally his father beat him—all in one night! It had to have been both physically painful and mentally debilitating. There was rarely a "sparing of the rod" in the Little household, but this was just one instance of the violent spanking that Larry found himself on the receiving end of as a child.

"One day, my mom and dad went to school with me," recounted Little. "One of my teachers was named Miss Dorothy Graham. She was the meanest teacher that I ever had in my life. She had me suspended another time. Again, I was playing hooky. The principal's name was Ms. Grace Albert. She asked me, 'Do your parents know that you are suspended from school?' I said 'Yes.' So, we went into her office. Miss Graham came down, and when she was talking, I looked at her, and I rolled my eyes at her. My dad jumped up and slapped me. He said to me, 'Don't roll your eyes at Miss Graham without my permission!' Then Ms. Albert asked my parents, 'Do I have your permission to beat him?' And my parents said 'Yes.' So, that was another beating that I got."[13]

These corporal elementary school whippings could be described as ones that certainly got out of hand. But Larry Little could not predict what would happen at the start of his examples of playing hooky. He was in a situation where he had to pay a price, and where he would at the very least obtain a tougher mindset. . . a mindset which involved dealing with a physical beating, regardless of who was giving him that beating. But there were other factors involved regarding his reasons for playing hooky in the first place.

"I wanted to avoid getting bullied," Little said, "and one thing led to another. I can look back on it, and that was what happened."[14]

Today it is called street cred. Back when Little was roaming around the crowded inner city of Miami's poorer neighborhoods, it may not have had a defining name. But the youthful minority citizens knew how a tough reputation and mean credentials could become your saving grace along the streets, where the saving of anything was not very common. Whatever it took to stay alive and to avoid getting hurt, injured, or killed. . . that was the end goal of that group of people. To some, that was all that they could hope for.

"If I didn't grow up fast as a kid, I wouldn't have grown up at all," Little admitted. "Mostly, we ran down the streets. ... from guys with knives and cops with guns. But I never did something I'd needed a lawyer for. What helped me out of that fool stuff was my parents."[15]

That innate desire of Little's to stick with the sport of football may have gotten its start when he played street football in his neighborhood before he went to high school. It was there that he was introduced to the sport in an active way, and it was on the streets where he found enjoyment in imitating the football players that he saw playing the game on television. Street football was a rough brand of football to be sure. But it went a long way in toughening up a growing Larry Little. Those street football games gave him an opportunity to form a heart for the game.

"One street would play another street," Little recalled. "It was teams like the 19th Street team playing the 14th Street team. It was teams like that. I was on the 19th Street team. It was tackle football on a cement parking lot. . . a broken-down parking lot. At one time there would be rocks and broken glass out there. We would play tackle football out there. And it was organized football."[16]

Little's interest in the game developed and grew while playing in those sandlot games, and it provided him with a yearning to be a part of something formative. . . something productive. This sandlot action gave Little a rudimentary taste of football, and a foundational knowledge of the game. These contests were at first intended to be fun, and indeed they were. But they would also give Little some knowledge of how teamwork proved to be the most important element in the sport. It was here that Little and his teammates learned that they had to work together to achieve any measure of success in football.

Buoyed with this primary knowledge, Little moved on

to bigger and better things, as he grew older in his scholastic environment. He started to mature as a young man, and he made the most of whatever opportunity came his way. Even though the chances for him to show what he could do on the football field were few, he decided to be as prepared as he could be, in the hopes that his chances to play would soon increase, and in the hopes that someone in his near future would give him a chance to display his abilities.

One other thing that Larry Little saw with his own eyes was an introduction of sorts, to what would eventually be a glimpse of his future. The game of professional football appeared to Little by how it initially was observed by most youngsters who grew up in South Florida. He first saw the sport on television broadcasts, and even though those broadcasts were sparse in number, they collectively planted a hook in the young man's mind. He felt a natural attraction to the game. It stayed with him, and it became a perceivable and important part of him.

"You know during those days, we didn't see much professional football down south," recalled Little. "Down south, the only games that we could watch on television were the Washington Redskins [now known as the Washington Commanders], because they were the team that was the farthest south than any other team. That was when Eddie LeBaron was their quarterback. So, we saw them play. I was a big Baltimore Colts fan. The reason why is because the Redskins at that time didn't have any black players on their team, but the Colts did. They had people like Lenny Moore, Big Daddy Lipscomb, Jim Parker, and Lenny Lyles playing for them. I remember Jim Parker when he was at Ohio State. He and Big Daddy Lipscomb were my idols. Those were the players that I would follow as a kid.[17] Now we didn't have a TV until I was around eleven or twelve years old. That's when I saw my first televised football game."

Football may have preoccupied Little's mind at this stage of his young life. But his high school days at Booker T. Washington High School would provide him with a somewhat different vantage point. He started to see his life with a new vision. . . a little more worldly viewpoint. He was searching for his own individual identity, mind you, all while observing a group of his friends who were doing the same thing. Little was in the yearning stage of his young life. All young kids go through this stage, each looking for some avenue or another where he or she can move ahead in his or her life, and where he or she can obtain at least some measure of success in addressing the new challenges that they face each day. For Larry Little, those challenges during his high school years involved the idea of fitting in with both smaller and larger groups of classmates, all of which comprised his environment in the early 1960s in Miami. And not surprisingly, many of those challenges involved his lifelong desire to play football.

"When I went out for football, I was like thirteen, going into the ninth grade," remembered Little. "I was still young and kinda timid. There were some big guys on that team. If they saw that they weren't going to have anybody to beat down in practice, they'd beat on me. I made up my mind that [despite those beatings] I would never give up."[18]

Once Little made the decision that he wanted to devote his energies to football, he never wavered one bit from that pronouncement. It sounds simple enough, but that was not the case. Not quitting required a huge amount of personal strength and fortitude.

"I just wanted to be a part of something," Little assessed. "When I first went to Booker T. Washington High School, which went from the seventh grade to the twelfth grade, you couldn't play football until you went out for the team in the ninth grade. I did that, and I hung in there. I was told that I would never be a good football player. I was called 'sorry.' I was playing and going up against these guys in practice, and some of them were upperclassmen who were nineteen years old. Some of them may have been even twenty years old." Little laughed. "One of them was actually a professional boxer who I went up against. And they were beating the hell out of me, and I was only thirteen. Some of those older guys were held back a grade, and some weren't, some even had come to play for us from another city. I was still a boy going up against some men. But I wouldn't quit.

"In my freshman year, I didn't play at all. I would be sitting on the bench. The coaches and the upperclassmen never gave me anything. Some of the upper-class kids would come along and put dirt on me to make it look like I had played in the games, even though all I did was sit on the bench." Little laughed again but reflected on his treatment during his first year playing. "I was a chubby kid at that time. They were trying to ridicule me. It was tough, but I stuck with it. Everyone else my age on that team quit. But I didn't."[19]

"In the tenth grade, I played a little, but not that much," remembered Little. "In eleventh grade, I played, because one of the assistant coaches had seen something in me, where other coaches before him hadn't seen anything in me. He was actually the men's basketball head coach, but he played football in college. His name was Cecil Harris. He had a defense that he called 'Harris' Raiders.' And they gave me some pride because I now had a name. I was a part of Harris' Raiders. I now had an identity, and a part of the team that I could identify with. I was now a part of something."[20]

That new identity as a member of an esteemed group fell right in line with Little's dreams and ambitions to play football. He knew that it was a major steppingstone in his young life, and he made the most of it. When he was just a kid on the streets, he was just another kid on the streets. But the connection that Little felt with the sport just grew deeper and stronger with Harris' Raiders, and by this time, there was no turning back. He now felt important to his teammates and to himself. Indeed, if he had not quit throughout all the abuse that he received in his earlier years playing the game, he certainly was not about to quit now as he prepared to enter his senior year in high school. He was prepped and ready to make his final year in high school his best.

By this time, came his fondness for reading about football, and about many sports in general. Even to this day, Larry still feels that the greatest gift that a young student can possess from elementary and high school is his or her ability to read. He believed the ability to read presents the possibility of success. Larry recalls his mother frequently glancing over at her son to see Larry pouring through the local newspapers every morning while she was making breakfast.

"We got the *Miami Herald* at my house," proclaimed Little. "I read it every day. I've always loved sports, always followed sports, always read about sports."[21]

Reading about sports may have been a slight motivator for Little. But there were other influences in his young life beyond the printed word. Larry Little was seemingly always having to look over his shoulder at people and at situations that were not of his making. Take for example the situation with his older brother, George. Little grew up with a sibling who was supposedly smarter or more gifted than he could relate to in high school. A tinge of jealousy can sometimes become a motivator, but for Little, it was accompanied with a touch of wanting to earn something more for himself.

"My older brother George was a genius," affirmed Little. "When I went to high school, I kind of rebelled. Because even though he was four years older than me, George was one of the most popular people in my high school, because he could do it all. He was a great actor, he was a great singer, and he was smart. He had an A average. The teachers that I went to. . . the ones whose classes he had attended, would always ask me, 'Why aren't you more like your brother George?' You know I heard that enough, and I rebelled.

"And the only thing that we had in common was that we both sang in the school choir." Laughed Little. "He could do it all. And then in the school yearbook, people were telling him that he could be the next Sidney Portier, because he could act so well. That's how great he was. He even went to Howard University on a math and chemistry scholarship."[22]

Seeing his older brother accomplish so much gave Larry Little a dual sense of pride for his brother, and perhaps also a secret internal wish that he had—or would someday achieve—similar feats in whatever walk of life he was destined to follow. But somewhere, in the back of his mind during his high school years, Little eventually came to the realization that all good things take time. He abruptly came to know that life was not always fair. . . assuming that it ever is. He acknowledged that some things just come easier to some people, like they did for his brother George, than they did for himself and for other people. Larry knew by now that his dreams would take a lot of dedication to become a reality one day. The only worthwhile career that he could envision at this stage of his young life involved football. With that fact in mind, he set out to make his dream of one day becoming a pro football player a reality. . . one step at a time.

With this determination, Little grew ecstatic as he was set to play on the offensive line when he began twelfth grade. This is where he would experience his first lessons in the position he would excel at for the rest of his life. Soon after the school year began, practice at the field would have Little under the teachings of the offensive line coach, Cleveland Paulk. "We called him 'Coach Nasty Mouth.' That's because it seemed that every word out of his mouth was a profanity." Little chuckled. "But he was a hell of a line coach, and he only weighed 165 pounds. One of the things that I remember about Coach Paulk was the fact that he had a paddle, and he would beat all of the linemen's butts in the locker room at halftime." Little laughed even harder. "He ended up beating me too because I wasn't playing!"[23]

Coach Paulk would stress the fundamentals of effective offensive line play for Little like no one else had before. Both in pass blocking and run blocking, Little's knowledge of how to ward off pass rushers and how best to open holes for runners in the game grew, thanks in large measure to the efforts of "Coach Nasty Mouth." Little was certainly not a completely polished offensive lineman yet at this stage of his young life, but he was firmly walking on the road toward that goal. And that was a good aspiration for his focus.

During his final year of high school, Little spent his time outside of school, besides the hours that he spent on the football field, involved in the normal and somewhat mundane parts of his complete scholastic experience. His typical days included activities in which practically every kid during those times participated.

"Well after school, basically I went home, and if I had homework, I would do it," Little remarked. "But I would just hang out with the guys. Maybe not at my house, but at another friend's house where a lot of us hung out at. My parents were sticklers in me and my brothers and sisters in getting good grades in school. In high school, I usually earned Cs and C plus grades."[24]

Little's mother, Ida Mae, would have probably wished that Larry's grades were higher than the C range, but she had to have been proud of him, nonetheless. She obviously knew how much he enjoyed playing football during those years, and she loved it when he showed off some sign of fulfillment with something that brought him so much happiness. His father, George C. Little, however, was a whole other story.

"Well, my mom really pushed me to believe in myself," Little said. "But my dad was an alcoholic, so I didn't listen much to him. My dad had a job, but he was a bad alcoholic, and he was very abusive. In my senior year of high school, my dad said that he wasn't going to pay any more rent. He wasn't good to my mom."[25]

But fortunately, Little had also been dealing with the legality of rules and fairness in the sport of football. Those feelings of right and wrong had taken a strong and growing hold on his mind and his thoughts all throughout his time in high school. He realized that the interpersonal examples that his father set before him were not good ones, and ones that he was not going to repeat if he would ever get the opportunity to become a husband and a father himself. But despite that frame of mind and that strong conviction, he still had to deal with the serious and downright bad examples that his father was exhibiting in the daily lives of his family.

"My dad would get so drunk sometimes, he'd forget where he put his money," Little remembered. "I was always the one to find it for him. I remember my brother having one of those old foot lockers that they used to have. Well one day, I hid my dad's money underneath that footlocker. But I didn't know that one day, that footlocker was broken, and my dad had sent it out to be fixed. One of the repairmen came to get the footlocker, and he took the $300. When my dad found out that the $300 was gone, he beat me, and he beat me, because he thought that I had taken the money. I told him 'Daddy, I did not take your money!'

"Then to make a long story short, we went on vacation that summer. My family and I were going to visit my grandparents up in Georgia. And we were at the Greyhound bus station waiting for the bus. My father came and took me into the bathroom, and he searched me. He was still thinking that I had taken that money. Well, I didn't have the money, and his search of me proved that. That may have been the only time that he felt that I did not steal his money. And I never did. The people who came to move that footlocker. . . they were the ones who took that money.[26]

Finally, Larry Little had reached a point in his life where he had endured enough of the treatment that both he and the others in his family received from his father. He was an upper classman in high school by that time, and he had grown up, both in physical stature and in maturity. He was now ready to take a stand against his father.

"When my brother George left home to go to college, that left me to be the man of the house," said Little. "And I had to keep my father from coming home drunk, and I had to keep him from wanting to fight my mom. I had eventually grown bigger than him because he was only five-foot-eight. He came home drunk one day, and I said, 'To hell with all of this.' I said to him, 'No more, buddy.' I went and put his stuff out on the front porch, and I wouldn't let him in the house."[27]

Little's definitive stand against his father's actions marked a turning point in the young man's life. He had the strength of his convictions of what was right and what was wrong, and that determined approach to his home situation was indeed important. Nevertheless, his stance of sticking up for his mother and his siblings was tempered somewhat by what was happening all around the nation at that time. Though kicking his father out of the house was extremely traumatizing, he had also grown numb to it. He had to numb himself to a lot of things. Even when facing struggles at home, and the adversity met by his own family, Little still had to face it when he walked out his front door. The unjust specter of racism had reached exasperating levels all throughout the 1960s, and Larry Little had seen it develop, even in the game of football. Some of the elements of racism regarding the sport, and the aspects outside it, were blatant and impossible to ignore, while other segments of it were held just barely under the cover of something else.

"We could walk from my house to the Orange Bowl," recalled Little, "because I lived so close to the Orange Bowl then. But because of segregation, we weren't allowed to sit in the stands. We black folks had to sit in the bleachers at the Orange Bowl."

Little had to stomach the acceptance of the viewing experience at the stadium, the only silver lining was being able to watch his team.

"Booker T. Washington had one of the powerhouse high school football teams in the state back in the 1950s," remembered Little. "By the time that I played football there in the twelfth grade, Alkin Hepburn was my head coach. Those guys were my heroes. By the time that I had graduated high school, I was on a team that won just ten games in four years."[28]

The shame of losing more than half of his team's games did not help the feeling that Little felt when contemplating the unfairness of the Orange Bowl's seating restrictions.

Nevertheless, the addition of Coach Hepburn to the Booker T. Washington coaching staff was undeniably a change for the better for the team. True, the football team did not win a lot of games. But Coach Hepburn owned an impressive legacy at the school, having been an athlete for their football team while he himself was a student there. He also developed a fair reputation as a pretty good quarterback when he attended college. For his part, Little was developing into a pretty good offensive lineman under the tutelage of Coach Hepburn and Coach Paulk. Little's actions at practice showed how much he was willing to sacrifice to play the game. His determination was undeniable.

Little was getting bigger and stronger by his late teens. As a lineman, he was generally expected to be bigger and stronger than most of the other young men who played different positions on the team. In order to gain girth and strength, Little ate a lot of food. But his speed on the football field never really suffered, regardless of how much he weighed.

Little's teammates could not help but notice his growth. But they also noticed his willingness to become a team leader. By the time that the growing lineman had reached his senior year, he was selected as a team captain. The honor was not lost on him.

"The coaches didn't make me a captain, but they thought that I showed leadership ability," said Little.[29] Little's leadership capabilities would come a long way.

Coach Hepburn knew well enough to judge Little's heart for the game. He knew that his young lineman had an unquenchable desire to play football. It is something that a coach cannot develop or explain. A player either has that desire, or he does not. The bottom line often comes down to something as simple as that. Larry Little was the type of player, indeed the type of person, who was not going to give up on his dreams.

He now seemed to get the better of the hits that were delivered during his senior year on high school football fields. He managed to escape injury for the most part, except for one head-to-head concussion. It would be the only concussion that he would receive in all his twenty-four years of organized football action as a player. Looking back, Little finds it an astounding accomplishment, considering how deficient the equipment was back then compared to the safety advancements of today's helmets and padding.

But overall safety was not on Larry Little's radar when he stepped on the gridiron as a youngster in high school. To say that the 190-pound lineman who never made any All-City teams in high school had become a ferocious blocker by this stage of his life was perhaps a little premature. It was accurate, however, to state that he had made the most out of his opportunities while in high school as a lineman for the Booker T. Washington football team. Being on that team gave him a sense of belonging to something important. He had somehow made it through a poverty-stricken area of Miami, the struggles of his upbringing and instability of his home life, to walk across the stage at his scholastic graduation while being part of a team he was proud to have joined.

In the end, Larry Little wanted much more than just a high school diploma. He wanted to continue onto the next logical step toward his dream of becoming a professional football player. That step involved going on to becoming a student-athlete at one college or another. He immediately fixed his mind and his sights on that next logical step toward his dream.

CHAPTER 2

A PRODUCT OF GOOD FORTUNE

With all the bad luck and unfortunate circumstances that became a regular part of his early life, it was perhaps only fair that Larry Little would eventually get to experience some good providence for a change. He would finally benefit from his hard work on the gridiron, as he would get a chance to continue playing football in college.

But what college would that be? Little did not receive a lot of attention from any college back in 1963. For his part, it was assured that if he did get at least some amount of correspondence from any school, he would be eager to follow that up with his own inquiries Unfortunately, the actual collegiate attention that he received in the early 1960s revealed that scouting by the Historically Black Colleges and Universities (HBCU) was woefully inadequate for the number of outstanding gridiron talent that could be found at most of the high schools in the southern states. Little quickly realized that he had to play the cards that he was dealt in advancing to a college. When his future was in limbo, Little was seemingly just an innocent bystander when different college coaches came to his high school to observe several football prospects.

"When coaches from Bethune came down to Booker T. Washington to look at me and another guy, I only weighed 210 pounds," Little recalled. "The other guy weighed 240 pounds. And I think that they were mostly looking at him than they were looking at me. But I think that my high school coach [Alkin Hepburn] told them that if they wanted a football player, they should take a look at that quiet one sitting in the corner [me]."

"In my freshman year, we had what was called a 'Grant in Aide' back then," said Little. "I thought that I was going to go to college on a football scholarship. I knew that my high school coach Alkin Hepburn wanted me to play football in college."[1]

Little had been recognized by Hepburn as a significant football player at Booker T. Washington. Little was a lineman that could support his team through and through, He was a player worthy of praise. Hepburn made it his mission to have Little be chosen by a college scout. "Only two colleges were on table that were looking for a kid like me, Florida A&M and Bethune-Cookman University. Jake Gaither was the head coach at Florida A&M. He and another coach from that school came down and visited our high school. Coach Hepburn didn't want to recommend me to go to Florida A&M, even though he went to Florida A&M. He didn't think that I was good enough to play for them."[2]

Florida A&M was a juggernaut during those years, and they were a devastating opponent to deal with. Their lineup was simply loaded. Coach Hepburn accurately realized that if Little went to that university, the only time that he would get into any of their games would be with a couple of minutes to play in the fourth quarters, when substitutes were doing mop-up duties for the first stringers after the outcomes of those contests were already decided. But Hepburn knew that Little could grow into becoming a quality lineman, however, especially for a college that had a need for one, and a college where the young man would get a fair chance to play in their games.

Enter Bethune-Cookman University in Daytona Beach, Florida. That school was situated just ninety miles south of Jacksonville. Coach Hepburn made some telephone calls, and some coaches from Bethune-Cookman took a 260-mile car trip to Miami to meet Little and his coaches at Booker T. Washington high school. Little did not run any drills for those coaches, nor did they watch any films of him. Instead, they listened to what his high school coaches had to say about Little's abilities.

"The Bethune-Cookman coaches Jack 'Cy' McClairen [the head football coach] and Lloyd 'Tank' Johnson came down to see me," remembered Little. "Another assistant coach by the name of Ralph Burns, told Coach Hepburn and Coach McClairen that 'He [Little] is a late bloomer. He can make the Bethune-Cookman football team.'"[3]

The coaches in attendance, which included his high school offensive line coach Cleveland Paulk, thus came to an understanding and an agreement. Little was recommended by them all to attend Bethune-Cookman University. It was a brand-new door that was opening for the still-growing student-athlete. Practically every teenager who gets to go to college experiences a similar feeling of excitement, nervousness, and perhaps downright happiness. Many youngsters who found themselves in similar situations to Larry Little's were often awed by the experience. But that was not really the case for Little. He knew that he was going to go to college on the prior establishment of his ability to play his favorite sport during his high school years. He took a stationary role on both the offensive and defensive lines during that time, so he felt that he had a good, all-around skill set from which to draw upon for many potential colleges.

As soon as the gun sounded at the conclusion of Little's final football game in high school, Larry Little's football life—unlike that of many of his classmates—was far from being over. He was going to get a chance to continue his dream in college.

"I never thought that my last high school game would be my last football game ever,"[4] admitted Little. And this thought ultimately proved to be true.

Little's decision set the ball rolling. There was much more for him to experience than just the proximity of that school's location to his family, however. There were factors that involved the plans of Bethune-Cookman's football team, as well as some considerations regarding the good fortunes that were headed Little's way, unbeknownst to him at this time. Worth noting is the fact that nothing in his high school background prepared the future college freshman for what he was about to experience at Bethune-Cookman. He was going to get a quick education in the ways and means of the school. He was also going to hear some chatter from other schools.

Little's decision to attend Bethune-Cookman proved to be both a beneficial one and a wise one. He would be staying within driving distance of his home, as Daytona Beach was only about five-hours' drive from Miami. The other school that made a similar offer to Little was Saint Augustine in Raleigh, North Carolina. But the closeness of remaining in Florida proved to be too much and too important for him to ignore. He stuck with Bethune-Cookman.

"It was the best decision that I made as a teenager," Little recalled many years later. "Because in my senior year in college, Saint Augustine dropped their football program. I would have missed out on my senior year of football if I had chosen Saint Augustine, which would have made it even more difficult for me to get drafted in the pros. So, it was very beneficial to me that I chose to attend Bethune-Cookman."[5]

So Little's college career began, and one of the first steps along with starting classes, was meeting back up with very coaches who recruited him.

"Coach Jack 'Cy' McClairen and Coach Lloyd 'Tank' Johnson were my only two coaches while I was in college," stated Little. "Coach McClairen was an ex-pro player. He played for the Pittsburgh Steelers as a tight end. He was the first Bethune graduate to go pro, and he even made the Pro Bowl one year. Well, they practiced in the gym at training camp, and when I got there to meet them, the whole group of coaches were cutting guys from the team at the door to the gym!"

"I was looking around at all of the other coaches, and then I saw those two coaches who had recruited me."[6]

As it turned out, Little's coaches were looking for him too. But they could not seem to find him. That was because Little spent the summer away from Florida, and he had gone through some visible changes during his absence from the Sunshine State.

"I weighed about 215 pounds when they recruited me in high school," Little confirmed. "I wasn't big back then. But that summer when I went to training camp, one of the coaches was looking around and saying, 'Where's that Little kid from Miami?' And I said, 'That's me, Coach.' I had gotten up to 240 pounds that summer. I had gone to Georgia that summer where my grandparents lived, and I was eating all that country food in the country. And I picked up a lot of weight."[7]

Little was then welcomed to the team, and his freshman year of college finally began. He would eventually gain two more coaches by his senior year. Not only with the joining of his new team but also starting classes at the college level. Proving to be a challenge not only in curriculum, but what his degree would be in. The college coursework was naturally more demanding and intense. But Little rose to that challenge. He would—through hard work—manage to improve upon his grades. His most common high school grade was a C or a C plus. In college, however, with a tougher curriculum load, he somehow improved his grades to the low B neighborhood. That type of result was due to his diligence. He came to the realization in college that success in the classroom was similar to whatever he would achieve on the football field. It would take his devoted time and effort to earn good grades during his time in Daytona Beach.

"If I didn't quit when I was in the ninth grade, then I wasn't going to go into college and quit," affirmed a dedicated Little in a 2022 interview. "If I didn't quit when a bunch of older guys would beat me up every day at practice, and when I was the only ninth grader who would stay on the football team without quitting, then I wasn't going to let something like the toughness of my college classes get to me. I was going to grow."[8]

Larry Little's first taste of college was typical of most freshmen, and it featured the same expectations that are visible in practically every college setting in America, even to this day. He had to adjust to a whole new lifestyle like all young students, and he had to rely on his own accumulated wits to get by and adjust to the increased amount of classwork that he was required to complete for academic success to be achieved.

"I took fifteen hours of classes every semester," remembered Little, "and that enabled me to graduate on time. I didn't take any more than fifteen hours in any semester. I graduated in four years, but in order to do that, I had to go to summer school one summer.[9] I really don't remember too much about my first day at college, though. I was just taking the basic courses—the core courses—that freshmen take."[10]

College subjects are different from what one sees in high school, as anyone who has ever taken college classes will agree. After you get through with your core classes, you then focus on classes that will enhance your understanding of your major plan of study. For Larry Little, his major in college was Sociology, and that subject intrigued him because of his interest in human nature. Little's idea in college was not just to help him further his initial goal of one day becoming a pro football player. He also wanted to excel as much as possible as a student in college. He was all about challenging himself. Furthermore, he also owned and demonstrated a can-do attitude.

"I was optimistic at that time," admitted Little. "I felt that my attitude was that I could do it. As a matter of fact, I was the parliamentarian of the class. For every year from my freshman year to my senior year, I was the parliamentarian."[11]

His academic success in college and his optimistic outlook had to have their origins in his willingness to work hard. Little knew early on in his freshman year that he was going to have to expend a lot of hard work if he was going to prosper, both in his college classrooms, and on the football fields of the Southern Intercollegiate Athletic Conference (SIAC). He was certainly not the least bit afraid of putting forth that kind of effort. Moreover, the college environment was something that Little just seemed to welcome. It was like the grand opening of a brand-new house, where numerous rooms were large and brilliant, and where to reach the next room, all one had to do was study hard.

"My college instructions and lectures were more intense than what I experienced in high school," admitted Little. "But everything was. In college, you were more so on your own. When you had to study, you basically were on your own. We didn't have a tutor at that time either. You had to study on your own and fend for yourself. I was a "C" student. I wasn't a great student, but I was an average student. I had Cs and Bs. I don't think that I got any As in college."[12]

Little espoused a basic and simple guideline when it came to his core classes, which proved beneficial to his efforts in earning a higher grade-point average. He quickly decided to stay away from classes—namely mathematics—that he knew he would have difficulty in passing. He did at least attempt some of those classes, however.

"There's no thinking about my most difficult classes," admitted Little in a most definitive way. "Math. Algebra. My professors saw how I was struggling in those classes. But my professors were thoughtful. I had mixed professors. Even though Bethune-Cookman was a HBCU school, I had both black and white professors, and for my Spanish class, I had a Cuban professor. My professors were very diverse."[13]

To decide upon what his major point of study would be, Larry Little relied on both his earliest backgrounds of reading newspapers as a kid, and on observing the tenor of the times of the 1960s in America. He enjoyed learning about current events by exploring the printed word, and he saw firsthand how history was being made right before his very eyes by living during one of the most turbulent decades in American history. Little wanted to observe and examine how his mind worked through questions and decisions in the face of right and wrong, hence his decision to study Sociology.

As a caveat to that subject, Little also developed a keen interest in the mechanics of rules and laws, on both a local level, as well as on a broader, more nationalistic level. He wanted to explore the makings of not just how laws were made, but the reasons behind the laws in America. To further those curiosities in his mind, Little began enrolling in classes which gave him answers to his deeper questions.

"I did really well in government. . . American government," acknowledged Little when recalling his collegiate subjects. "I did well in civics. Basically, American government and civics. I've always been interested in the branches of government. . . the rise of government, and things like that. I follow politics, and those classes helped me to better understand politics."[14]

Understanding his fellow classmates would be an ongoing process for Little, however. He received a small taste of the variety of different people that he saw and heard from in his numerous college classes. Be they professors or students, there was a common thread, that of the differences between everyone. An intuitive guy like Larry Little was quick to notice those distinctions.

"In college, in a segregated college, we learned from people from all different walks of life," Little explained. "They may have been more well off than I was. Their parents may have been professionals, or whatever. And I mingled with a lot of them too, you know."[15]

Little also got to mingling with a variety of current events while he was in college. The civil rights movement was competing with the Vietnam War for the attention of most citizens in the nation during the 1960s. Both topics were situated front and center on the evening news, and both stories got front page headlines in the newspapers. For young African Americans like Larry Little, avoiding the conflict in Southeast Asia was one thing, but there was simply no dodging of the struggle for fairness between the races in America during that time. You could not be a fence sitter. Little got a small taste of a chapter of it, and of the personalities of the issue, while he was a student at Bethune-Cookman University.

"In college, Stokely Carmichael had spoken at Florida A&M University." Stokley was a national civil rights leader during the 1960s. "He was leaving Tallahassee and coming to Daytona Beach to speak at our campus at Bethune-Cookman," Little explained. "Our university president had some of the football players make sure that we didn't let anything or anyone come onto our campus in order to make sure that nothing bad happened to him. I was as active as I could be, only to find out that on the way to Daytona Beach, he [Carmichael] said that two white people tried to run him off the road with their car."[16]

Neither Little nor his teammates could be responsible for what happened to Carmichael while he was traveling to their college. But this episode of Carmichael's life did give the young football player another taste of what many African Americans across the southeastern United States had to deal with when race relations were in question. Little did not really need another example of the disparities between the races in Florida, but he received one, nonetheless. At times, it appeared as if the problems that the civil rights issue was dealing with would never be rectified. But even though it was often difficult to see, the country would be moving slowly but steadily toward a sense of fairness and equity in the differences between skin colors in America. Little and his teammates were postured witnesses to the beginning of this societal change, as evidenced by the Carmichael incident in college.

"I was saying at that time that there's a right time and a wrong time to protest," said Little. "What I meant was that it was okay to protest, but it was not okay to riot. It was okay to focus on nonviolent protests. That's what Martin Luther King was preaching."[17]

The beginning of Little's college football life, however, was ranked as quite different from anything else that he saw or experienced at Bethune-Cookman in his lecture hall settings or the picket lines. In the 1960s, the idea of "student-athlete" was sound, with collegiate academics remaining the most important part of the equation. Things have changed over time, naturally, as today's college football players are held in higher regard for what they can accomplish on the gridiron than what they can achieve in their classrooms. Larry Little came to a quick realization as a college freshman in 1963 that the reason why he was able to get a chance to earn a college degree was due to his abilities as a football player. Nevertheless, he was determined to work just as hard at studying for a political science test as he did on blocking an opponent along the line of scrimmage. Quitting at anything was not a part of Larry Little's DNA. He certainly came too far and tolerated too much all throughout his high school years to ever give up on playing football at the college level.

Little's earliest memories of playing for the Wildcats came from his freshman year. Bethune-Cookman had far fewer coaches than they do in this current day and age. Because of this, every player had to make the most of whatever time he got with whichever coach wanted to explain techniques and strategies to him. And as a player, he had to make himself stand out to the coaches. Being noticed was an important element in Little's hopes of becoming a successful college football player. Ironically, in being noticed, Little pulled a hard-hitting repeat of sorts from a moment of one of his high school practices.

"I remember my very first football practice at Bethune," related Little. "The freshmen came in before the upper classmen, and I remember us practicing in the gym. The coach called for us to run a sweep. And I was a guard, and there was a guy holding a blocking dummy in my path. And I hit that dummy so hard, that I knocked it down some steps next to the floor."[18]

"I give my college coaches a hell of a lot of credit," said Little in a 1972 interview. "We only had two coaches where some schools have ten or twelve. Tank Johnson worked with me until dark many days and Coach McClairen wanted to make me into an outstanding player. He was a great tight end himself for the Pittsburgh Steelers in the 1950s."[19]

Little absorbed the knowledge that his coaches would give him, and he remained focused on his ultimate goal—to get into the pros—just as Coach McClairen had done. But the tenuous nature of college football did not escape him, however. In the 1960s at Bethune-Cookman, Larry Little discovered that to attend his college classes, he was going to have to first excel as an offensive or defensive lineman for the Wildcats.

"If you didn't make the team, you were going to be sent home," said Little. "You didn't know if you were going to get a scholarship or not. If you got cut from the team, then you would lose your scholarship. You could then go home or pay for your own classes at school. If you made the team, then you would keep your scholarship. Sometimes losing a scholarship was too tough for some of the guys, and they would sneak out at night. You could hear the sound of them dragging their suitcases down the steps in the dormitories."[20]

On paper, it appeared to be simple. Make the Bethune-Cookman football team, and you will be allowed to stay in school. But Little had his back to the proverbial wall. No other school in Florida had offered him a scholarship or even a partial scholarship. So, it was all or practically nothing for him at Daytona Beach. He was going to have to make the Wildcat football team. A player in such a situation at any level with so much at stake can either work his butt off and give it all he has, or he can fail to make the team. It was a time for no excuses for Little. Everything that he had prepared for, and everything that he had worked for during his high school years, was now going to be evaluated for its worth. Despite enormous odds going against him, Larry Little did not quit his high school football team. Now he was going to have to repeat that effort to make his college football team.

Little succeeded in this effort thanks to his own simple desire. He wanted something better for himself than just the life that he left during his childhood and high school years. He wanted to be able to make his own way in the world, to obtain and earn a quality education, and to someday make enough money to buy the things that he never had owned during his earlier life. His college years would thus become the obvious next step to climb on the ladder toward his future accomplishments. And all that was dependent on his worthiness to be a part of the team.

Little would be picking up a starting spot on the team's roster. Few are the freshmen football players in colleges across the nation who manage to start for their teams, but Little had two important factors going for him in his favor to become a starter. One, he had the physical tools with which to excel at his two positions along the offensive and defensive lines. Two, because of the small number of only thirty-eight players on the Bethune-Cookman team, Little's addition on the squad would greatly be required for the team to have some depth on its roster. Despite his overall lack of experience, he was going to play. Today, a college football team with only thirty-eight players would be either laughable or hard to believe, but back in the 1960s, such a low number was common for some of the smaller schools like Bethune-Cookman.

"I ended up going against guys that already had two and three years on me, and I was competing with them," said Little. "I called myself a late bloomer."[21]

Regardless of how long it took Little to adapt to the rigors of college football, it was still going to be a challenge. Bethune-Cookman was a school that was a member of the HBCU. The stereotype back in the 1960s stated that the players who attended the traditionally southern HBCU schools were believed to be not as good as the players who were recruited to play at Division 1-A schools. Such was not always the case, however. Many great athletes played for HBCU colleges for several valid reasons. One, many of these schools were closer to the homes of these athletes, which was important for their families. Two, many of these schools would tend to offer a student-athlete a full scholarship, as opposed to a partial scholarship that may have been offered to the player at a Division 1-A college. And finally, there was a sense of familiarity with the HBCU student athletes, as many of the players knew each other from their high school years. This chemistry with their team members, along with the stability of their home lives and scholastic careers, Little discovered, would be a resolving advantage on the field for Bethune-Cookman.

Little took advantage of all the playing opportunities that were made available to him at Bethune-Cookman. He was becoming more worldly at this stage of his life. He was being inundated with information, both in and out of the classroom. All throughout this time, he was also chalking up numerous experiences, which have provided him with fond and at times solemn memories of his collegiate years.

One of those memories involved a subject of national importance with a collective feeling of tragedy amongst all the country's citizenry.

"I remember it like it was yesterday," said Little in a recent interview. "It was during my freshman year in college. It was November 22, 1963. We were on the bus to go to Tallahassee to play Florida A&M. Then we got word as we got off the bus in Tallahassee from some of the Florida A&M football players that John F. Kennedy had been killed. My initial reaction was that I was shocked. And then there were rumors going around that the game against Florida A&M, which was scheduled for the next day, which was a Saturday, wasn't going to be played."[22]

The game between the Bethune-Cookman Wildcats and the Florida A&M Rattlers was held as scheduled, however, despite the somber mood that was felt by the players and the fans all throughout the stadium.

On the day of the game, Bethune-Cookman was more than familiar with the sheer strength of Florida A&M, their team winning a majority of the games they played in a given year. These views were shared virtually by every player who suited up for smaller schools. Those recollections were indicative of how much stronger the Rattlers were than practically any other HBCU team in the Southeast.

"When we played Florida A&M, we only had thirty-eight or thirty-nine guys on our team," remembered Little. "Florida A&M had like four different teams! We came out of the locker room at the same time to stretch and go through our warm-ups before the game. When we were done stretching, some of the Florida A&M players were still coming out of their locker room onto the field to begin their stretching! They had more depth on their team, no doubt about it."[23]

During Bethune-Cookman's 1964 meeting with Florida A&M, Larry Little also got a chance to meet an acquaintance from the neighborhood where he spent his childhood. In Little's sophomore year, he brushed up against Archie Williams.

"Williams grew up in the same neighborhood that I did," Little explained, "and he went on to play college football at Florida A&M. In 1964, he was their center, and I was playing nose guard for Bethune. Well, I was making a lot of tackles that day, and we eventually got into a fight with each other. I got thrown out of the game for that."[24] The Rattlers were a dominating team that year and they easily defeated the Wildcats, 38-14.

Throughout Little's four years in college where he went up against strong schools and not-so-strong schools, he continued his football progression. He got the basic foundations of playing the game during his high school years, where he began at the ground level. Then in college, he received more advanced lessons and knowledge about the strategies of the sport from what would often be better and more experienced coaching staff. Finally, if he was truly lucky enough to reach the highest level of professional football, the coaching staff in the pros were generally regarded as the best of the best. Indeed, many pro coaches in the 1960s as in this current day were also pro players themselves. A coach will typically obtain increasing amounts of knowledge from the game at every school or team wherein he coached. Then he would make use of that knowledge by teaching those lessons to his young players.

Larry Little's college football lessons at Bethune-Cookman were valued and important. The Wildcats posted a respectable 6-3 record during both his freshman and sophomore seasons (1963 and 1964). That included a 4-3 record of SIAC games each of those two years. Before his second year in college concluded, Little would experience more victories than he had in his four years of playing football in high school. His junior and senior seasons in college were a tad different, however. Bethune-Cookman did not win as many games in 1965 and 1966. The Wildcats won five contests in both of Little's junior and senior years at the university. But they only entered a loser's locker room twice in each of those seasons. Also worth noting is the fact that during his first three years at college, Little played on both the offensive and defensive lines. In his senior year, however, he remained solely on the team's defensive line, where he was named to the All-American team. His future solely as an offensive lineman would have to wait, and it would remain in question if Little would ever play on the offensive line again.

But the moments that he spent on the defensive side of the ball would prove to be beneficial to him over time. He would gain practical knowledge as to the types and variances of moves that typical defensive tackles would make in any given situation. Little would eventually use that information when he made it to the pro ranks. He would recall those defensive moves that he was taught in college, then figure out ways to counter them in his years playing the game on the offensive side of the ball in the pros. Naturally, he could not foresee what he would do after he hung up his shoulder pads at Bethune-Cookman for the final time. Nor did he know for sure if he was destined to continue playing the gridiron game.

Nevertheless, despite any uncertainty about his future that he might have felt, Little was by nature a confident fellow. He preferred to look at his own situation in a positive light, where his own efforts would result in some measure of success, if not immediately, then somewhere down the road. If for nothing else, he had grown up in a difficult and poverty-stricken environment, and yet he had somehow by his own efforts and diligence made it to college. That was quite a hurdle to clear, but he cleared it. He had followed in the footsteps of his older brother George and his older sister Betty, both of whom attended college. Now he was about to step outside of his siblings' shadows and make a name for himself. Now it was time to prove his worth, to his college coaches on the football field, and to his college professors in the classrooms. It was time for him to see if he could measure up to all his fellow college classmates.

"I did grow up in some respects because I was away from home. I had to grow up quickly. My momma wasn't there to wake me up to go to school every morning. You had to do that on your own if you had a class in the morning. I think that was beneficial to me.[25]

"But I definitely formed a bond with the members of the football team, because you went there and practiced together before the rest of the school opened. And when we went up there, it was about a three-hour bus ride, and we got to know each other by riding the bus up there together after we met up at the bus station in Miami."[26]

A couple of bus-riding stories are worth mentioning from Little's memory. They speak of the tenor of those times, where the Bethune-Cookman team—like most of the HBCU teams—did not operate with a wealth of wealth. Now that is not saying that the football program was a completely bare-bones operation, mind you. They just did not possess the big money that bigger Division I schools were fortunate to have. The lack of gridiron funding was evident, even while the team was journeying on their road trips.

"When I was in college and me and my teammates were traveling on a bus, our bus didn't have a bathroom in it," Little recalled. "The bus driver had a roll of toilet paper in a compartment on the bus, and he would pull over to the side of the road, give us the roll of toilet paper, and we would go out in the woods to do our number! And then one time, I had diarrhea, and my teammates were cussing me out, because the bus had to keep stopping!"[27]

It was not all laughter on the Bethune bus back in those days, however. The ugly remnants of prejudice and racism were aptly present in the rural sections of many Southern States during the 1960s. If Larry Little did not get enough of a view of it while growing up in Miami, he certainly got an eyeful of it on occasions while traveling with the rest of his college buddies.

"I remember one time we were playing a team called Lane College [in Jackson, Tennessee]," said Little. "And on our way back from the game, the bus driver had to stop and get gas. Now mind you, we weren't supposed to use the bathroom at that gas station, because we were all black. Well, one of my teammates and I decided that we were going to use the bathroom anyway. But we never did get to the bathroom. The man running that gas station pulled a shotgun on us to keep us from using the men's room. I can't recall exactly what he said, but it was along the lines of 'You can't go in there,' or something like that. So, me and my teammate turned around and went back to the bus. And our coaches panicked, and they cussed us both out, because they didn't want anything to happen to us on their watch."[28]

Moments like these were scattered around Little's experiences from early childhood to even his college years, challenging him to adapt, to acquire behaviors, and acclimate to his surroundings. These stark contrasts of acclimations were always prevalent, whether at home, out on the streets in Miami, or in school. Some of these being the adversity that he learned to shoulder as he got older, while others reflected similar behaviors he held back when he was a child. Back to when he was in the Little household. When it came to the Bethune-Cookman team, one of these behaviors was ironically his eating habits. He went from 215 pounds as a freshman to 240 pounds as a sophomore. His hunger and his weight increased to 250 pounds as a junior. Finally, by the time that he graduated from college, Little tipped the scales at 260 pounds, which was perfect at that time for a quality college or pro football lineman.

"I was fast as a kid and the increasing poundage didn't seem to bother me," said Little. "I always ate pretty good at home and after a couple of years at Bethune, my weight began to catch up with me."[29]

These behaviors and habits reminded Little of home. He would think of his siblings, but more often, he would think of his mother. Unfortunately for Little's family, his mom, Ida Mae Little, was never able to see her son play football in high school or in college. Part of the reason why was because she was often busy working on the days and nights when Larry was playing football. The other part of the reason for missing her son's football games resided with her duties at home.

"She was either working during the games or she was at home watching my younger siblings," remembered Little. "She got a car right after I went to college. She eventually went back to school to become a nursing assistant. She did not see me play football until I got to the pros."[30]

Despite these melancholy thoughts, Larry Little improved with each passing year. His offensive blocking techniques became more sound and more dynamic. When he was switched to the defensive side of the line of scrimmage as a senior, he had accumulated enough football knowledge to excel on the defensive side of the ball as well. The Wildcats did not fare well against most of the teams that they played during Little's time at the school. Nevertheless, he succeeded enough to know in his heart and in his mind that he stood a pretty good chance at continuing his football career in the professional ranks. It was one of his main goals, after all, and it was within his sniffing distance of obtaining.

"I did feel that I was worthy of a shot at the pros," affirmed a retrospective Little. "There were a lot of teams that sent scouts to come out and look at me."[31]

The pro scouts may have come to Bethune-Cookman University to take a closer and more critical look at Little, but they also would see the Wildcats as a team that was improving on a regular basis during the years that the big lineman suited up for them (1963-1967). Those scouts would observe strong play along both sides of the line of scrimmage, where most football games are either won or lost. As far as Little was concerned, he felt that his team was able to show strength in most of their games.

"We had a strong rivalry with South Carolina State," recalled Little. "Beating them was big because they were one of the better teams in the SIAC at the time. They were also one of the bigger schools with the most students. But I think that we matched up pretty well with them. We matched up pretty well with everyone. . . except for Florida A&M."[32]

In college football, every team occasionally deals with a school that, on paper, has the edge on them. Sometimes, those types of colleges were simply in a more competitive conference. Little and the Wildcats had to deal with such a team like that in their contests with Florida A&M University during the 1960s. But even bigger and better teams were left off the Bethune-Cookman schedule, perhaps for the benefit of the Wildcats. Those schools just possessed a wealth of talents at practically every position. Moreover, they also laid claim to a huge amount of depth on their roster, something that was impossible for most of their opponents to ignore.

"South Carolina State was the only state school that I think was on our schedule that year [in 1966]," recollected Little. "You see, we were a Methodist school, and most of the other teams that we played were from church-believing schools. So, we were right around all on the same level.[33] Even though we didn't have a losing record when I was in college, we still only played schools on our level. We never played the so-called major black colleges at that time. We never played schools like Grambling, and we never played Southern University. Instead, we played teams like Morris Brown, Allen. . . schools like that."[34]

Regardless of the level of competition that he observed in college, Larry Little saw a lot of eye-opening things during his collegiate years (1963-1966). He was a member of a team that accrued a 22-10-1 overall record while he suited up for them. He had gained a plentiful amount of knowledge during that time, and he had proven to many of his earliest detractors that he was good enough to play football well beyond his high school years. Now the challenge that was set before him was to prove to several more doubters that he could also play the sport at the professional level.

CHAPTER 3

A HANDSHAKE WITH A HIGHER BIDDER

Larry Little would find himself one big step closer to one of his childhood goals just a couple of months after his final season of college football ended. It was time for the annual selection of college seniors by the professional football teams, otherwise known today as the NFL Draft. But in 1967 when Little became eligible to be chosen by a pro team, there would be more than just one league who might vie for his services. The American Football League (AFL) sported nine teams that year, and any one of them were eligible to pick Little, along with any one of the sixteen NFL teams.

Little was familiar with how scouts would be looking for a player like him. A typical scout would watch films of a player, read any newspaper clippings about them, then call his coaches, and ask them questions about the player's abilities. The scout might then go to see the player in person, perhaps in a game, and if enough interest in said player materialized, after the season was over in an organized workout, an offer could be available to them. Usually more than one scout would connect with other scouts from other teams to watch just one workout of the player at the same time.

But perhaps the two most important factors when one considers the relationship between scouts and players involve luck and connections. Little knew that good luck was almost always a requisite when players from small schools got scouted. As luck would have it, Little was considered a diamond in the rough, and even though he might need some polishing, he would one day turn out to be a worthwhile gem that a team could point to as being an important part of their roster. But there would always be a risk of being wrong about taking chances on players from smaller schools.

The other factor that stood out to Larry was the relationship and connections between a scout and a player. Are there scouts that know anyone from his college? Would a scout trust his coach's opinion of him if this was possible? Lucky again for Larry, this was a reality.

"My coach [Cy McClairen] had some teammates in Pittsburgh who were scouts," Little said. "And those scouts came down to see me. And I was even promised by a scout from the Houston Oilers that I would probably be drafted by the tenth round. And then a scout from the Rams told me that I would probably be drafted."[1]

Hearing several scouts tell him that he would probably be drafted by one pro football team or another was music to Larry Little's ears. They were statements from several people who were professionals, and who supposedly had an inside track as to what ways the pro teams were leaning when making decisions on who to draft. Little felt a surge of optimism as the time came nearer to the draft.

Larry Little found himself in Florida on the day of the 1967 pro football draft. He was still on campus at Bethune-Cookman on that day, and it was a safe bet to say that he had to have been anxious to some degree. The nervous anticipation waiting for a phone call was—and still is—not unlike that of a person awaiting a job offer, or that of a teenage girl waiting for a boy to call her on the telephone. For Larry Little and for countless other college football players hoping to get a shot at playing pro football, that phone call meant a chance at fulfilling a dream. It meant the change in the road along the path that their future would take. Draft day for Little was filled with worried expectations, occasional prayers, pacing back and forth across the floor of his dorm room, and wishing for that doggone phone to ring.

"On the day of the draft, I was sitting in the dorm by the phone," Little recalled. "I was a captain of the team, and the phone was right by my room. And I wouldn't let anybody use that phone on the day of the draft. I was waiting for a call. . . the call that never came."[2] The draft lasted an incredible seventeen rounds back in 1967, but despite that, Little was ignored by every team.

He was awestruck. How did this happen? How could he be visited by several pro scouts and not be selected by *any* of the pro teams during the draft? Trying to piece together the vagaries of that draft, Larry found himself in a whirlwind of events that befell practically every college football senior at that time.

There was no foolproof way of figuring out who was drafted, when they were chosen, and which team selected them. The only thing that a player had to go on was a telephone call from a team's representative. And in some cases, such phone calls were far from infallible. For instance, several teams could call a player and inform him that he would be their pick if his name was still not taken off the board by a specific round. Unfortunately, this story would be a similar one among players in the draft. The prospective team often finds interest in another player. Perhaps that team has coaches who desire a different player at a different position. Regardless of the reasons why, many college grads seem to be sold a bill of goods by one team, only to be let down by them. Larry Little would have been forgiven if he did not feel at least a little bit depressed and at least a little bit deceived with the results of the draft. He was not chosen by any pro team in either the AFL or the NFL. Little was certainly not the first college football player who counted the hours going by on draft day, only to not hear his phone ring at all, and he would most assuredly not be the last.

There was still hope for Little. By his final year at Bethune-Cookman, he had earned a ranking as an All-American defensive tackle, and as such, he was almost guaranteed to receive some attention from some pro teams despite not getting drafted. There were options, even at this point. His dream to play pro football was not over at the end of the draft, but rather, it was just taking a detour. He was still on the road, but only now, it would be up to him to determine which road he would take on the map as a free agent.

He was now able to accept any deal that any team would offer him if he wanted to do so. Or he could wait for a better offer if he felt that one was to be had. His connections from the scouts who had previously looked at him had some connections of their own, and that phase of this process, where the communicating of friends, and the calling of friends of friends, was just beginning.

"I was contacted by scouts from both the Miami Dolphins and the San Diego Chargers of the AFL and the Baltimore Colts of the NFL," said Little. "The Colts scout called me first, and you know, I'm being Mr. Bigshot, and I would ask him what kind of bonus they were going to give me. And he said that 'We don't give free agents bonuses.' Then somebody from the Chargers contacted me, and I asked them, 'What kind of bonus would I get to sign with you?' They told me that they would give me $750. And I jumped on it, because $750 was a lot of money back at that time. So, I committed to the Chargers."[3]

Timing has a lot to do with negotiations and personnel signings in the world of pro football. Good timing is especially treasured by anyone who has something to gain in this environment. Larry

Little was just such an athlete. He knew that his position in this process was lessened by the fact that he was not drafted. But he was also smart enough to realize that he was still wanted by a couple of teams, and his common sense pointed to him taking the best deal available. But this little episode was not completely finished at this point, however.

"Well guess who called me the next day after I signed with the Chargers?" Little asked. "It was the Miami Dolphins! Joe Thomas, the Miami general manager, called me and said, 'Hey Larry, how are you doing? I'm Joe Thomas with the Miami Dolphins. How would you like to come back and play for Miami? How would you like to come back and play for the Dolphins?' Well, I asked him, 'How much bonus money are you going to give me?'"[4]

Most pro football players who were not regarded as superstars did not receive the million-dollar contracts that are familiar in modern NFL. Quite the opposite, in fact. For players who were undrafted free agents, as Little was, their salaries would be for even less money than the amount the rookies who were drafted received. As a result of this fact, most players had to get whatever extra money that they could acquire, usually in the form of a bonus for signing a contract. In 1967, that extra money might mean the difference between agreeing to a contract or not, and meeting their financial obligations (i.e., making ends meet) or not. There was always a certain amount of negotiation between the player and the team before signing the contract.

"Joe Thomas said, 'We're going to give you $500,'" recalled Little. "I told him, 'Well Joe, I signed with the Chargers yesterday for $750.' I honored my commitment to the Chargers. . . no doubt. Plus, I had always wanted to see the West Coast. I had never been out there before. And I signed with San Diego. I signed my rookie base salary with the Chargers for $12,500."[5]

But Little had another issue to deal with that might have

been even more worrisome to him than his first pro contract. Just because he signed on the dotted line did not mean that he was automatically a member of the team. He—like all rookies—would first have to make the team, and that would take perhaps the greatest effort that he would ever give up to this point in his young life. It would not be easy, because there were dozens of other young men competing against him for a chance to make a pro football roster. The size of those rosters in 1967 stipulated that each team could have forty active players on their team. Little would have to fight for his dream to continue, and it would begin with a process that the young lineman was not all too thrilled about. Little read in a newspaper that he was one of the free agents ordered by San Diego head coach Sid Gillman to report to training camp a week before the drafted rookies.. Regardless of what reasons Gillman might have had for that decision, it did not make much sense to Little.

"That really got to my pride," said Little. "They were rookies like I was. There was no reason for me to report a week ahead of them.[6] I didn't realize that I had to report early until I got there. I was disappointed that I wasn't drafted, and I didn't like it that I had to come into camp ahead of the drafted rookies. That was another blow to my pride, but it did give me an advantage. I had some good practices, and they did like my time in the forty-yard dash. I ran a 4.9 in full pads and at 273 pounds.[7] I was wearing a jersey, shorts, and shoulder pads. . . let's put it that way."[8]

Those forty-yard dash numbers are impressive even by today's standards. The Chargers, like football teams, tried to find the best use for the talent that they had. In Little's case, Gillman was not really sure where he would best fit in. He was indeed big enough to play somewhere on either the offensive or the defensive lines, but Gillman was both an innovator and a tinkerer. He was not above trying to do some things that were out of the norm, so to speak.

"Sid had signed me as a defensive tackle," said Little, "then he put me in at fullback. At times, during half-line scrimmages, I'd be playing offense fifteen minutes and defense fifteen minutes. I didn't want to play fullback, but I would have played anywhere else to make the team.[9] And I remember running pass patterns, and getting passes thrown at me." Sid Gillman was widely known for his intense desire to throw the football. He simply wanted to throw the ball as much as possible and to whomever was open. "I was there for one day when Joe Madro, the offensive line coach, said, 'I want you to play offensive line.'[10] He saw something in me and asked Sid to move me over."[11]

But Gillman hesitated on moving Little over to the offensive line. He was still undecided as to where his big rookie fit in best. It is not that easy for a player, regardless of how intelligent he is, or how versatile and athletic he is, to learn a whole new position in a very short amount of time. And Little was bouncing around from a defensive line position, to fullback, then back to the offensive line. It had to be a confusing mess. Gillman knew that Little possessed plenty of potential. But where could Little provide the team with the best outcomes? So, the thought process continued, at least until one day, when. . .

"I had a bad practice one day, and I was on defense," said Little. "But my defensive line coach when I went to San Diego was Bum Phillips. So, I told Bum. . . I said 'Coach, I'm not going to be able to make it. I'm going home.' He said, 'You're doing what?' I said 'Yes.' So, late that afternoon, Sid Gillman comes over to me and says, 'Listen up Big Fella. . . if you talk about going home again, I'm going to break your neck.' And that simple remark gave me all kinds of confidence. It let me know that I was going to be there some way."[12]

Despite how Little felt after he received that jolt of encouragement, he still could not help but realize that the odds for most of the rookies were slim at best. And they seemed to be getting slimmer each week, as Coach Gillman continued to bring in more players into camp. Several free agents were given tryouts practically every week in San Diego during the summer of 1967. At least one sportswriter felt that out of twenty-one free agents who came to camp, only two or three might still be around to compete against the drafted rookies. It was simply survival of the fittest for rookie and free agent alike.

But Little seemed to have carved his niche. Once he was officially moved to the offensive line in his very first pro training camp, he would never play on the defensive line or at fullback again. In fact, Little often commented that he really did not enjoy getting hit as much as fullbacks generally get hit on every play. He much preferred to do the hitting, which he would certainly get to do, while playing on the offensive line. Moreover, he learned a lot more about honing his blocking craft from assistant coach Joe Madro, who was quite a unique individual in his own right, and who had his own distinctive ways to get into Little's head.

"Joe used to stay on my back so much," remembered Little, "there were times I could have hit him. But I learned quite a bit from Joe. He had his ways, but I can laugh at it now.[13] Joe was a really good offensive line coach. He was like five-foot-five, and he wore his t-shirt on backward. And he always had something to say. I mean, he was a motormouth. And I would end up hiding from Joe during training camp, because he would always want to work me out on the field, and he would come looking for me every day and yell out 'Laaarrryyy! Laaarrryyy!' And I would be hiding somewhere in the sauna most of the time. He never did find me until I wanted to come out. By that time, I'd lost about two pounds."[14]

The evading of Coach Madro in summer camp continued, as did the hitting along the line of scrimmage. Lots and lots of hitting. These required physical exertions, mind you, were all being held at the height of the turbulent 1960s in America, when the civil rights era was in full force. There was unfair treatment of African Americans on many pro teams. Some Southern cities where games were scheduled to be played during the early part of that decade offered stiff resistance into allowing the black players on some teams to stay at the same hotels with the white players. It was an unjust mess, and nobody with a conscience could—or would—accept it. For his part, Larry Little rarely dealt with many Caucasians as he grew up in Miami.

"I never hit a white guy in my whole life until I started playing football in San Diego," Little quipped.[15]

But despite mixing it up on the gridiron with men who had a different skin color than his own, a hit was coming Little's way as the 1967 summer training camp was nearing its end. The small number of players that each team was allowed to suit up each week meant that more athletes would be cut from the team, and for most, that cutting effectively ended their dreams of playing pro football forever. Larry Little was among those who were cut by the Chargers, but only for a moment. That is because pro football teams had decided—in their infinite wisdom—to realize that forty players were just not enough to get through an entire season from a physical health perspective. So, each team was allowed to have a handful of players on a separate squad, who could be called up to the regular roster, should a member of that regular roster get traded or injured and have to be placed on an injured reserved list. That separate group of players form what is known today as a practice squad. They could practice with the regular team during the week, but on gameday, though they could be standing on the sidelines, they were not allowed to be in uniform.

In 1967, the practice squad had a different name, commonly referred to as a "taxi squad" or a "cab squad." That small group of players (usually no more than five or six men) got their unique name originally during the 1940s from Hall of Fame Cleveland Browns head coach Paul Brown, who designated several of his most promising players who did not make the team, but who were allowed to be kept as reserves. To avoid payment rules from the league, Brown used his share of local connections to provide a solution to his problem. Those reserve players were instead paid by a local taxicab company, Yellow Cab of Cleveland. They were a business whom Brown had developed a friendship with over the years. Now, keep in mind that those reserve players never actually drove any cabs. But they were allowed to stay with the team as reserves, while still making a partial wage under the guise of taxi drivers. The league eventually caught on, and because Paul Brown was so influential, they permitted each team to have a reserve list of players to remain a part of their teams, albeit not being allowed to suit up or play on Sundays. But the label of "Taxi Squad" or "Cab Squad" stuck around for many years.

That was the situation that Larry Little would find himself in at the end of the 1967 summer training camp. But despite the relief of knowing that a player has at least made the taxi squad, there also came the predictable issues of economics and the cost of living. Some places in the country were (and still are) cheaper to live in than others. Keep in mind that a vast majority of the players during Little's rookie season were not making a whole lot of money to begin with.

"At first, I did not make the regular roster," said Little. "I was cut by the Chargers, and after I cleared waivers, I was put on the taxi squad. . . or the cab squad."

Once a player is waived, a bulletin goes out to every other team in pro football, notifying them of that fact. Then any of those teams has the right to claim that player within twenty-four hours, usually for the sum of $100. If no other team decides to claim that player, then he remains the property of his original team, who can then give him his outright release, or keep him on as a member of the taxi squad.

"And when they cut you," continued Little, "they tell you to stick around for a little bit, and we'll see. Then they would negotiate, and then they called me into the office. And then they told me that they would give me $250 a week."[16]

The sum of $250 a week, even in 1967 dollars, was not much. When one considers the high cost of living in California, $250 can get spent very fast. But that was the predicament that Larry Little found himself in as he attempted to play pro football in his rookie year. He was not alone, however, as other young players who had not reached superstar status found themselves in similar circumstances. The most obvious question that revolved around Little's mind at this time dealt with how he was going to make ends meet. Fortunately for him, he had a bargaining chip upon which he could rely.

"I told them that I can't stay here in San Diego for that amount of money," declared Little. "Now some of the guys who were playing for Bethune Cookman before me were also playing in the semi-pro league called the Continental League at that time. I had like three teammates who were playing on teams in that league. So, I told the Chargers that I could go and play in the Continental League for that much money [$250/week]."[17]

The time had come for Little to do some bargaining with the San Diego management. He also had to try his luck as a poker player too. But Little was not bluffing. He was serious about using the Continental League option to get the Chargers to see things his way. In the end, it all boiled down to money. San Diego wanted to keep him on their team as a practice player. They certainly did not want to see him play for another club in the AFL or in the NFL for that matter. Both the player and the team wanted to give and get Little's services at an equitable price that both sides would be satisfied with.

Coach Gillman and the Chargers were adamant in keeping Little on the team's taxi squad, however. They were not ready by the end of summer training camp in 1967 to move him to a spot on the active roster. The team needed to somehow convince Little that spending some time on the taxi squad would be beneficial to him. From his viewpoint, Little had an open mind. But he also had to do some convincing of his own.

"I was negotiating my butt off down there," admitted Little. "So, I told them that I would stay in San Diego for three-quarters of my salary. And so, I signed to play for San Diego on the taxi squad for three-quarters of my salary. Now mind you, my salary was $12,500 [a year]. After state tax and federal income tax in San Diego, you can imagine what my final check [take home pay] was like. Especially out there in California. So, I was on the cab squad for the first four games of the regular season."[18]

As a player on the taxi (or cab) squad, Little was required to participate in all the team practices, film sessions, workouts, etc. He was expected to be as prepared as possible, just as if he was a backup player, which he was not. On game days, he was stationed on the sidelines, but not in uniform. It is the NFL's version of being in limbo. He was part of the team, but in a more real sense, he was not really an active part of the team. He was making much less money than all the other players on the team's roster.

The main goal of every reserve player in pro football is to somehow be named to the team's active roster. Once achieved, their main goal then turns to actual playing time. Larry Little's situation was similar to every taxi squad member. He had to bide his time, be as prepared as possible to play, then if his opportunity to play came about, he had to be able to succeed on the field to the point that the coaches would be satisfied enough to keep him on the team's active roster. That is exactly what happened to Little following San Diego's fourth game of the 1967 regular season, a 31-31 tie at Boston.

Pro football rosters are rarely set in stone. As a typical regular season continues, numerous changes in personnel take place. Injuries are the main cause for a team's coaching staff to remove a starting player from the list of starters. Then, to keep forty men on the active roster (in 1967), a trade for another player from another team can take place, or more often, a player from the taxi squad gets moved up to the active roster. Thus, the dreams and hopes for the athletes on the practice squad could eventually be realized. Larry Little's desire to finally get a chance to play pro football occurred through this situation, albeit with a little change in the reason why. Fellow San Diego lineman Ed Mitchell was cut from the team, and Little was promoted to the active roster to take his place.

"I recall that it was Joe Madro who informed me that I was going off the taxi squad and onto the regular roster," said Little. "He [Mitchell] came to training camp very much overweight. He wasn't my best friend on the team, but I looked up to him. He could have been a great football player if it wasn't for his weight. And he showed me a lot of things. He helped me out a lot. I was sorry to see Ed go, but I was happy about my opportunity. I was very happy. . . I was ecstatic that I would be getting a regular paycheck instead of a taxi squad paycheck. From that point on, I was determined to keep getting better and to keep playing professional football as a member of the actual roster. My jersey number was seventy-three while I was playing in San Diego."[19]

But just because Little was officially wearing a Chargers uniform on Sunday afternoons did not necessarily mean that his new situation was going to be a fair one. It was now time for him to get a taste of the micromanagement that went on in pro football.

"Well, I was already upset because the Chargers would start another guy, then put me in the lineup during a game to replace him," Little recalled. "So, I would play just enough downs to get my bonus. And I was upset. I just played in so many plays in a game. So, it was the equivalent of five [total] games. I wouldn't necessarily start in the games, but they would put me in later in the first quarter."[20]

The way that San Diego regulated Little's playing time was witnessed by many players all throughout the league. Some teams did not want certain players to receive the bonuses that they signed for, especially when those bonuses came in the form of clauses where overall playing time was concerned. Such actions were valid proof that pro football was run like many businesses and companies, where the bottom line dealt with winning and losing, but also with cost-benefit analysis. It was an eye-opening move that Larry Little got his first taste of in 1967, and it soured him to a degree that the sport had devolved into the world of checkbooks and calculators, rather than first downs and forward passes.

During his rookie season with the Chargers, Little also got another taste of something else, and his teammates' eyes were definitely opened to view his actions. Little had always enjoyed eating food ever since his childhood, and his appetite was as robust as anyone's appetite could possibly be. But as a lineman in pro football, eating had become a requisite activity for him to partake in. On his first night during training camp, he sat down amongst several of his teammates and began eating a delicious chicken dinner. He ate, and he ate, and then he ate some more. It was as if there was a perpetual vacancy sign inside his stomach. His teammates were astounded as to what they were witnessing.

"Brady Keys, who played for the Steelers, had a place," recalled Little. "Joe Beauchamp, Gene Foster, and me went there one night, and I ate two half chickens."[21]

The legend was born. Other players on the team considered watching Little eat chickens as a spectator sport in and of itself. Teammates would call their friends and invite them to come and watch him eat chickens. According to columnist Bill Braucher of the *Miami Herald*, "Little approached 300 pounds and attained a measure of fame as Chicken Little. It was reputed that he could absorb the entire daily product of Thompson's Poultry Farm in Escondido, California, where the Chargers trained."[22] Generally speaking, only Little's friends called him "Chicken" to his face, and they referred to him with that moniker only because he enjoyed eating chicken, and not because the sky was falling or because he was afraid of one thing or another.

As Little ate increasing amounts of chicken and as he grew larger, so did the Chargers' victory totals. The big rookie would play in ten regular season football games in 1967, during which time San Diego went 5-5. That season ended up in the worst possible way, however, as the Chargers lost their final four games against Oakland, Miami, Houston, and the New York Jets. The team managed to put up some impressive statistics, however.

"We had a great offensive mindset on those Chargers teams," admitted Little, "with Sid [Gillman] as our head coach. We had great players there. We had a great quarterback in John Hadl, and of course we had a great wide receiver in Lance Alworth, and a great running back in Paul Lowe. We had some great talent on that team. We had a great offensive line with Walt Sweeney, and Ron Mix, who is in the Hall of Fame. Ron and I have remained good friends to this day. I was Walt Sweeney's backup in San Diego, and one year in the Pro Bowl, Walt was my backup. He was a good one, and I learned a lot from Walt. Although we weren't winning championships in San Diego, we were still winning.[23]

"Sid was so innovative with the passing game. We threw the ball I think more in San Diego than we ran the ball. Besides Lance Alworth, we also had Gary Garrison as a wide receiver. So, Sid was an innovator. Right now, they said that a lot of teams later on did the same things that Sid was doing back in the day."[24]

Despite all the individuals who possessed outstanding abilities, San Diego as a team was outshined by the other competitive teams in the AFL. Oakland, Kansas City, Houston, and the New York Jets typically put together successful efforts, and it was those clubs who made the playoffs, not the Chargers. Yet over the many years since the late 1960s, it was the players and the coaches who are still readily remembered today. Mention the likes of Sid Gillman and Al Davis, and every football historian and every longtime fan knows their legacy to the game. Those two innovators also shared a past with each other. Moreover, both also could list paranoia as one of their least desirable behaviors.

"Al Davis was an assistant coach for Sid Gillman when the Chargers first started playing in the AFL," said Little. "When Al left to go over to the Raiders, they did not trust each other. And one day before we were going to play the Raiders, we would be on the practice field, and there was a plane that flew by kind of low. Sid Gillman would stop practice. Well, Sid thought that it might have been Al Davis, spying on us to see what we were doing. And once Sid even caught a guy up in the mountains in a tree because he thought that he [the guy in the tree] was spying on us. You see, we were practicing in a mountainous area. Sid stopped practice to go over to the guy to see who that guy was."[25]

This football version of spy versus spy has been going on for years, at all levels of the sport, from junior varsity high school teams all the way up to the NFL playoffs. Most of these stories were nothing more than rumors. Nevertheless, there were many coaches who took them seriously enough to question their legitimacy and to spend valuable time investigating these supposed antics of their foes.

The pressure to win football games is undoubtedly the root cause of whatever paranoia exists in the game. Every single person involved with a pro team acutely feels that pressure. If a player for whatever reason does not feel the pressure, usually their coaches help them to at least observe it. Sometimes threats are involved, which often include the potential loss of one's starting position on the team.

The Chargers managed to deal with the pressure and earn winning records during each of Larry Little's seasons with the team. But one day, during Little's second year with the Chargers in 1968, the pressure to win eventually got the best of both Gillman and his young offensive guard. The episode occurred during a regular team practice, when Gillman was watching members of his blockers, including Little.

"On one play, I trapped a guy real hard and I knocked him on his butt," Little described. "And then Sid said to me sarcastically, 'It's about time that you hit somebody.' I expressed my disagreement with his remark. Then the guys on the team told me that after voicing my disagreement with Coach Gillman that I was going to be sent out of San Diego. At least the veterans did. All because I had a disagreement with a coach. I never hit a coach. The veterans had been around there longer than I had been, and they knew how stuff was there."[26]

Larry Little did not do any favors for himself when he caustically disagreed with his head coach in San Diego. But he was not doing his body any favors either since his earliest days on the West Coast. It was then that Little had begun the practice of smoking cigarettes. The term "secondhand smoke" had not been invented yet, and the dangers of smoking to one's lungs and heart were not completely disclosed among the populace. Moreover, Little was joined by many players and coaches who smoked.

"I smoked cigarettes up until 2018," admitted Little in a 2022 interview. "I was smoking while I was playing. I started in my rookie year in San Diego. The veterans there were smoking, so I thought that it was a cool thing to do also. That's when I started smoking, and back then, you could smoke in the locker room. The last thing that I did when I was smoking as a player, I would be walking up to the locker room door with my helmet in one hand and a cigarette in the other, right before I ran out onto the field. We smoked in the locker room before the game, and we smoked in the locker room at halftime. In fact, some of our coaches used to bum cigarettes from me.

"In 2018, I had a health problem, and I went and quit cigarettes cold turkey. But it wasn't easy. What happened is that I had heart problems, and they gave me a patch when I was in the hospital. Later on, I was just laying in my bed one day and I said to myself, 'Larry, you know what? You don't need this patch.' So, I threw the patch away, and I never ever thought about smoking again. But like I said, there was smoking all over the locker room when I played."[27]

The rest of Little's life in San Diego also included dealing with his immediate offseason from football. Back in the 1960s and 1970s, Little noticed that the cost of living continued to rise steadily all throughout America. The only solution to making ends meet for most pro players was to get a second job, which is what Little did.

"I didn't have to get a second job in the 1970s, but I did in the 1960s," said Little. "After my first year in the AFL with the Chargers, I worked at what we called the Youth Hall down there. It was a home for delinquent youths, and those kids lived there on the property. I worked there as a counselor. Then when I went back to Miami, I taught middle school during the offseason at Homestead Middle School. I was what they call a permanent substitute. And my third offseason, I did the same thing. . . teaching at that middle school. And then I started making a little bit more money playing pro football, and I didn't have to work a second job in the offseason."[28]

Teaching young kids was not an easy job for Little, and there were moments when he had to question the various elements in the society in which his students grew up. The racial attitudes of the late 1960s and the early 1970s had managed to seep rather drastically from some of the adults down to their kids. One of those moments that sticks out in Little's mind occurred when he had to confront those racial attitudes and stereotypes in the mindset of one of his students.

"When I came back to Miami, I was teaching in Homestead, Florida," said Little. "The kids down there were lacking as far as dads were concerned. In one year, they were just beginning integration, and there was a fight almost every day between the white and the black kids. One day when I was teaching, a white kid called me 'boy.' I wanted to beat somebody upside his head and beat the hell out of anybody who would call me that. I had him up against the wall and I told him that if he ever called me 'boy' again, I would kick his butt, his daddy's butt, his brother's butt. . . anybody's butt. I tried not to use foul language."[29]

Foul language and various epithets were commonly heard during the late 1960s in America, and there appeared to be no cure for the racial anger and bitterness that pervaded the country, especially in the inner cities. One incident on April 4, 1968, was seen and felt all throughout the nation, and it was one that Larry Little vividly remembers to this very day.

"I was sitting down at a watering hole that I used to frequent in Miami, and they had some TV sets in there," said Little. "And they had a newsflash that came on TV that Martin Luther King Jr. had been killed. And I remember going home to my mom's house. . . I didn't have my own place yet in 1968. And my older brother was there at the time. And I told them that Dr. Martin Luther King had been killed. . . assassinated. It was a shock."[30]

That shock led to action a few days later, when several of the poorer sections of Miami saw sign-carrying protests, then legitimate riots, which included rock throwing, burning of buildings, and looting. Doctor King's assassination may have been the spark that ignited all those actions, but the anger among the African American communities of the city had been developing for years. The main causes were poor jobs, poor housing, and lying politicians who annually made promises to minority citizens that they were never able—or willing—to keep. Sadly, it was the violence of that era which saw the city of Miami become another location for the saga of continued poverty and distress.

Larry Little dealt with that terrible news as best he could, but he would have to feel one more shock following his second—and what would be his final—year in San Diego. It would be a shock that would change his life and his future.

CHAPTER 4

BACK TO THE OLD NEIGHBORHOOD

The San Diego Chargers were on the verge of challenging for the top spot in the Western Division of the AFL as Larry Little prepared to play his third year in pro football. The idea of staying out on the West Coast greatly appealed to him, with its temperate climate, its robust nightlife, its numerous opportunities for recreation, and its second-to-none scenery.

"I loved it out there," admitted Little. "I was planning on moving out there."[1]

Little was taken somewhat by surprise when he heard the news that disrupted his plans, however. Following his brief but explicit remark to San Diego head coach Sid Gillman during a team practice earlier during the 1968 season, Little was traded to the Miami Dolphins prior to the 1969 football season. Getting traded to another team follows no set pattern or ritual. It is a different procedure for practically every player who has ever been traded. In Little's instance, Coach Gillman was shopping him around when Joe Thomas, the general manager of the Dolphins, began to show some interest. In the not-so-distant past at this point, the Dolphins had almost signed Little as a rookie, but they came up short on offering a lesser signing bonus than what the Chargers offered him. Now it was time for Thomas to rectify that mistake.

The story of how Little landed a position back in the town of his youth involved a third party. Larry Csonka was a young fullback who had just finished his rookie season with the Dolphins. His recollection of how his future offensive guard was given a contract began when the two men had a chance meeting that was either a brush of good fortune, or a destined blessing of fate for Miami. . . whichever you believe.

"I met Larry Little at Edelin Buick in 1968, right after I suffered a concussion at the end of the 1968 season," remembered Csonka. "I was going into Edelin Buick to get a car that I had recently damaged and had repaired. There was a glass door at their establishment, and it was a shaded kind of glass door. It was a two-way door, and I was trying to push my way in, but there was a guy trying to push his way out. When I opened the door and looked up, I saw Larry Little."[2]

Sometimes, and in some unusual situations, you get a feeling about a person from the very first time that you lay eyes on that person. It is well within reason to believe that Csonka experienced one of those feelings upon seeing Little for the very first time. It was a moment where the gears in Csonka's mind instantly informed his brain that Little was going to have some important role in his life, in one way or another.

"I immediately asked him, 'Who do you play for?'" continued Csonka. "And he said, 'Well, San Diego.'"[3]

The young fullback instantaneously saw the benefit of having Little on his team. It was as if Csonka got a sudden vision of a cost-benefit analysis in his head. Adding a rather huge figure like Larry Little would equate to a lesser number of concussions that he would personally have to endure. And that was a good thing as far as Csonka was concerned.

"Then I asked him," recalled Csonka, "'Do you live here in Miami?' He said, 'Yes.' Then I asked him, 'Wouldn't you rather play here?' He said, 'Well, yes.' So, I got his name, and it's kind of funny that we jammed the door against each other at the same time."[4]

That dual door jamming was somehow meant to be. The time was now at hand for Csonka to spring into action. He knew that he had to do something about this chance meeting with Little. He had to see this fateful encounter through to one conclusion or another.

"Well, I turned around, and did not keep my appointment for the car," Csonka admitted. "I turned around and got in the car, drove the thing to 330 Biscayne Boulevard [the Miami Dolphins' front office headquarters], went up to the eighth floor, or the seventh floor, or whatever it was, to Joe Thomas's office, who was our personnel director. And I went in to see him. His secretary was trying to keep me out, we exchanged some unpleasant pleasantries, but I managed to get myself in there. I wanted to see him right then, you know, while it was still fresh in my mind."[5]

What do the red highlights indicate? I have no idea what they mean, what they pertain to, etc. I would like to know what these thick red highlights mean. "To make a long story short, I just walked into Joe's office," said Csonka. "He says, 'What can I do for you?' I said, 'I think that we should sign Larry Little.' He said, 'Yes, I'm working on trying to get him. Have you met him?' I said, 'Yes. . . I just met him at Edelin Buick in a doorway.' And then he said, 'Well how in the hell did you know that we wanted him?'"[6]

Truth be told, Larry Csonka did not have any idea that Joe Thomas was trying to sign Larry Little to the Miami roster. The mere fact had to have given Csonka some degree of optimism and proof that he did the right thing by forcing his way into Thomas's office to discuss the matter with him at this specific moment.

"He then asked me, 'Do you have any idea how well Little

blocks?'" said Csonka. "I said, 'Joe. . . look at my eye.' I had a black eye from my concussion. And there was no white in my eye. It was all red. I said, 'Look at my eye.' He said again, 'How well do you know he can block?' I said, 'I don't care how well he can block. If nothing else, I can hide behind him.' He said, 'Well I'm working on it [Little's possible contract with the Dolphins]. I'm down to the nitty gritty. We're just a few thousand dollars apart.' I said 'Joe. . . I've got a deferred signing bonus. I'll pay half.' He said, 'You'd go that far?' I said again, 'Look at my eye, Joe. I'm starting to sound like a broken record here.'"[7]

His persistence with Joe Thomas certainly proved to the general manager that Csonka knew a good thing when he saw it, and that he was determined to see the team's running game improve.

"As it turned out, Joe Thomas signed Larry Little, and they never used any of my deferred bonus or anything," concluded Csonka. "I meant what I said, and Joe Thomas. . . he laughed. And as I started to leave his office, I said, 'Joe, I'm serious about signing him.' He said, 'Well I'm serious too.' I said, 'Joe, we're on the seventh floor. Unless you can fly, you better sign him.'"[8]

It was a deal that would benefit both Csonka and Little for many years, to the point that both men ended up becoming perpetual teammates in the Pro Football Hall of Fame. For the record, Thomas traded a little-used defensive back by the name of Mack Lamb to obtain Little. In an ironic twist, Lamb was a former high school teammate of Little's at Booker T. Washington. No known evidence of a similar trade for former high school teammates has been heard of occurring before or since in the annals of pro football's storied history of player acquisitions. The trade of Little for Lamb at the time, however, was termed by several critics as "a nothing for nothing trade."[9]

In the end, the trade would make the San Diego front office

personnel look like a group of short-sighted failures, and it made
Joe Thomas look like a genius. The Chargers would soon regret the
trade. Lamb was cut by San Diego before the 1969 regular season
even began, and he would eventually go on to play pro football
in Canada. Little, on the other hand, went on to a distinguished
career with the Dolphins.

For Larry Little, the trade to Miami represented the best of
both worlds. He received a small pay raise to play for the Dolphins,
but it was a pay raise, nonetheless. And he got a chance to play
in front of his family and friends in Miami. But throughout it
all, Little was nevertheless grateful for his opportunity to play
pro football for the Chargers. The city of San Diego welcomed
him with open arms, and he returned their embrace during his
brief two years there.

"It was a good thing for me to go to San Diego," opined Little
many years later. "It helped me to grow more as a man. It was a
good turn for me because it gave me more understanding. I was
actually pretty disappointed when I was traded to Miami, because
although we never won any championships at San Diego, we still
had a pretty good football team with a fair amount of good talent.
When I got traded to Miami, it was like taking a step back. The
Dolphins weren't that good in my first year there."[10]

That feeling that the Dolphins were not that good was similar
to how many people felt about the whole AFL. The understanding
of many people during the 1960s was that the AFL was nothing
more than minor league or bush-league football. History has
proven that not to be true, but many folks had that prevailing
notion at that time. Larry Little, however, did not concur with
their beliefs. He knew that he was playing bona fide pro football
in the AFL with the Chargers.

"I was happy to be getting paid to play pro football," affirmed

Little. "It didn't affect me one way or the other playing in the AFL. I knew that San Diego was a good football team when I went out there. As long as I was getting paid, that talk didn't matter to me. When I was with the Chargers, we scrimmaged against the Saints. The Saints would train near San Diego. And we had a preseason game against the Rams. So, no. . . we weren't inferior to them."[11]

Little would soon prove to be not inferior to any offensive guard in pro football. That acclaim did not happen overnight, but it would happen. And at least one person in San Diego openly regretted the day that Little was traded to Miami. Joe Madro, the San Diego offensive line coach who drove Little crazy with his rantings and his humorous searches throughout the team facility for Little during 1967 and 1968, saw the potential for greatness that Little possessed. Madro would get a chance to meet up with his former lineman when the Chargers went out to Miami to play a game there in October of 1969. It was a meeting that Little remembers to this day.

"Joe could put them down a little bit, with the bottle," Little recalled. "When the Chargers came out to Miami to play the Dolphins [in 1969], I went to the hotel where they stayed at to see all of my old teammates before the game. I saw Joe, and Joe had a few drinks, as usual. And when Joe saw me, he started crying. He said, 'I didn't want you to go. I didn't want you to go.' He called Sid Gillman 'the old man.' He said, 'It was the old man who wanted you to go.'"[12]

While it was good to get back in touch with his buddies on the Chargers, Little knew that those days in San Diego were behind him now. His current focus was on making his new team, the Dolphins. They gave him a new jersey number. He wore number sixty-five in San Diego, but in Miami, it would be number sixty-six. The equipment manager supposedly told Little "that he would make number sixty-six famous one day."[13] Little knew that the media did not expect much from him, so he had a mindset to prove that he was worth trading for. He looked around and saw that Miami's roster was growing with accumulating talent on both sides of the line of scrimmage. But to look at their team during the 1969 season, most observers would be hard pressed to see that talent showed itself. That was probably because the head coach, a man by the name of George Wilson, was not really the type of coach that young ballplayers needed.

Most of the players on the 1969 Dolphins roster were young men. They were excellent athletes, but they lacked overall game experience. But mostly, they lacked a head coach who would drive them with persistence and with fervor. Coach Wilson, however, was the type of head coach who was not really interested in getting his players to work hard. He was not a lazy man, mind you. But he just lacked a desire—for whatever reason—to force his players to practice a whole lot in the hot Florida heat.

"I played for George Wilson in my first year at Miami," said Little. "George had previously won the NFL championship [in 1957] for the Lions when he was the head coach in Detroit. He was an old-time coach in Miami. You know on a hot day, when George was coaching us, George would say, 'Aw hell. . . go jump in the swimming pool. No practice today.' [Future Miami head coach] Don Shula would never say anything like that. I thought that George was a pretty good coach. Where he was different from Shula was in how he prepared his team. George liked to have fun. Now Shula liked to have fun also, but he was a disciplinarian, and George wasn't."[14]

The George Wilson-led Dolphins were not what you would call a very competitive team. Not by a longshot. They earned a 3-10-1 record in 1969, good enough for last place in the AFL's Eastern Division. But they did have a nucleus of great athletes.

When Little first met his new teammates as a member of the Dolphins, however, he was briefly surprised by some of their appearances.

"When I came back to Miami, they had a lot of guys who were from the south on the team," Little recalled. "I'll put it this way. . . they had a lot of white guys on the team. And all of these memories come back at you, and I'm thinking that I'm going to a Ku Klux Klan rally. I just looked at them, and they looked that way. To see them all walking together, going to lunch, chewing tobacco. But those players didn't treat me like that. And then I got to be friends with them. They welcomed me."[15]

The 1969 version of the Dolphins would have welcomed anyone of Little's caliber to their team. They were an expansion club in their fourth year in the old AFL, and like any expansion club during that era, they suffered from a seemingly requisite number of mistakes on both offense and defense. They rarely looked impressive in any of their three victories, and in some of their other games, they looked downright pitiful.

The Dolphins did show some fight and determination when Buffalo came to town on October 26, however. It was deemed "Victory Sunday" by the fans, and the game was undeniably the team's best effort on both the offensive and defensive sides of the ball all season long. Miami dominated the contest from the second quarter on, and Dolphins quarterback Bob Griese threw for 232 yards in this, the team's first win of the season. It was indeed "Victory Sunday."

Unfortunately for the Dolphins, the win over Buffalo was only repeated two more times in 1969. They lost five of their final seven games, and they were never able to develop any reasonable amount of momentum all year long.

But despite all of that, Larry Little was nevertheless glad to be back home in Miami. The familiar surroundings did wonders for him. Moreover, all his friends and family members were glad to have him back at home. They could all finally get a chance to see him play pro football in the city's stadium, the renowned 80,000-seat Orange Bowl. By the time that he joined the Dolphins, members of the black race could finally sit in any seat that they could afford at the Orange Bowl. It almost seemed as if a new era was dawning in Miami as the 1970s neared.

The sport of football might have had a lot to do with that. Increasing numbers of young boys of all races attended the games of the late 1960s and early 1970s, when admission prices were quite less than the high prices that you will see for modern NFL games. Those youngsters got to see these big players up close. It would not take them long to emulate the men that they considered to be their heroes. The addition of more and more African American players helped to turn some pro teams into winning pro teams.

Winning, however, was not on Miami's radar in 1969. One reason for their failures was injuries. While it is true that every team suffers from injuries every year, Coach Wilson saw no less than twenty-six of his forty rostered players miss at least one game or more because of injuries. That fact alone made it nearly impossible for the squad to make any headway in the AFL Eastern Division standings throughout the 1969 season. Starting quarterback Bob Griese missed the final five games of the year because of injuries, and four other Miami first stringers, including wide receiver Howard Twilley, were out for the entire year.

Larry Little himself could not avoid getting hurt in 1969. He suffered a knee injury which kept him sidelined for two games that year. All in all, it was not a banner year for staying healthy in Miami.

But a banner of another sort began flying as soon as the

1970 season beckoned. There were numerous neighborhoods in and around the city wherein Little was raised that continued to deal with abject poverty. Little had seen it and felt it during his youth. But now, as a professional athlete, he realized that he was looked upon by the kids as one man who came from Miami, and who made his young life a success. Little felt a deep connection to those youngsters, and he, along with several of his friends on the Dolphins, decided to do something that would—even in some small way—help the urban situation and perhaps leave a positive mark among the local community and its young boys. That was the original idea of coming up with the Gold Coast Summer Camp, as it was called.

"Actually, it was not my idea," explained Little in a 2022 interview. "It was an idea from one of my Miami teammates, a guy by the name of Dick Westmoreland. While we were talking about it, we wanted to do something for the community. Then Dick was traded to the Minnesota Vikings. But I had two other partners, and they were Freddie Woodson, who was a Dolphin at the time, and Rudy Barber, who was my college teammate. . . the three of us agreed that we were going to try to keep this thing going."[16]

"This thing" turned out to be a template for future sports camps for underprivileged kids in underserved neighborhoods and in troublesome inner cities. It may not have been the first summer sports camp in America, but it was unique to Miami-Dade County. The emphasis and main goals of the camp were simple. Larry Little and company wanted to keep the kids off the crime-ridden streets, even for just one week during the hot Florida summer. The camp also gave many of those youngsters in Miami a learning structure outside of school for the first time in their lives. Moreover, it offered a daily routine of discipline for many kids who desperately needed it. Many of the boys who attended the camp were the product of single-parent households, and quite a few of them grew up without a father figure in their young lives. Little, Westmoreland, Woodson, and Barber were in effect trying to fill that role for their adolescent charges.

The camp's beginnings, especially during its first year, did not have a wealth of financial backing. Little himself had to use his own funds to buy food for the kids. Nevertheless, the idea of the camp was sound, and the desire to make a difference in a bunch of kids' lives meant everything to the camp's counselors. They knew that those kids had lacked attention all their young lives, and this camp would give them some attention. . . mixed with sports.

"It's not just a football-oriented camp, but a sports-oriented camp," admitted Little in a 1974 interview. "And we also try to teach the kids discipline. We don't stand for no nonsense. Fred Woodson once caught a kid gambling, and he took him home. This year we caught a kid stealing, but we gave him another chance. I tried to show him how stealing can lead to robbery and then to much worse."[17]

But perhaps the most inspiring aspect of the Gold Coast Summer Camp involved its foundation. All during his childhood years, Larry Little astutely observed the numerous Christian examples of kindness and love that his mother, Ida Mae, had bestowed upon him, his siblings, and even to the kids of the neighborhood.

"My mom enjoyed working with kids," said Little. "She would help them put on different plays. . . Christmas plays. She liked doing stuff like that. I think that carried down to me because I enjoyed working with kids too. It was something that I was interested in for a long time. I was an underprivileged kid myself."[18]

The camp was a work in progress, where new ideas were introduced on an annual basis, many of which worked out for the benefit of the kids. It started with a basic structure, and once established, that structure remained steady for all fifteen years that the camp was held.

"When I and my partners were starting that camp, we didn't want it to be a one-day camp, where the kids would come in that day and go back home that same day," explained Little. "Our camp was five or six days in length. They would come in on a Monday and then stay until Saturday. We wanted to get them out of the environment that they were accustomed to. A lot of the kids that came to our camp had never been out of their own neighborhoods before. But once they came to our camp, they would live on a college campus, eat three square meals a day, have a snack at night, and they would meet other kids from other locations. And that was our main goal."[19]

It was a culture shock to be sure for most of the boys who participated in the camp. They had to adjust to the one-week change in their lives, but the camp itself also changed over time. Westmoreland, Woodson, and Barber were not destined to actively play pro football for too much longer. Eventually, Little was the only man left in the pro game from the original four who began the summer camp. As a result, they all agreed to rename the annual summer event the Larry Little Gold Coast Summer Camp. And it certainly helped matters that Little had long been a familiar face from the neighborhood. His name recognition, combined with the camp's positive results and evaluations, helped to annually make the camp one of the most successful of its kind in the State of Florida.

Any guarantee of success was not assured during the first year that the camp was held, however (in the summer of 1970). There were just too many intangibles involved, where the planning and the monetary funding were not what they would be in the future summers that the camp was held. The staff simply had to learn the hard way as to what they were doing, as well as the best way to go about doing things. They also made their share of mistakes. In that regard, the age-old trial and error method was constantly in play.

"The first year that we had it, we were on South Beach," remembered Little, "and we had tents for the kids. And then it happened to rain. It was intended to be a day camp for a week, before we had them stay for the nights too."[20]

A college friend of Little's who worked with the United Way was asked to see if the organization could support the camp. The United Way soon got involved by donating funds, which in turn helped the camp to grow and succeed. A major organization such as the United Way helped the camp operate in a firmer setting. But with their donations, the United Way also managed to have its say in how the camp was organized and scheduled. The old saying of "too many cooks in the kitchen" appeared to be an appropriate phrase on this occasion.

"Once the United Way got involved in it, they tried to change our format, and our bylaws, and our goals," said Little. "You see the way we had it, we would keep the kids for a whole week. One group would go home on a Saturday, and the next group would come in the following Monday. And then the United Way wanted to make it a day camp, and they wanted the kids to go back home at the end of each day. But we had no way of doing that.

"And it wasn't just a football camp. It was football, but it was also track and basketball, and swimming contests too. On the Friday nights they would put on a talent show. We would give the kids a good talk every night. And we also had guest speakers. Angelo Dundee, who was Muhammad Ali's and Sugar Ray Leonard's trainer, came out to talk to the kids, to build up their confidence and their self-esteem. And then Ferdie Pacheco, who was Muhammad Ali's doctor, also came out to talk to the kids."[21]

Anytime that a volunteer venture such as Little's camp is held
annually for more than a dozen years, one knows that someone
is doing something right. The kids who participated in the camp
were the obvious beneficiaries of all the hard work of Little and
his friends. The ages of the kids ranged from eight to fourteen,
but those age limits were not necessarily etched in stone. The kids
were not only receiving attention from adults, but they were also
having fun in the structured environment. Most of those kids
had never received that kind of care before. Sure enough, many
more kids wanted to participate than there were available spots
for them all.

"It's hard to say 'no' to a kid," said Little in a 1980 interview.
"We normally use the schools from all over Dade County, and we
try to use low-income guidelines. However, there are times when
those exact guidelines don't cover all the human needs we might
see in one youngster's case. If we feel there is a real need. . . then
we consider a little leeway on the guidelines. You know, sometimes
a youngster may not be as bad off economically as some but really
be hurting and needing some kind of parenting or need a proper
male image. We just give a little leeway to those youngsters."[22]

The focus of the camp had always been on the kids and how
their lives were affected by interacting with Little and his squad
of camp counselors during those one-week sessions. But in all
of the years that the camp was held, Little was also benefiting
from the camp. He certainly saw flashbacks of his youthful life
as he dealt with the boys in his camp, and as a result, he could
better understand their lives and at least some of the difficulties
that they faced.

"We're doing it because we enjoy it," admitted Little back
in 1980. "We enjoy working with kids, and I don't think anyone
has done it [hold a summer sports camp] as long as we've done

it. Secondly, we give kids an opportunity and we give them discipline."[23]

Anytime that you have any kind of organized activities where adolescent boys are concerned, you must impose a series of rules. For some of those kids, the Larry Little Gold Coast Summer Camp represented the first representation of any kind of rules in their young lives. Call it "tough love" or finally dealing with a dose of reality. Little and his camp coordinators were forced to address disciplinary factors that many of these youngsters sadly were deficient in learning from their earliest days.

"First, we do not condone profanity," confirmed Little. "We tell all our youngsters that by the time they're eight or nine, they've lived long enough to learn a decent word. If such a youngster is using profanity, he needs to be 'seen to' right away, and we do exactly that. Also, every youngster knows there is no stealing. If a kid steals, he's going home. If his parents can't come and get him, we'll take him home. This is made clear to them on the first day, and we rarely have a problem.

"Finally, we won't tolerate insubordination. We know, when a kid gets frustrated, he may get a little 'hyper' about certain things, and we do give him a chance to calm down. We see what kind of a kid he is, and we can deal with that. But, if he continues to be insubordinate, he's out!"[24]

The benefits for kids involved in the camp proved far and away worth their efforts to conform to the rules of the camp. This was an opportunity that many young boys in Miami were not able to take advantage of, and by word of mouth from those who did manage to attend the previous years' camps, it was an occasion and a prospect in which they also truly wanted to take part.

"One thing that we do is establish that we do things as a group," said Little back in 1980, whose camp typically had several hundred boys attend every summer. "We tell them that for one week, we are a family. They are our children for a week. We do things as a family; we eat as a family. We play as a family. And they are learning a lot more than we put into words for them. Some of them had never slept in an air-conditioned room before. They showed their appreciation every day by thanking us.

"At the end of the week they spend here, we make sure that just about each and every one of them has received an award of some kind that has been earned. We try not to let a kid go home empty-handed. I think we give away probably more awards than any other camp around. Then, we ask them if they had a good time, and they're unanimous on that. We indicate that their time in camp has been made possible by people who took their time and effort to offer them direction and show some concern about them as people. Then I tell them, 'All we ask is that some day in your lives, you give up some time and effort for somebody else.' It's a linkage, a bond each to each that we are seeking."[25]

That linkage was important to Little. He saw how many kids who attended his camp over the years got their very first taste of teamwork and camaraderie. Perhaps the most important aspect of his Gold Coast Sports Camp was the opportunity for a bunch of kids to meet so many other kids, and so many influential adults as well. In 1970, the year the camp was formed, Larry Little would get a chance to meet a specific and significant adult also, and that person would have a defining role in changing the young camp counselor's life.

CHAPTER 5

A WHOLE NEW EXPERIENCE

The Miami Dolphins were your typical pro football expansion team during their early years. They would lose more than their share of games during the last half of the 1960s. The main goal for all expansion teams back then—which consisted of mostly young players—would be to obtain some measure of experience. Under head coach George Wilson, however, on-field experience was something that did not get much exposure in Florida.

Although their first year in the old AFL was back in 1966, you can legitimately mark the origin—or the genesis—of Miami's ability to compete with the other teams in pro football. That ability was born in 1970. That is when team owner Joe Robbie decided to fire Wilson. As a replacement, Robbie hired Don Shula, the former head coach of the NFL's Baltimore Colts. Shula was a spry forty years old when Robbie hired him, and he stood out as the opposite of Wilson. Shula had led the Colts to Super Bowl III in 1968, but he had fallen out of the good graces of his former boss, Baltimore team owner Carroll Rosenbloom. There was plenty of intrigue and questionable deal making in the Dolphins' signing of Shula.

"I think that Joe Robbie was about ready to get rid of George Wilson anyway," suggested Larry Little. "There was a sports reporter for the *Miami Herald* by the name of Bill Braucher. He and Shula went to college together at John Carroll University in Ohio. And for some reason he got the word that Shula might be available. And I am told that someone told that to Joe Robbie, and that's what got the ball rolling. We knew that Shula had a winning reputation before he came to Miami. You know he had some great teams in Baltimore."[1]

The addition of Shula was not only great for the Dolphins as far as a huge increase in victories was concerned, but it was also great for Shula himself. In having Robbie as his new boss, Shula would get a chance to be his own man, and coach his own way, with no interference from Robbie. When he was in Baltimore, Shula had to regularly deal with Carroll Rosenbloom's input. That new breath of freedom that Shula would inhale would be important to developing future success in Miami.

Little was at this time keen on the fact that pro football was a business, and not just from the players' perspective. He knew that a coach who does not oversee his team winning games on a regular basis is just as quick to be on the unemployment line, indeed just as much as the players who get cut from the team for not playing well or not producing enough. George Wilson's exit was proof of that postulate.

Larry Little was hoping for his new coach to obtain more success in Miami than Wilson had achieved. To that end, the big offensive lineman decided that he would try to meet Shula and get to know him. Little wanted the relationship between himself and his new coach to begin on the right foot.

"The first time that I met him, he was having a press conference," said Little. "I drove downtown to meet him, and after the press conference was over, I went up to him and said, 'Coach Shula, my name is Larry Little, and I'm your right guard.' Now I weighed 285 pounds at the time. And that was during the time that linemen weren't as big as they are now. You know

I was big for an offensive lineman in 1970. The first thing that he asked me was, 'How much do you weigh?' He just walked off. He didn't say another word to me. I said to myself, 'Why did I come down here?'"[2]

Before Little and his teammates could prove their worth to their new head coach, however, a problem made its appearance in Miami, and in every other NFL city as well. The NFL Players Association, otherwise known as the NFLPA, decided that 1970 would be a prime year to test their solidarity in the face of the owners' stand on player pensions, disability payments, widows' benefits, and dental benefits. The strike was the first major players' strike in NFL history, and it was held just in time to have some quality training time canceled. It was not a long-lasting strike in terms of days and practices missed, mind you. But it did affect the number of practices that Shula had scheduled for his new team. To catch up to where the new head coach felt that his players should be at during this time on his performance calendar, Shula immediately proved to everyone that he was no George Wilson.

"You know that we believed in Shula," said Little, "but we didn't go to training camp until just before our first preseason game. And I thought. . . we're supposed to play a game on Saturday, so we won't be working that hard. Man, we were in for a rude awakening. We got out of the meeting on that Sunday night, and we started going over Shula's schedule. So and so time, you'll be on the field. So and so time, you'll be back on the field. So and so time, you'll be back on the field again. And again, we'll be back on the field again that evening. Then we would have a meeting after that."[3]

It was termed "four-a-days," meaning four on-field practices each day. Brutal was probably the most accurate adjective to describe it. Anyone in the know would undoubtedly call the 1970 Miami Dolphins summer training camp the toughest ever in modern pro football history. Coach Shula's training regime was derived from the time lost during the players' strike. When discussing a crash course in learning Shula's playbook, you had to start with that very first Shula training camp in the summer of 1970.

"It was no lie that he was the toughest coach to play for in the entire NFL, especially during summer training camp," admitted Little. "He also yelled at everybody. . . all the time."[4]

Miami fullback Larry Csonka realized what Shula's intentions were. Csonka knew that a big reason why the Dolphins were not competitive enough in previous years was simply because they were not tough enough themselves to deliver a stronger brand of competition to their opponents. Csonka could see that Shula intended to change all of that immediately, through the extreme rigors of his summer practice sessions.

"From the day that Shula arrived, you were asked to sacrifice," Csonka explained. "He told us that we would utilize the Florida heat, and become camel-like, to be able to go into the fourth quarter when other people [on other teams] couldn't, because they hadn't practiced four times a day in ninety-degree or above heat. Now there's two ways to look at that. You either worry about getting heat stroke, or you gun your motor and go straight up the hill. You know, damn the torpedoes. And that's what Shula's idea was. He wanted us to go full speed ahead. My response to him was, 'Well Coach, that'll work. . . if we live.'"[5]

The players who did make the team did in fact live, and most of them would regard Shula's training camp as a particular brand of hell on earth that they would never forget. Many others did their best to adjust their health status to compensate for the drills and demanding heat of Miami's sweltering temperature and humidity. To make matters even worse, Shula forbade his players to drink water or Gatorade during the practices, as he believed that the consumption of such liquids would induce cramps. The lack of fluids, however, just brought about numerous bouts of dehydration. Today's practices would never be held without the aid of liquid refreshment, but many years ago, Shula and some other football coaches across America withheld those drinks during training camp.

The bigger men, such as Larry Little, would naturally have a tougher time dealing with the stress that the camp delivered. It did not take him too long to question, at least in his own mind, the sanity and/or the reasoning behind all those practices. Little finally reached a day when he decided to do something about it.

"On the third day, it's still early in the morning, and we're in a walk-through in shorts," Little described. "Then in the evening, we're again in a walk-through and in shorts. But in between during the hottest part of the day, we were in full pads. On the third day out there, I told my roommate Freddie Woodson, who ended up being one of my best friends to this day. . . I told Woodie, 'Man, you know what? I'm not going to let this man [Shula] kill me. I'm going down tomorrow.'"[6]

To consider even briefly going down to the turf with a fake injury speaks to how truly hellish Don Shula's 1970 summer training camp was to the Miami players. To those who dared to think about such an action, they undoubtedly must have believed that their very lives were in jeopardy during those practice sessions. Every man—even the kickers and punters—sweated more than they ever sweated in their lives, to the point that they could sweat no more by the afternoon. Well, the closest facsimile of those days was ultimately being trapped in a hotbox that was twenty degrees hotter than a sauna. It is important to note that any member of the Dolphins who reached the point of falling out of a summer Don Shula practice session by fainting could not really be blamed for doing so. Larry Little had reached that mindset.

"At about 10:30 that morning," remembered Little, "it was pretty hot out there. So, about an hour into the practice, I started reeling and hit the ground like I passed out. I remember that the trainers came to me and surrounded me. They put me in an old station wagon to take me into the locker room. I'm lying on my back for an hour, watching what's going on through one eye. When I get into the locker room, they immediately start packing me in ice—and they've got an air conditioner going in there too."[7]

Little's body temperature had undoubtedly gone from overheated to chilled in a matter of minutes. It was at this time that Little was now faced with the question of how this whole scenario was going to play out. What would be the solution to the situation that he had made for himself? Could he somehow get himself out of this mess?

"And I then said to myself, 'Oh hell. . . I've got to make a Plan B now,'" recalled Little. "I decided to act like I was having hallucinations to get that ice off of me. I told the trainers to 'get all of that ice off of me now! Throw it out!' I finally came to and then they wanted to send me to the doctors. They sent me to one doctor, and he couldn't find anything wrong with me. Then they sent me to another doctor, and he couldn't find anything wrong with me either."[8]

By this time in this situation, Little's back was against a wall. He knew that the team would eventually run out of doctors and specialists to send him to see. All the while, the gears in his mind had to have been churning faster than they ever had before. How was this going to end? The worry that had pervaded his thoughts was now getting the best of him. He had to "save face" with a valid excuse for his "fainting" during practice.

"Then they finally sent me to an internist," said Little. "When I went to the internist, he looked at me, checked me all over and everything, and said to me, 'Hey Larry. . . there's nothing wrong with you. You're the healthiest human being that I've ever seen.' I told him, 'But Doc. . . you've got to find something.' He said, 'Well you do have a slight sinus problem.' Then I said, 'Well put that on the report!' So, I was fine, and I was in shorts for the rest of the week. And then that Saturday, I started the preseason game in Jacksonville, against the Steelers."[9]

You know that you are in one difficult situation in pro football if playing in the actual games is easier than going to your team's practices. But that was the position that Larry Little and the rest of his teammates were in during the summer of 1970. Those preseason games had to be a picnic compared to Don Shula's workouts. Perhaps it was Little's untimely fainting episode that convinced Shula to take things a little easier on his players. Maybe it was just the physical pounding that his men were being subjected to which led Shula to believe that he might not have enough healthy players to suit up for their preseason games. Regardless of the reasons why, Shula to his credit did eventually begin to limit the length of the practices during the 1970 preseason.

"See back in those days, we had six preseason games," said Little. "We practiced after the first preseason game, that first week of practice. I figured one more week of four-a-days, then after that, we were going to play a preseason game on the weekend. Then we went down to three practices a day, up until the last preseason game. Then we would get down to what is considered normal for a normal practice. We were more in a regular schedule for the regular season."[10]

But one thing that Shula did not do without was a specific conditioning activity, one that everyone on the team had to participate. It was a twelve-minute run that was designed to help some of the overweight players shed their extra pounds. It also tested the endurance of every man, which showed the coaching staff in no uncertain terms who wanted to make the team and more importantly, who might quit on the team when the going got tough. The run, however, was not really a true indication of how well a player would perform in an actual game. Take Larry Little, for example. He would become a very important part of Miami's offensive attack. But for all his worth, he had more than his share of difficulty with Shula's runs.

"I never made a twelve-minute run," admitted Little, "and you had to make it in a certain amount of time. It was five and a half laps around the field, and you had to do it in twelve minutes. And I always had to run it in the late morning. But we were already tired from practice by the time that I would start running it. I would have to stop and throw up when I was running it. Now I don't know what it was about that twelve-minute run that got to me, because when I was working out by myself during the offseason, I always made it with no problem. But whenever I had to make it with the team and in practice? I never made it on time. So, I had to run it early in the morning at six o'clock in order to make it. Now Shula adapted to things when he saw the need. But I knew that Shula knew that I wasn't making that run."[11]

Another aspect of Shula's practices involved another ritual that Little often had difficulty with. It was the weekly weigh-ins, a device that Shula used to determine whether a player was losing weight or gaining weight. Shula wanted Little to get down to 265 pounds, and that was a challenge that Little had to accept if he wanted to remain on the team.

"We had weigh-in every Thursday before the games," Little recalled. "And Shula would tell me how much I was required to weigh. And every Thursday I would make my weight requirement. . . except for one time. Assistant coach Carl Taseff. . . he took pride in weighing us. He went to college together with Shula, and they even played in the pros together. Carl was our running backs coach. Well one Thursday, he discovered that I was a half-pound over my required weight. And Shula said, 'So, you're a half-pound over, huh?' And I said, 'What? Coach, I'm not a half-pound over.' So, I was walking into the meeting, and Shula was walking into the meeting, and then he said, 'You know, I get tired of you guys moaning. I'm gonna get somebody else to weigh you guys in. I should turn it around and give somebody else the job of weighing you guys in.'"[12]

Despite the strenuous runs and the untimely weigh-ins, the preseason wore down to its end, and the Dolphins and all the other NFL teams had to cut their rosters down to forty active players. Larry Little managed to get his weight down to a manageable 265 pounds during the 1970 training camp. He also remained on the active roster, mainly because he was able to show Don Shula and the rest of the coaching staff his worth as a blocker for the Miami rushing attack. The Dolphins ended that first preseason under Shula with a record of 4-2. Somewhat surprisingly, they played all their exhibition games in the State of Florida, as they participated in two away games in cities that did not have NFL franchises yet, Tampa and Jacksonville.

Regardless of the state where Shula's team practiced or played, one of his assistant coaches whom Little wanted to impress the most was the team's new offensive line coach, Monte Clark. Whenever a new head coach is named, he typically gets the right to bring in his own assistant coaches. Shula realized the abilities of Monte Clark, whom he hired in April of 1970, following glowing recommendations from Cleveland Browns head coach Blanton Collier and San Francisco 49ers head coach Dick Nolan. As it turned out, the hiring of Clark—who previously played as an offensive tackle for the Browns—proved to be one of the most important decisions that Shula made during his early career in Miami. The Dolphins offensive line would never be the same again, because Clark helped to transform it into one of the greatest offensive lines in pro football history.

"Monte Clark was the best offensive line coach ever," affirmed Little. "He was the one who got the best out of me. You know that everyone on our offensive line were all castaways from other teams. We all came from other teams that didn't want us. We possibly became the best offensive line that ever played the game. I'm going to say the best.

"Monte was really strict on blocking technique. He helped to fine tune the way I played guard in the NFL. Doing things the right way. You know, basic stuff. . . like making sure your feet were in the right place in order to keep your balance while blocking. Making sure that your technique was right. Yeah, he was the one who got the best out of all of us on the offensive line."[13]

Aside from Little's obvious allegiance to his team, his teammates, and his new offensive line coach, this was a group of men who were put together from the ground up with hardly any fanfare, and that was fine with the likes of Shula and Clark. They were one of the youngest teams in the league, averaging twenty-five years of age. They wanted to play the surprise role when they went up against supposedly stronger teams during the 1970 season. Unfortunately for the Dolphins, it was they who were surprised in the regular season opener at Cambridge, Massachusetts. There, they would go up against the upstart Boston Patriots, a team comprised of even younger players than those on Shula's roster. The Patriots' defensive line managed to blow through Miami's blockers to the tune of eight quarterback sacks. The Dolphins suffered a 27-14 defeat, proving that preseason games and preseason won-loss records had little significance to what a team was able to accomplish during the regular season.

"That was Monte Clark's first regular season game as our line coach," remembered Little. "Giving up all of those sacks. . . it was so bad, that Monte's blood pressure went up. I think that they were about to take him to the hospital after that game, because his blood pressure was so high."[14]

Fortunately for Clark, his blood pressure eventually lowered to normal levels, and the players on his offensive line gave him a reason to feel healthier. Blockers like Larry Little, Doug Crusan, Norm Evans, Wayne Moore, Bob Kuechenberg, Jim Langer, Howard Kindig, and Bob DeMarco had what for most of them was one of the best seasons of their lives, up to that point, in 1970. Langer is a member of the Pro Football Hall of Fame, right alongside Little. Many people feel that Kuechenberg deserves that honor as well. Collectively, they all added to Miami's offensive strength.

"Both Wayne Moore and Norm Evans were mostly technicians out there," asserted Little. "Norm had great technique. Wayne had bad knees, but he gutted it through even with his bad knees. Both Bob Kuechenberg and Jim Langer were tough as nails. Bob DeMarco and Doug Crusan were a couple of smart veterans, both of whom eventually became quality backup players when younger players won starting jobs on the team. DeMarco eventually was traded to Cleveland when Langer took his place as our starting center. Langer was the best center in the game as far as I'm concerned. Howard Kindig was basically a long snapper, and he was an excellent long snapper."[15]

Coach Clark simplified the blocking assignments and the blocking techniques for all these players. The new strategies helped to take advantage of each athlete's best assets, and the results were hard to ignore. After the loss to the Patriots, Miami's offense began improving on a weekly basis, and their victories increased as well. The 1970 Dolphins owned a 4-1 record by October 24.

When Miami came home to the Orange Bowl after their opening game, the playing surface was changed from natural grass to Poly-Turf, which was a special brand of artificial turf manufactured by a company called American Biltrite. During the 1970s, more than half of the pro teams—and many of the nation's college teams—had altered their playing fields to some brand of artificial turf. Some stadiums had Poly-Turf, some had Tartan Turf, and still others had AstroTurf. Yes, all the fake green fields looked nice, and they looked clean. The players would end the games without any mud or grass stains on their uniforms. Moreover, the players—especially the running backs and the wide receivers—would have more traction on the artificial surfaces than they would on natural grass fields. NFL Commissioner Pete Rozelle made no secret of the fact that he greatly approved of additional artificial playing fields throughout the league. But if you asked 99 percent of the players in the game, minus the placekickers, they would all come up with a much different opinion than that of Commissioner Rozelle's.

"There were no good artificial turf fields in pro football when I was playing," declared Little. "None. They were all bad. It was like running on concrete. And the artificial turf that we had at the Orange Bowl, when it got hot, it was slippery. And when it rained, it was slippery.[16] It was as hard as a rock, and it would scratch you up. Plus, playing on that turf in Miami, it was like twenty degrees warmer than playing on natural grass. Now when they started to improve artificial turf fields, you could move faster on those turf fields than you could on natural grass. But I would rather play on natural grass. . . I'll make that short."[17]

Regardless of what surface they played on, Shula expected his players to deliver their best efforts in every practice and in every game. No excuses were tolerable. Shula expected results. He expected success. He demanded success. He was a volatile man who would never be described as "soft" on anything. Most importantly, he wanted his team to develop that same persona on the field. Shula tried his best to form a team into a dynasty. He wanted his Dolphins team to change history in Miami.

According to Larry Little, that was a goal that Shula eventually would achieve, and he would use any method possible to do so.

"The addition of Don Shula was the main reason why we were able to start a dynasty in Miami," Little said in a 2022 interview. "There's no doubt about that. I'll tell you what else he did. He had us taking advantage of the Miami heat. We switched sidelines at the Orange Bowl. We would now be on the sidelines where the shade showed up for half of the game, and the other team would be on the sunny side of the field. They would be in the heat of the day more than us so we would get that advantage. He wanted our opponents to deal with that hot sun all game long."[18]

Little soon discovered that Monte Clark was also a man of similar means as Shula. Clark was tough and demanding, and like Shula, he was not one to accept excuses. But Clark was also a teacher of his craft of blocking. He did whatever he could to get his points across to his offensive linemen. He wanted them to succeed.

"Monte had a way of having you to believe in yourself," Little said. "The belief that you could get it done. We took a lot of pride in ourselves as a unit. I'll always remember that every time that we broke the huddle before a game started and warming up, we would say to each other 'The Best in the Business.' And that was the kind of pride that Monte instilled in us."[19]

Clark delved deep into the many nuances of quality offensive line play to bring out that sense of pride in his blockers. He took what worked for him as a former player and delivered similar techniques to his young linemen. The activities of conversing with each other along the line of scrimmage, mixed with efficient film study of their opponents, were daily occurrences for Little and his mates.

"We were great at communicating with each other on the offensive line," commented Little. "We had our secret calls that we would make, so that none of the other teams could pick them up. For instance, when we would snap the ball on the first sound we would go to the line of scrimmage, and I would confirm the count with Jim Langer. He would say 'A.' I knew that was the first sound. If it was 'B,' I knew that was the second sound. No defense ever picked up on that. Also, there was a third sound for the snap count. If it was one, then we used a color, which was red. If it was two, it was white. And if it was three, it was blue. Red, white, and blue. It sounds simple, but it worked."[20]

Once the members of the offensive line showed that they could mesh well with each other and coordinate their efforts good enough to establish their strength on Sunday afternoons, the team started seeing positive results. Every man along that line would credit Monte Clark with providing the changes that brought about the successes.

"That was Monte Clark being Monte Clark," said Little. "He had us really study our opponents. Find out what their best move was, then try to take that best move of theirs away from them. And then in practice, I would have [Miami defensive tackle] Manny Fernandez go over and simulate the moves that the guy who I would be playing in front of the next week, and he would face me with tactics they liked to use, to get me prepared for the game on Sunday.

"But what I worked on mainly was setting up quick. Not necessarily my footwork in pass blocking. I felt that if I could set up quick, I could always counteract what the guy in front of me was doing. If I could set up quick enough and deep enough, when we were playing against teams that liked to run stunts and games, like an end-tackle game or a tackle-tackle game, I could read it while it was happening. So, I wouldn't let them catch me by surprise."[21]*

By being ready for any of his opponents' moves, Larry Little's weekly improvement in his abilities to ward off a defensive tackle or a defensive end was important for the overall improvement of the Miami offense. For Little, that meant spending the time needed to improve on every aspect of his tasks. Ask any Hall of Famer what it takes to make it to the Hall of Fame, and it is almost a guarantee that he will respond with something to the tune of "it takes the willingness to work hard and the desire to sacrifice all of your efforts toward the goal of success." Most of the men who ever make it in the pro ranks will also comment in a similar manner when it comes to advancing to the pros from the college ranks. Little was no different. He did whatever he could to stand out as a superlative blocker. His techniques and his study habits were all part and parcel of those efforts.

Little needed all his abilities in the early 1970s to handle a unique move that defensive linemen had in their bag of tricks which aided their efforts to get to the opposing quarterback. They would not use it on every play, but they would use it regularly, especially if it resulted in a successful pass rush. That move was simply called, the head slap. It occurred when a defensive lineman took one of his open palms and whacked the side of a blocker's head, hence the name head slap. It was outlawed in 1976, as it was deemed too dangerous, as it often resulted in concussions.

"Well, what I did when I studied film of my opponent," explained Little, "was that I studied to see when he liked to use the head slap, especially on passing situations. I was watching to see what hand he would use. He would typically use the hand that was not down. If he was in a three-point stance, the hand of

---

* Author's Note: A stunt is a name given for defensive linemen crisscrossing their pass rushing lanes to confuse the blocking assignments of the opposing offensive linemen.

his that wasn't down on the ground was the one that he would use the head slap with. So, what I would do, when I knew that he was going to use the head slap, I would block that head slap with my opposite arm. And I would hit him in the gut as hard as I could, with my other fist. You would hear him go 'Ugghh!'"[22]

Larry Little quickly became a student of the game, even more so than he had ever been before Monte Clark introduced a wealth of vital knowledge to him, and to his credit, Little was a sponge. He just soaked up all that basic and advanced information, then he used it for his benefit on his opponents.

"As long as you have good body position, you can be a good blocker," Little concluded. "I just concentrated on basically just doing my job. I figured that if I could do my job, and do it right, then everything would fall into place. I was one of the fastest guards in the league at the time. Being big and quick were two keys toward being a good offensive guard back then. Because there was more pulling back then in those days, than there is now.* Well, what happened then was that we were not able to use our hands like they do today. It wasn't until 1978 that we could actually extend our arms while blocking. Before then, we weren't allowed to grab the defensive lineman's shoulder pads with our hands like they can today."[23]

Regardless of what blocking techniques he was being taught, Larry Little was now, in 1970, seeing firsthand how he and his team were improving. He realized that fate had brought him to Miami to play for Shula and Clark. It was here where he was destined to become the type of football player that he always wanted to be. Being a member of the Dolphins in 1970 was what you might call being in the right place at the right time.

---

* Author's Note: Pulling denoted an offensive lineman leaving his stance along the line of scrimmage, running behind the line, then leading interference for the ballcarrier up field.

"At this point, I'm feeling that this is where I'm supposed to be," surmised Little. "This is better than being in San Diego. I was able to be around my family by playing in Miami. You know my mom didn't really have a chance to see me play a lot when I was growing up or in college. She didn't have an automobile then to drive to Daytona Beach to see me play when I was playing at Bethune."[24]

Larry Little had finally reached a point of security in his life. No, he was not making a superstar salary. In fact, he was only making $17,500. But he was back home in familiar surroundings, and he was an important member of a winning team. Just at that midway point of the 1970 season, however, the winning came to a screeching halt. The Dolphins would fall to 4-4, as they lost three games in a row in the middle of the 1970 season. They were all debilitating losses. First, they were wiped out by the Cleveland Browns in the Orange Bowl, 28-0. Things got worse the next week. Miami paid a visit to Coach Shula's old stomping grounds in Baltimore. The Colts welcomed their old coach back with a 35-0 butt whooping. Two straight games, and two straight shutout losses. But the losing was still not over.

On November 8, 1970, the Dolphins lost to the Eagles in Philadelphia, 24-17. Yes, they finally scored some points to break their string of being shutout. But they lost to the lowly Eagles, a last-place team that was 0-7 going into their game against Miami. To say that the Dolphins and Shula were embarrassed was an understatement. At this time in their schedule, Shula could have berated his players, and he could have delivered an angry tirade in the team's meeting rooms. But Shula had a sense about him that told him that his players were feeling the dejection and the embarrassment of their losses just as much as he was. So, the head coach chose another approach.

"Shula tried to keep us motivated during our losing streak in 1970," Little remembered. "He tried to keep us focused on the positives. But he also talked about the negatives too, even when we won. He would find something negative to talk about, even if you won big. . . he would find some negatives to talk about. But he was always basically on an even keel though. If we won, you know we were great. If we lost, he would always be mad at the meetings. Shula wasn't going to let us feel sorry for ourselves, even though we went ten quarters without scoring a point during our losing streak. We got shut out by Cleveland and Baltimore, and we went the first half in Philadelphia without scoring. But he would not let us feel sorry for ourselves, and he told us that if we kept working hard, we could turn things around. But on the field, he could be on one side of the field, and you could be doing something on the other side of the field, and he would notice it, and then you would hear him yelling at you."[25]

Everyone would notice the tone of Shula's voice from time to time if they were around the Dolphins practices and games of that season. Some games indeed had to gnaw at Shula quite a bit, in particular their three straight losses in 1970. Shula probably felt the most upset, however, after his new team lost to his old team. That 35-0 spanking that his Dolphins received from the Colts was something that Shula never wanted to see happen again. And it did not, at least not anymore in that season. Baltimore would be making a visit to Miami to play the Dolphins in the Orange Bowl two weeks later, and Shula made sure that his players were ready for that contest. Shula wanted some payback. To get Shula off their backs, the Dolphins players did too.

"Coach Shula really wanted to beat Baltimore," explained Little. "He had it in the back of his mind as a revenge factor to beat Baltimore. Baltimore was our rival, because of Shula. We were in a big slump that year, but even after those three straight losses, we still felt that we were a good football team. We did have talented men who were determined to win. We didn't feel like we were not good enough. Instead, we kept a positive attitude. Shula made sure that we kept a positive attitude."[26]

The Dolphins faced the Colts in the rematch between these two American Football Conference (AFC) Eastern Division teams on November 22, 1970. This time, however, the game was played at the Orange Bowl, and that home field advantage proved to make a big difference. Miami took a 31-10 lead into the fourth quarter and coasted to a 34-17 victory. It was the Dolphins' second straight win, after besting the Saints the previous week, 21-10.

The Dolphins won their final six games to close out the 1970s regular season. For his part, Little knew that he was being relied upon to deliver key blocks during that victory streak. This was especially true while Miami was running the ball on the ground.

"I would say that I was better at run blocking than at pass blocking," Little assessed. "We were more of a strong side running team because they always ran behind me. . . at least 85 percent of the time.* We had one of the best blocking tight ends that has ever played the game in Marv Fleming. We ran sweeps to the strong side, with Marv blocking."[27]

Miami would advance to the AFC Divisional Playoffs in 1970. Their opponents in the postseason would be the AFC Western Division Champion Oakland Raiders, a team that the Dolphins had defeated in the third week of the season at the Orange Bowl, 20-13. But this playoff contest would be held in Oakland, and both teams would have a tough time dealing with the weather and the field conditions at the Oakland Coliseum. A downpour of rain occurred before the game, leaving the field a muddy mess. It was a quagmire, actually. Players from both

---

* Author's Note: The strong side denotes the side of the offensive line where the tight end lines up at.

teams were slipping and sliding all over the place, and by halftime practically everyone on the field was wearing brown uniforms due to the immense amount of mud. Many years later, Larry Little reflected on that game.

"I believe that my most memorable game from that 1970 season had to be that playoff game against the Raiders on that muddy, muddy field," Little said. "There had been rumors that in order to slow our wide receiver Paul Warfield down, that [Oakland owner] Al Davis had his field crew use a water hose to water down the field. That field was wet. Your feet sunk so far down on it. On one play, I had to do a trap block on [Oakland defensive end] Ben Davidson, and when I trapped Ben, he went backward. . . on his keister."[28]

Little certainly did his part in this contest with the Raiders. He kept savvy Oakland defensive tackle Tom Keating far away from Dolphins quarterback Bob Griese all afternoon. Miami just made too many mistakes which inevitably cost them the game, and which cost them a chance to move forward in the playoffs. Griese threw a third-quarter pass that was intercepted by Oakland defensive back Willie Brown, who returned the ball fifty yards for a touchdown. Then Dolphins cornerback Curtis Johnson was burned by Raiders wide receiver Rod Sherman for an eighty-two-yard score which produced the winning points. Oakland defeated the Dolphins, 21-14, thus ending Miami's 1970 season.

"Well, we knew that we had a better football team than the Raiders," proclaimed Little. "But Oakland beat us."[29]

Despite the loss to the Raiders in the playoffs, Little and his teammates had come a long way in their first year under the tutelage of Don Shula and Monte Clark. They were naturally disheartened by coming so far to the cusp of the conference championship game, only to fall just one step short of that lofty position. Little would be quoted as saying after that game that "we should have beaten them even on the floor of the ocean."[30] But Shula was not going to allow his players to focus on defeat in the locker room after the loss to Oakland.

"I can't rightly recall offhand what Coach Shula said to us after we lost to Oakland," said Little, "but I still think that it was something positive. Shula had a knack in having us believe in ourselves, where we could do anything that we wanted to do. Where we could beat anybody that we wanted to beat. You know we never felt good losing a game, but there were still seeds on the field for us to grow on. There was still a strong feeling of optimism in our locker room."[31]

Miami's optimistic growth would come fast, and it would be greater than any of the players thought could so rapidly be attained. The 1970 season had seen this young team succeed to the point of going to the playoffs for the first time in the franchise's history. The Dolphins went from a lowly 3-10-1 record in 1969 under George Wilson as their head coach to a robust 10-4 record in 1970 under Don Shula. The 1971 season, however, would see them go much farther than that.

CHAPTER 6

GOING TO THE BIG DANCE

The year of 1971 would be one of the most important seasons in Miami Dolphins' history. It would also be very important to Larry Little. The big guard worked hard all spring and summer to keep his weight down to the 265-pound limit that head coach Don Shula required. That was a job in and of itself, with all the sweating, straining, running, and dieting that one could imagine for several straight months. He was as lean as he had been in several years, and he was ready for the 1971 season to begin. Little was also ready to discuss his salary with Miami general manager Joe Thomas, because he felt that he was worth at least a decent pay raise, if not a hefty one.

"My first contract with the Dolphins was $17,500, or something like that," Little remembered. "If I was playing today, I would be getting $17,500 a minute. So, I went to see Joe Thomas. I said to him, 'Joe, I started last year, and I want to get a raise, to $20,000 a year.' And Joe's office was on the eleventh floor of an office building in downtown Miami."[1*]

Now it was the job of all general managers across the league to make money for their team's owner. To do that, Joe Thomas was the guy in charge of shelling out the money to the players.

---

*   Author's Note: Joe Thomas apparently had his office moved from the seventh floor, where Larry Csonka claimed that his office was in Chapter 4 of this book, to the eleventh floor.

The less money that he gave to the players in the forms of their annual contracts and their bonuses, the more money would be left over to go into the owner's wallet. So, in all actuality, Thomas was as much of an accountant as he was a football talent evaluator. Keep in mind that this was before the age of the NFL's salary caps, where today's general managers have a certain amount that they are allowed to spend, and no more. Thomas had to be able to discern what a player was worth, what the team would be willing to pay for his services, what free agent players to sign to the Dolphins, what players to draft coming out of college every year. . . indeed, Thomas needed to wear a lot of different hats to do his job successfully.

His meeting with Larry Little in the spring prior to the 1971 season was not uncommon. There were many players each year who would try to get a pay raise from him. There were also times where a player might speak to Thomas through his own agent. Thomas—indeed all general managers—had to be great communicators, great listeners, and great at evaluating the goals of the team and all its players. In short, a pro football general manager was not an easy occupation.

But Thomas was prepared to confront Little when the two men met to discuss Little's salary. He probably realized that Little was deserving of more funds, but he nevertheless had to toe the company line, and represent the team owner, Joe Robbie, first and foremost. Little continues the story:

"And Joe said, 'Before I would give you $20,000, Larry, I would jump out of this eleventh floor window," Little recalled. "And then I said, 'Well Joe, then you better get some wings.'"[2]

It was not uncommon for players to describe in detail their meetings with Joe Thomas to each other, to help each other with their future discussions with the general manager. It was all part of the teamwork that helps players bond with each other.

"I started to see the business aspects of pro football better during the time that I tried to negotiate my contract with Joe Thomas," Little explained. "I wasn't making that much money in San Diego, only $14,000 a year when I was traded to Miami in 1969. Now, it's important for me to say that the business side of the sport did not take away from my enjoyment in playing pro football, because I was still playing the game that I loved."[3]

Little was playing his favorite game well enough, apparently. Thomas eventually relented and gave in to Little's demands. The big offensive guard would now be making $20,000 a year as his base salary with Miami. It was the most money that he had ever made playing pro football, at least up to that time. Besides the increase in money came the word from the NFL Players Association (NFLPA) that Little was named the outstanding offensive lineman in the AFC for his exemplary work in the trenches in 1970. Anytime that your peers, and especially your opponents, vote for you as the best in your position, you know that you have accomplished something great. Larry Little was entering the category of greatness as far as his own productivity as a guard was concerned.

"Larry took a giant stride forward last year. . . when he was recognized by the players," remarked Don Shula after the 1970 season. "It's a tremendous honor. After that, you had to know more and more people were aware of his ability. Larry's been consistent. I think he wants to be one of the really good guards in football. He's got everything you look for."[4]

Little had thus convinced his head coach of his worth to the team. And with his new contract now behind him, Little was set to focus his attention on the 1971 season.

The Dolphins' overall focus on that year was to naturally improve upon what they accomplished in 1970. Their summer training camp was once again another episode of extremely hard work in the hot and relentless Florida sun. No, it did not involve the four practices per day that were seen during the first week of the strike-shortened 1970 training camp, but it was rigorous, nonetheless. The previous year's training camp may have been a shock to most of the players, but in 1971, most of the players were ready for it. They now knew what to expect from Shula, and because Shula was Shula, he naturally expected more from his men. That extra effort is what is usually credited as the key to making good athletes and good teams great ones. That was certainly Shula's mindset all throughout the 1971 summer training camp at Biscayne College.

But just prior to that season's camp, Larry Little had some other business to do at Biscayne College. For the second straight year, his Gold Coast Summer Camp was held, and it was quickly becoming a major event for a lot of young boys in the Miami area. This year, however, Little was going to get some help with the camp. Some big-time help.

"Coach Shula came out to visit our camp one day that summer and he saw what was going on," remembered Little. "He then told Joe Robbie about it. As soon as he did, the Dolphins organization became involved with it. Joe Robbie started footing the bill for it."[5]

Robbie's generosity and benevolence toward those youngsters, all of whom were a world's distance from the Dolphins owner as far as affluence and wealth was concerned, was certainly inspiring for anyone involved with the camp. The kids in the Gold Coast Summer Camp were now able to benefit from the organization's stronger foundation, improved equipment and facilities, and increased popularity. Several hundred young boys attended the camp in 1971, and that number would grow exponentially almost every year. Larry Little's efforts with the camp earned him the type of recognition that he had never had before. In less than two years, Little was named a finalist for the NFL's prestigious Man of the Year award. He also would by season's end receive an honorary degree from Biscayne College, that of a Doctor of Science and Human Relations.

"It is a great honor," affirmed Dr. Little back in the spring of 1972. "First of all, you don't find too many guys my age [twenty-six at that time] receiving an honorary doctorate. And secondly, it's odd for a professional football player to receive such a degree."[6]

The honors would continue to roll in for Little. By the end of the 1971 season, he would be named by his peers for the second straight year as the outstanding offensive lineman in the AFC. He also was named to the All-Pro squad by the Pro Football Writers of America (PFWA), *The Associated Press*, by the staff and writers at *Pro Football Weekly*, and from the folks at *The Sporting News*. It was indeed an abundance of positive attention that Little may never had thought possible—and he probably never even dared to dream about—when he was a kid struggling to get on the football field at Booker T. Washington high school.

"I've got more awards this offseason than I've gotten all together in my life," claimed Little after the 1971 season.[7]

But all would not be good news for Little in the summer of 1971, however. Little would be hit with disheartening information about one of his family members in the midst of all of the excitement and expectations of the Miami Dolphins summer training camp at Biscayne College. It was the type of story that would be heard practically every day in the Miami neighborhood where he was raised. Only now, it would involve one of his own family.

"I was in training camp," Little stated, "and what happened was, my older brother George was so smart, that I think he may have outsmarted himself. He became a drug dealer. But he had a regular job back then too. He just wanted to make some extra money, that's all. And then he became a drug user, and he got hooked on heroine. He ended up living in this sleazy hotel in Florida. I was playing professional football at the time. And I would go to see him, and I would see his drugs on his bureau, and I would take them from him. And he would beg me to give them back to him."[8]

The basic lines of right and wrong, good and bad, get blurred somewhat and are difficult to discern when you are talking about a member of your own family. You hear them pleading with you about how things are going to change, and how they are turning over a new leaf. They just need a little bit of help. . . that's all. They just need a little bit of understanding, and because you are in a better situation than they are currently in, either financially, or mentally, or whatever, you do what you can to help your family member. It is a story that has affected millions of families in America. Unfortunately, the story does not always have a positive message or conclusion. The lessons do not always get learned until it is too late. Sometimes, family members can only do so much to help.

"And I just said one day," remembered Little, "while he was begging me to give his drugs back to him. . . I just said, 'The hell with it.' And I just threw them down on the floor and walked out. And he grabbed them and ran down the hallway. I didn't give it no mind. I just left. And then one day, he had gotten so bad, I picked him up and drove him around and talked to him. And he would be hallucinating. He would say that people were watching him. It was a very sad case. Unfortunately, he didn't have a happy ending."[9]

Little knew there was a reason why authorities and adults from all walks of life try to explain to young kids why they should not open the door to drugs. Many older people have seen what can happen to those who are younger who allow themselves to partake in drugs. Bad news is often the result. Little has seen newspapers filled with tempered stories of people who have sadly met their ultimate—and usually premature—demise, when they were involved in some way with drugs. His family also could sadly not escape that reality in the summer of 1971.

"My brother George was killed on his thirtieth birthday, on July 29, 1971," Little remembered. "The day after he was killed, I was on the practice field. And our equipment manager, Danny Dowd, was a former policeman. So, the cops would come out and hang out during training camp with Danny. Well, the cops came out that day, and they said that they needed to talk to Larry Little. I walked over to them after practice, and they asked me, 'Do you have a brother named Frank Henry Little?' I said 'No. . . but I have a brother named George Franklin Little.' One of the cops then said, 'I believe that he was killed last night.'

"Every Thursday, we would have the night off, and I would go over to my mom's house. Well, I went over there, and my mom asked me if she had heard from my brother. He had called her earlier and told her not to forget his birthday the next day. And that was the day he was killed, and my momma had just started a new job."[10]

The circumstances surrounding George Little's death were not unusual for the times. George Little unfortunately became another statistic. He was another young African American man who was caught in the wrong place at the wrong time.

"The cops said that he was stealing a carton of cigarettes from out of a store," said Little. "The store owner just shot him in the street as he was trying to get away." Little having been in a similar situation himself while in college, at the end of someone's scope, it was a terrifying reality to relive. "The store owner was found not guilty. Yeah, it was a sad story. And the other thing that got me too was when I took my mom to go to the morgue after football practice was over, to identify his body, I wouldn't let my mom go in. I told my mother, 'Mother, I'm not gonna let you go in. I'm going in.' So I went into the morgue, and they pulled out the slab, and it was George. I said, 'That's my brother.' So that took a lot out of my mom. He was the second oldest in the family."[11]

That traumatic experience would naturally hit everyone in the Little family hard. Losing a person with so much talent, ability, and intelligence as George Little was a disheartening reminder of how drugs can adversely affect everyone. . . even the brightest of people. The shock of losing his brother was at the forefront of Larry Little's thoughts during the summer of 1971, but he knew that he had a separate outlet for his thoughts, and he was wise to use that outlet.

"You know to keep my mind from being on my brother's death so much," Little remarked, "I continued to go to practice. I kept my mind on playing football. We even had a scrimmage on that Saturday that I participated in. All because I didn't want to keep my mind on what happened to him."[12]

Perhaps it was best for Larry Little to focus on football. His head coach, Don Shula, practically demanded it, and not just from his star offensive guard, but from everyone on the team. Shula knew that he could not control the timing of tragedies. The only thing that he could control was keeping his players in a state of mind where hard work was their main priority. Shula was great at that. He was a disciplinarian of the highest and most indignant quality, to be sure. Yes, the price to perform during those Miami summers was high, in the form of physical and mental strain. But so too was the price of not satisfying the head coach. That price could—and for many players in summer training camp did—result in being cut by the team. Little was not going to slack off one bit in the wake of his brother's death. In fact, that solemn tragedy may have inspired number sixty-six to work even harder to honor his late brother.

In retrospect, and now over fifty years since his brother's death, Larry Little's Gold Coast Summer Camp also uniquely and somewhat unexpectedly served him in the process of overcoming that shocking and painful loss of his brother. By focusing his spare attention on a bunch of young kids each summer, Little was accomplishing a couple of things.

First, he reconnected with his home community in a unique way every year, by helping the local boys stay off the crime-ridden streets, even if for only a week. Second, he was disseminating valuable information to those kids, in the hopes that at least some of them would eventually develop an appreciation for the hard work and the discipline that they observed in Little and in the other camp counselors. Little could not keep his brother from the scourge of drugs and the violence of the streets, but perhaps his annual efforts with his summer camp could plant some seeds of hope in the minds of these youngsters. Maybe those seeds could one day grow in them for their positive and promising futures.

The immediate future of the 1971 Miami Dolphins regular season began on the road in Denver, Colorado. The Dolphins on paper were a better team than the Broncos. On the field, however, Miami did what a lot of favored teams seem to do to this very day. . . they played down to the level of their opponents. Their lackluster performance permitted Denver to stay in the game, which belonged to the Broncos all the way into the fourth quarter. Then, just when it appeared as if Miami was going to lose another opening game, the offense clicked. Dolphins quarterback Bob Griese managed to see his best wide receiver, the future Hall of Famer Paul Warfield, sprinting toward the Denver end zone on a slant pattern with just over two minutes remaining in the contest. Griese hit Warfield with the ball right in the pass receiver's hands from thirty-one yards out. Warfield then eluded a diving attempt at a tackle by Broncos' safety George Saimes and sprinted into the end zone for a touchdown. Miami escaped the Rocky Mountain State with a 10-10 tie.

"What I remember about that season opener at Denver," extolled Little, "was that I had been to Denver before when I played for the Chargers. They had that high altitude out there, and everyone breathed heavy out there. I remember Denver coach Lou Saban telling the press after we ended up with a 10-10 tie game that 'A half a loaf is better than none.'"[13]

Shula's attitude after the season opener in Denver could not have been a good one. His team was out gained in yardage by a club that was considered a lower-echelon team. Indeed, Denver would go on to win only four games in 1971. But Shula had been through all this before. Despite the tie with the Broncos, he knew that he had a good team, and he realized that it would take time until they started to develop consistency and momentum. The Dolphins would indeed be tested somewhat during the first month of the 1971 season. Miami would shuffle up to Buffalo in the second week, and they managed to attain their first win of the season over the Bills, 29-14. The following week, however, the Dolphins lost their home opener to the New York Jets, 14-10. A key error by Miami's punt return unit in the fourth quarter resulted in a big turnover, which led to New York's winning touchdown. Despite their 1-1-1 record, Shula kept his team on an even keel.

"Shula never let us get down on ourselves," remembered Little. "We believed in him, but I know that he believed in us too, because he knew that the talent was in us. We knew that he was a winning coach when he came to the team."[14]

The winning was soon to be seen in Miami in very robust clarity. Following the unexpected loss to the Jets, the Dolphins reeled off a total of eight straight victories. Eight straight wins! Shula had to be doing something right, because the team had never in its young history been able to conquer that many opponents in that long of a victory string before.

The basic strategies that Shula and his offensive line coach Monte Clark employed were paying big dividends by this time. The Dolphins were dominating their opponents, particularly in their running game. Quarterback Bob Griese would regularly hand the ball off to his running backs (Larry Csonka, Jim Kiick, and Mercury Morris), and between those three divergent ball carriers, Miami would garner first down after first down, which accomplished two things. First, it ate up time off the game clock, which in turn gave their opponents less time to possess the ball. Secondly, the Dolphins rushing attack would usually—by the fourth quarter—wear down their opponents' will and abilities to stop them.

"I like the running plays," asserted Little in a 1972 interview. "It even ups your tools with the defensive man. You can unload on him. Knocking people down is my business. My pride comes from throwing blocks and seeing the game films where the other party got up slowly. . . if at all."[15]

The violence in pro football is most evident on every play in an area known as "The Pit," a small portion of space where offensive and defensive linemen do battle on every snap of the ball. Physical strength is the most common denominator of the men who tangle with each other along the line of scrimmage. Larry Little possessed the kind of strength which made him one of the best offensive guards in the business. He was strong enough to do the hitting that he needed to do to keep his opponents from penetrating into the offensive backfield. But Little also had something else going for him that was prized almost as much as his muscular force when the play began. Little had a lot of quickness. His feet and legs moved probably faster than any offensive lineman in the league in 1971. He was also quite successful at breaking away from his stance and leading the

Dolphins running backs downfield.

"All I'm interested in is knocking people off their feet and making them respect me," Little expressed in 1972. "When those number twenties and thirties show up in front of me, I sorta feel good. I know they are probably fifty or sixty pounds smaller than me. If I hit 'em hard enough, the next time they might give ground, and it'll make the job easier."[16]

Another player who was smaller than Little in physical stature was one of his teammates, the fleeting, dashing, and darting tailback, Eugene "Mercury" Morris. Most pro football running backs throughout time have employed their own unique style of carrying the ball, and that was certainly true of Morris. One look at him toting the pigskin, and you could tell that his style was distinctive to say the least. His feet barely spent a fraction of a second in contact with the ground. It was as if he was running on the surface of the sun as he tried to jump off the turf with every one of his steps. Yes, he juked many defensive opponents in his efforts to avoid their attempted tackles. But he also combined those juking movements with forward and sideways bursts of speed, which would often result in fans witnessing the flailing arms of numerous defenders.

But while the opposition may have felt frustration in trying to tackle Morris, so also did Larry Little on occasion in trying to block for Morris. This was partially due to Little's speed, as evidenced by the times that the big guard led Morris on sweeps. On more than one occasion, Little would get too far ahead of Morris on those running plays to the outside. The jitterbug-running Morris would in turn have to utilize his own unique way of "catching up" to Little.

"Chicken* was so fast and so quick at getting out of the

---

* Author's Note: Larry Little's nickname, "Chicken," may have been given to him in San Diego, but it stuck with him in Miami as well.

offensive backfield, and so was I," explained Morris. "We had these plays that Coach Shula designed. One was called Ride 38, and it was a touchdown-scoring play. Little led me, and I put myself in a position at a forty-five-degree angle off of his hip. Unless, of course, I had my hand down his pants. Not tugging on his jersey. Literally, my hand down his pants. I used to do that with [fellow Miami offensive guard Bob] Kuechenberg too. Because when they got too far away, then that means that they were passing up potentially the most dangerous man to get to their assignment. I didn't have to do it to Larry that much, but when I did it to him, he would yell at me to 'Get your hands out of my pants!'. . . as the play is going on!"[17]

Mercury Morris might have been the only Dolphins running back to try to get Larry Little to slow down a bit on some of the team's plays. But Morris was not the only Miami runner who benefited from Little's blocking prowess on those sweep runs to the outside. Burly fullback Larry Csonka was also able to carry the ball outside, albeit not as often as Morris. Taken as a whole, the Dolphins running attack, with a guy like Little opening holes for it on both inside and outside runs, was rapidly becoming one of the most formidable in the league.

"I didn't realize how fast he was until he was timed in the forty-yard dash," said Csonka. And that's when the idea formed in Monte Clark's head, that we could incorporate Mercury into the game, because with Little, we had a guard fast enough to make it to the outside and be devastating. The finer points of our weapons. I talk about players as weapons. You've got to know how to apply them. If you have the workings of a power running game. . . the fundamentals. . . a big and powerful offensive lineman who can get into a three-point stance and fire out and can actually move people. . . well, we worked in sync."[18]

That cohesive teamwork with the Miami rushing attack was

seen not just in providing strong blocking at the point of attack, however. Offensive linemen for Coach Clark had to display much more than a basic, rudimentary knowledge of how best to move the ball downfield. The members of the Dolphins offensive line all formed a collective measure of knowledge of their jobs in 1971. They were students of their craft, and they were relentless in their approach to opening up holes for the Miami runners.

"The second biggest thing that you have to have on the offensive line is intelligence," explained Csonka. "You know size and speed are very important, but without the intelligence to incorporate that into the teamwork that it takes to execute the power running game. . . well, it's not beneficial. But when we had a guy like Monte Clark, who came in as an assistant coach, and started to coordinate that, he could realize that those weapons were there, and he used them. And all he had to do was tell us how to coordinate those weapons. That's when it started to come into play. And that's when Mercury [Morris] started to play into the picture as well. And Larry was obviously by far our fastest offensive guard to pull and get to the outside. And then with Larry weighing 260 pounds plus, and him getting out there on a sweep with that kind of speed. . . it was devastating. Not using Larry's and Mercury's talents would be a great misuse, and a great miss of non-used power that was there. So, I think between Monte Clark, [offensive coordinator] Howard Schnellenberger, and Don Shula's willingness to recognize it, and having the intelligence to bring it forward, and the players being intelligent enough to use it. . . it became a team plan."[19]

Miami's "team plan" would focus on their running game, first and foremost. What was most incredible was the fact that all their opponents' defenses spent a very large amount of their time and efforts trying to stop or at least slow down the likes of Csonka, Morris, and Kiick, and yet failed for the most part to do so. The Dolphins ballcarriers would experience a great amount of success as the 1971 season wore on. During their eight-game winning streak that year, the Miami ground game accrued a total of 1,573 yards.

But to be considered as a team that was a credible threat to winning the AFC Eastern Division title, Miami was going to have to find a way to be able to beat some of their toughest competition. A couple of teams—the Los Angeles Rams and the Baltimore Colts—offered the Dolphins a formidable challenge during the middle portion of the regular season. Both the Rams and Colts were often involved in the postseason playoff discussion. Upsetting a recurrent winning opponent got the Dolphins on many teams' radars, if not on the headlines of the printed page.

"When we flew out to Los Angeles to beat the Rams," Little recalled, "I'll never forget reading the newspaper out there. The newspaper was the *LA Times*, and the newspaper columnist was Jim Murray. I remember the article where he asked, 'Who are these fish? Where are they coming from?' And the Rams were the team that had the 'Fearsome Foursome.' They had guys like Deacon Jones, Merlin Olsen, Lamar Lundy, and Jack Youngblood. And we went out there and beat them."[20]

Miami's 20-14 victory over the Rams was highlighted by a defense that allowed the Los Angeles offense to travel up and down the field on them but did not permit them to score that much. Indeed, the Dolphins defense proved that they were made of stern stuff.

In the midst of their eight-game winning streak, Miami would get another shot at taking on the defending World Champion Baltimore Colts. Beating Baltimore on November 21, 1971, would give the Dolphins the sole ownership of first place in their division.

"Shula didn't say anything about beating Baltimore, but I know he thought about it," Little confirmed. "I know that we prepared harder for when we played Baltimore than for basically any other team because of Shula. . . because he previously coached there. We may have beat them, but they still played us hard."[21]

There is an old sports cliché which claims that "to be the best, you have got to beat the best." That was Miami's focus against the Colts. A win over his former team would give Shula's young Dolphins a true sense of accomplishment as they bit into the meat of their schedule. Baltimore was a quality team with a lineup filled with veteran leadership. The Colts also had what a lot of pro football historians considered the greatest quarterback to ever buckle a chinstrap, the great Johnny Unitas. This meeting in the Orange Bowl would indeed be a bona fide measuring stick as to how well Miami was performing during the second year of Shula's head coaching tenure there.

The Dolphins had some unexpected help in this contest, however. A new tradition began in the stadium that day. A radio personality by the name of Rick Weaver noticed in several earlier games that a multitude of fans at the Orange Bowl would listen to the play-by-play of the game with their transistor radios. Weaver wanted to capture the emotions and the excitement of those fans, especially whenever Miami scored a touchdown. He came up with the idea of waving white handkerchiefs whenever he gave them a signal over the airwaves. So, all during the week prior to the Colts game, Weaver constantly reminded his listeners to bring their white handkerchiefs to the Orange Bowl. The sight of tens of thousands of white handkerchiefs waving in the stands would inspire the players. According to Larry Little, it certainly was noticed.

"Yeah, we could feel [the fans'] energy on the field with them waving their white hankies, for sure," proclaimed Little.[22]

The positive influence that the fans bestowed might not have been the sole reason for the Dolphins' momentum on that day against Baltimore, but it certainly did not hurt. Shula's team got behind early, then spent the rest of the game trying to overcome the Colts and take control of the lead. They eventually managed to do so in the third quarter on a one-yard Jim Kiick run up the gut of the Baltimore defense. Kiick's power surge for a score was thanks in large part to the halfback following Larry Little's crunching block on the middle of the Colts defensive line. The Miami defense then took over, and they paved the rest of the way to a big victory. They permitted Baltimore's prized rushing attack only 100 ground yards. They also forced three timely turnovers which helped to ignite a couple of key drives by the Dolphins offense. In the end, a twenty-yard field goal by Miami placekicker Garo Yepremian lifted the Dolphins to a pivotal 17-14 triumph over their division rivals. That victory permanently established the practice of hanky waving in the Orange Bowl, a tradition that continues at Dolphins games to this very day. Miami would not lose their grip of first place in the AFC's Eastern Division for the rest of the season.

But that did not mean that they would always play up to expectations, however. The Dolphins traveled to New England a couple of weeks after defeating Baltimore and seemingly laid down for the Patriots, 34-13. It was as embarrassing of a loss as the Dolphins had suffered all year long.

"We just didn't play well," Little bluntly stated. "You know it was one of those games where nobody could do anything right. Yeah, we just didn't play well. But we really didn't think about our record back then, or at least talk about it, because we knew that we had to prepare for the next game. We couldn't dwell on one game in which we'd get beat, because we had to move on. We had to get really prepared to play the next team that was on our schedule."[23]

That next game on Miami's schedule was none other than a rematch with the Baltimore Colts, who were intent on evening the score with their division rivals. They did just that in Baltimore's Memorial Stadium on December 11, 1971. The Colts took an early lead, then held onto it with a grip that was as strong as concrete. The Dolphins gained slightly more yardage than the Colts, but Miami committed two hurtful turnovers as well, which indirectly led to both of Baltimore's touchdowns. The Colts avenged their previous loss to Shula's team, 14-3. It was indeed a bitter pill to swallow, but by now, Little and his teammates knew that they had to put that defeat out of their minds. They had one more game left on their regular season schedule. If they were able to beat Green Bay at the Orange Bowl on December 19, they would win the AFC East title.

That particular goal was attainable, and the Dolphins played an inspired second half in order to claim their championship. They dominated the Packers in the final two quarters to post an impressive 27-6 victory. Miami thus finished the 1971 regular season with a stellar 10-3-1 record, which was a notch better than Baltimore's 10-4 mark.

The Dolphins were once again in the NFL playoffs, this time as a division champion, their first division championship in their young history. Miami's first opponent in the postseason would be the veteran Kansas City Chiefs at Municipal Stadium in Kansas City. It would go on to become one of the greatest games in league history. It was certainly the longest game in league history. This Christmas Day battle would last for an astounding eighty-two minutes and forty seconds of elapsed game time, and it was a contest that would not be decided until well into a second overtime period. A total of fourteen eventual Hall of Famers between the two clubs played in this game, and everyone who took part in it, or who was in attendance for it, or who watched it on television, would never forget it.

Like most sudden death overtime games back in that era, the first team to score would win. During the first four quarters, Kansas City would score, then Miami would counter with a score of their own. This trading back and forth of points eventually led to a 24-24 tie as the fourth quarter gun sounded. The extra overtime periods proved that this contest was a strength-sapping marathon. One noteworthy member of the Miami squad managed to stay in the game all the way until the final frantic play, even though he was not playing at 100 percent effectiveness.

"I injured my hip early in that game," remembered Larry Little. "I played over five quarters with a hip pointer. But you know that game was too important for me to leave, or to go out of the game. The training staff didn't give me any ice or anything. I just dealt with the pain."[24]

Little's assignment in this marathon epic was to block 6-2, 265-pound Kansas City defensive tackle Curley Culp, who prior to playing pro football was also a collegiate wrestling champion. Considering that Little had to deal with his ongoing hip injury, his performance against Culp in this contest was admirable by all accounts.

"I had never played six and a half quarters [the overall length of this game] in my life," Little said. "It's tough enough to play against Curley Culp for four quarters, and then to go and play against him for six and a half. . . is really something. I would try to attack him before he would get going real good, because of his strength. One time, Curley hit me upside my head. I said, 'Geez, Curley, what are you trying to do to me?' He started laughing. I didn't like to play in front of Curley. I could feel it in my entire body whenever I played in front of Curley. I had an advantage over a lot of defensive tackles because of my height [six-foot-one], but Curley was the same height. With taller guys, I could get under them. Not with Curley. Curley Culp was the strongest defensive lineman that I ever played against."[25]

One particular strong play enabled the Dolphins to prove their worthiness in this game, and it set up their ultimate winning points. Miami's running game was famous for its powerful, straight forward attack. But it was also developing a reputation for deception, especially during the most opportunistic times. Dolphins quarterback Bob Griese wanted to call a misdirection run earlier in the game, but he simply forgot to do so. Fortunately for his offense, he remembered at this most opportune moment to use the play, where fullback Larry Csonka would carry the ball off left tackle, while most of the other members of the offense ran deceptively toward the right. Leading Csonka on the play was Larry Little, who pulled from his right guard position, and who benefited from the fact that the play caught the Chiefs defense by surprise. Practically every Kansas City lineman and linebacker followed the fake handoff to Miami halfback Jim Kiick, which permitted Csonka even more room to run.

"You know we [Little, Csonka, and Griese] were talking about that play the other day," said Little in a 2022 interview. "It was a play that we hadn't run all year. It was called roll right, trap left. We hadn't run that play hardly ever before. But Griese saw something that they [Kansas City] were doing during the game, and he called that play. It took advantage of their alignment."[26]

Csonka's rambling twenty-nine-yard jaunt, where he followed Little downfield, was just one of the enduring images of this historic game. Perhaps the most noteworthy play of this marathon was the final play, however, where Miami placekicker Garo Yepremian booted a successful thirty-seven-yard field goal, thus ending the longest game ever played. The crowd at Municipal Stadium was for the most part shocked and silent that their team had just lost a double overtime playoff game to a much younger group of players.

Perhaps it was the Dolphins' youth, however, which proved to be the vital factor in their victory. Their younger bodies just seemed to have more energy as the contest dragged on and on and on.

Miami's contest the next week in the 1971 AFC Championship Game would present a similar matchup as what they dealt with against the Chiefs, in that their upcoming opponent had as much overall veteran experience as Kansas City. But unlike taking on the Chiefs, the Dolphins would be playing a familiar opponent on January 2, 1972. For the third time this season, Shula's men would be playing his former team, the Baltimore Colts, for the championship of the AFC. Both teams had defeated each other during the regular season on their respective home fields. This third meeting would be held in the Orange Bowl, amidst a capacity crowd of hanky-waving Dolphins fans. This game also proved to be more of an afterthought, however, when compared to the excitement that was seen against the Chiefs the previous week. So much so, in fact, that Little was hard pressed to recall any details from that AFC Title matchup versus the Colts.

"I don't really remember anything about that game," Little admitted. "I do remember that it was the game that we had to win to reach our goal that year. . . to get to the Super Bowl. We beat the Chiefs the week before, and we were fortunate to win that game. But we really needed to win the championship game against Baltimore. That game propelled us to go to the Super Bowl."[27]

Little and his teammates began their meeting with the Colts in the 1971 AFC Title Game by jumping out to an early lead in the first quarter. Star Miami wide receiver Paul Warfield broke free on a deep down-and-out pattern, snared Bob Griese's perfect pass along the sideline, then quickly turned up field. He then proceeded to outrace Baltimore safety Rick Volk to complete a seventy-five-yard touchdown play. As luck would have it, that was the only score that the Dolphins would need on this day. Miami won the AFC Championship Game by a final score of 21-0 over their toughest foe. The Dolphins were going to the Super Bowl, something that was completely unfathomable before Don Shula became their head coach.

With the frenzied celebrations going on all throughout the State of Florida following their glorious triumph over the Colts, Shula knew that his team had yet to reach its fullest potential. He refused to celebrate with everyone else, knowing full well that Super Bowl VI in New Orleans lay just a couple of weeks down the road. Shula felt that to beat Miami's upcoming opponent, the defending NFC Champion Dallas Cowboys, his players were going to have to forget about all their previous games and their earlier successes.

Larry Little's assignment in Super Bowl VI would be to block veteran Dallas defensive tackle Jethro Pugh, a man whose six-foot-six height was five inches taller than Little's six-foot-one frame. Pugh was one of the better defensive linemen in pro football, and he presented a quality challenge to any man who attempted to block him. But Little took his head coach's instructions to heart, and he prepared intently for whatever Pugh might present to him, from aspects like footwork to arm and hand movements. Indeed, whatever Little saw on film of Pugh, the Dolphins All-Pro offensive guard would be ready to address. As it turned out, he would show Pugh, the Cowboys' defense, the 81,023 in attendance at Tulane Stadium, and a nationwide television audience that all the accolades and awards that he had earned throughout the 1971 season were well worth the notoriety. Pugh did not get near Bob Griese all game long, thanks to Little's efforts on Super Bowl Sunday.

"I had to block Jethro Pugh in Super Bowl VI, and he had the longest arms I've ever seen on a man," confirmed Little. "I tried to keep his hands off me. I was satisfied with what I was able to do against him, because he did not have a good game that day."[28]

But similar success would unfortunately not be seen from most of the other Miami players against the Cowboys. The Dallas attack was relentless all game long, as their running game ran through the Dolphins defense to the tune of 252 yards rushing, a Super Bowl record at that time. Miami's offense, conversely, could not seem to get on track, as they committed three costly turnovers. Shula's prized rushing game could register only eighty total ground yards, a number well below their regular season average. The Dolphins lost Super Bowl VI by a score of 24-3. It was indeed a depressing end to what was the greatest year in their history, up to that point.

"We were so delighted to get into that Super Bowl, that we were not realizing that we still had to play the game and had to earn the win," commented Larry Csonka. "And I think that undermined us more than anything else. We had been through so much, and had been working to get up the mountain, and then finally when we got on top of the mountain, we couldn't hold the celebration. We started celebrating the fact that we were in the Super Bowl, instead of thinking about winning the Super Bowl. I don't think that we were ready to play that game, because we lost that Super Bowl so badly."[29]

The loss to the Cowboys ended what was a tumultuous season for Larry Little. It began with the terrible news of his brother's death, and it ended with his team's one-sided defeat in the biggest game of the year. But in between those two events was a mixture of big wins, a division and a conference title, along with numerous other team and individual successes. Little and his teammates would have to spend their off season dwelling on the good and the bad from 1971 and somehow make the most of what happened. They used that 1971 season as a building block for any future achievements that they would have.

"We may have lost Super Bowl VI," said Little after that year, "but we learned a lot.[30] You can say that I've come a long way, and we've all come a long way. I would say that I've still got a long way to go, and we've all got a long way to go. None of us will be satisfied until we've won it all."[31]

CHAPTER 7

A PERFECT ENDING

L arry Little had become in a very short time an NFL All-Pro, a team leader, and a team captain. He had shown Don Shula how much he was willing to work to keep his weight down, and to perform to the utmost of his abilities. The Miami ownership finally acknowledged Little's efforts and accomplishments on the field after the 1971 season concluded. He received a substantial raise, making him one of the highest-paid offensive guards in the history of the league up to that time.

"Larry has been recognized as the outstanding lineman in the American Conference by his fellow players," said Don Shula upon Little's signing of his new contract. "Today, in fact, he is probably recognized by many as the best guard in pro football. Larry has tremendous strength, speed, and balance. There's no question he's exceptional."[1]

Little's new financial deal with the team gave him a degree of wealth that he had never had at any other time before in his young life. His longtime dream of playing pro football had been realized, and now he was getting paid a lot of money to live out his dream. His new contract served as a reward for all the hard work that he had put into the sport since the time when he was a kid. . . when he was just getting to learn the game on the streets of Miami. Moreover, the timing of the signing of his new contract could not have been better.

"I'm definitely happy," Little said after putting pen to paper in the summer of 1972. "You could say I got a substantial raise. I had proved my worth to the team, and I got the money that I felt that I deserved to get. I'm also pleased to get it over with. Any ballplayer would rather be signed than have two things [their contract and actually playing the game] on his mind going into the season."[2]

Going into the 1972 season was on the minds of everyone connected with the Dolphins all throughout the months prior to the team's summer training camp. The expectations for the team were naturally very high. Going to the Super Bowl the previous year gave the players plenty of confidence that they could return to the big game. They knew the kind of sacrifice that it would take to make that journey again.

Larry Little did not get complacent as the 1972 season approached. He was opening holes increasingly wider in the early 1970s by the time that many games entered the fourth quarter. He was just wearing his opponents down. All that summer training camp conditioning that Coach Shula demanded from his players was paying off all along the line of scrimmage. Miami's running backs were the beneficiaries of it. They also profited from the innate talents and the reliability of a blocker like Little.

"With Larry, you knew that you could count on his block," affirmed Morris. "I could hit that hole like it was touch football, and that's what I tried to do."[3]

The 1972 season opener at Kansas City was not going to be as easy as touch football, however, as the Chiefs were smarting for revenge from losing their previous playoff game to the Dolphins. The rematch would be played on September 17, 1972, in the sparkling new Arrowhead Stadium in Kansas City. But it would also be played with a heated touch of South Florida weather which appeared to have moved westward. The temperature for the game sweltered over 102 degrees in the bright sun and even reached 120 degrees on Arrowhead Stadium's brand-new artificial surface. This was a climate that profited the Dolphins much more than it did the Chiefs. Shula's players were considerably more used to dealing with playing football in conditions of heat and humidity than were the men on Kansas City's roster.

A couple of other factors were also able to help Miami in this contest. One, the Chiefs were primarily an older, veteran team. The hot weather would take the starch out of them quicker than it would the younger Dolphins players. Two, Kansas City head coach Hank Stram inexplicably decided to have his team's bench on the side of the field where the hot sun would shine on them. . . all game long. By the third quarter, the Miami bench area saw nothing but shade. This unwise decision by Stram certainly did not help the overall stamina of his team. Miami took an early lead and held on to it. The Dolphins defense forced the Chiefs to commit four costly turnovers, most of which occurred in Kansas City territory. That meant that the Miami offense did not have to travel that far to put points on the scoreboard.

This game was more a mental contest than a physical one. Physicality would certainly have a role, as it does in every football game. But the will to win—or the striving to win—is often a mental prospect. Which team could endure the heat the best? Which team wanted to win this game more? Those questions would be answered more in the frame of mind of each of the players. Larry Little recognized very early that he would have another gargantuan battle with Curley Culp, one of the strongest players in the league. Little fortunately was not suffering from another hip pointer injury in this 1972 season opener as he did in the 1971 AFC Divisional Playoff game. So, in a battle with equal physical strength facing each other, Little decided to play a psychological game against Culp. . . during a timeout.

"I'll never forget that it was so hot. . . it was more than 100 degrees," remembered Little. "And I think that Shula mentioned this on one of his films where he was speaking. We were on our own twenty-yard line, and we changed quarters. I sprinted from one twenty-yard line down to the other, to get into the Chiefs' heads. And I'll never forgot Curley Culp, by the time that he walked down there, he said to me, 'What the hell is wrong with you?' That was my way of getting into their heads, you know? Knowing how hot it was. I sprinted. I didn't jog. I sprinted."[4]

Little's psychological ploy seemed to work. The Dolphins emerged from this sauna of an opening game with a 20-10 victory. It would turn out to be just the beginning of the greatest season in the team's history, and perhaps in the history of the league. Miami would come home the next week and defeat the lowly Houston Oilers, 34-13. But a bigger test came the following week up in Minnesota. The Vikings were a formidable group of veteran players with a prized defense. The Dolphins had their hands full all day long, and midway through the fourth quarter, Minnesota owned a 14-6 lead. Miami's runners could earn only a collective 120 yards all game long. To counter that, the Dolphins had to rely on the passing game.

Larry Little may have made his reputation on his ability to open holes as a run blocker. But his quickness and his nimble footwork proved to be most important in the team's passing game, to give quarterback Bob Griese enough time to drop back, spot a receiving target, and throw the ball. Little never seemed to get enough credit for his ability to block on the team's passing plays, but he was very good at it. . . especially in the clutch when a big pass or two were most needed.

"Well, that was my job," attested Little. "No matter what play we ran, whether it was supposed to go inside or outside, my job was to block for the running backs. And whenever we threw the ball, my job was to keep my opponents away from our quarterbacks. No matter what play we ran. I was good enough at running plays and at passing plays to get the job done."[5]

Little and the offensive line's efforts at Minnesota afforded Griese enough time in his pass pocket to connect with tight end Jim Mandich for the winning score. Miami had prevailed, 16-14, and were now 3-0. It was indeed a team victory.

"We would be on the sidelines late in the game," remembered Little, "and a team might go ahead on us. The attitude was, if we needed an eighty-yard drive, we knew we could do it. We expected to do it. We were almost to the point of being cocky."[6]

Coach Shula was never accused of being cocky, but he also was not above giving in to a feeling of satisfaction following the victory at Minnesota.

"The Viking victory was most satisfying," Shula felt following the completion of the 1972 season. "It demonstrated how we didn't collapse even though we fell behind. We never panicked and stayed with what we had, making the big plays when we had to. That game demonstrated how much character the team had. Maintaining poise and coming from behind are characteristics of a championship team. I knew we could go all the way after this game. The way the squad reacted in the face of adversity told me a lot."[7]

Miami was now the only undefeated team left in the NFL. But adversity would make another showing in the next few weeks. After beating the New York Jets in the fourth game of the 1972 season, the Dolphins would have to deal with a test of a different kind when San Diego visited the Orange Bowl the following week. In that contest, Bob Griese suffered an ankle injury and was carted off the field.

"My injury was a broken fibula," Griese recalled in a 2022 interview. "Actually, it was a cracked fibula and a dislocated ankle. There was no surgery involved. It just took time to heal."[8]

Some of the more pessimistic Miami fans felt that there would be no "healing" for the Dolphins for the rest of the season, thanks to the injury to their star quarterback. But such was not the opinion of the Dolphins players, however. Their second-string signal caller was a veteran journeyman by the name of Earl Morrall, a guy who previously played for Shula when the two were in Baltimore. Shula had decided to acquire his old quarterback from the Colts just prior to the start of the 1972 season. How would this "new" guy, who was at the ripe old age of thirty-eight, going to adjust to coming in for Bob Griese and taking control of the team's offense?

"No, Earl wouldn't let us panic when he came into the game," Little remembered. "When he came into the huddle, he told us to 'Calm down. . . everything is going to be okay.' And we on the offensive line all knew that we had to be better, especially at pass blocking. You see, Bob had the ability to run, where Earl was strictly a drop-back quarterback. We knew that we were going to have to maintain our blocks a little longer for Earl than we did for Bob."[9]

Morrall came into the huddle and took over without so much as a hint of worry. He proved to his teammates that he could handle the pressure that he was under. Miami's offense continued to produce just as it did before Griese's injury. Their offense was like an automobile. When one sparkplug broke, Shula just replaced it with another one. The result was more victories. . . every week.

The Dolphins, with Morrall leading the way, defeated the Chargers, 24-10. They then once again proved that they could come from behind in a game the following week when they edged the Buffalo Bills at the Orange Bowl, 24-23. The Colts were the next victim. Miami crushed them by a convincing score of 23-0. The Dolphins were now 7-0. They had reached the halfway point of the season and still had no losses. Could they continue this stretch of consecutive victories? What was being said by Shula to his team as these victories kept piling up?

"No, there was no mention of going undefeated," Csonka exclaimed. "Shula laid the groundwork for the 1972 season this way: He said that we are going to take 1972 by going one game at a time. We are going to learn to concentrate solely on what's at hand the week that it's going to happen. We will become so dedicated and so designated to that cause. In other words, we had to take each game very seriously. We can't celebrate before the victory. And that's what we learned in Super Bowl VI. And that's what he used as the main ingredient for '72. No, there was no mention of going undefeated. There was a mention, however, of treating every game as though it was a Super Bowl."[10]

Miami still had seven more regular season games to play. Quite a few of those contests were not considered "contests" at all by many of the critics, who have throughout the past several decades since 1972 derided the Dolphins as benefiting from a weak slate of opponents. One would be advised not to say that to Larry Little, however. . . at least not to his face.

"To me that's an insult," declared Little, "because we had to play the teams that were on our schedule. And what about the teams that we beat in the playoffs? They had a reason to be in the playoffs. They must be pretty good too. So, you know. . . they try to find everything that they can to cast a shadow on us, instead of just seeing why we were great, and that's that, we were just a great football team. Like I said, we had to play great teams in the playoffs. We didn't make the schedule up. The league made the schedule up."[11]

That schedule would continue with a rematch at Buffalo. The Dolphins' ground attack was churning on all cylinders in the second meeting with the Bills. Miami gained a total of 254 rushing yards which included 106 yards and two touchdowns from Mercury Morris. One of Morris's scores was a splendid twenty-two-yard circuitous journey through the Bills' defense, with Little leading the way. On most of Morris's outside sweeps, Little would be the one leading him, mainly because the big guard was fast enough to stay ahead of the speedy and shifty tailback.

Indeed, it was Larry Little's innate ability to make effective blocks on both inside and outside runs which showcased his greatness. A film study of Little delivering blocks during the early 1970s is a show of power, speed, and forceful determination. The films also show how Little was easily able to adapt—and adapt quickly—to whatever the opposing defenses were doing. You would often see him adjust to the stunts that the defensive linemen were running. On other occasions, Little could be seen penetrating through his fellow blockers and getting in the way of the opposing linebackers, and thereby shielding them from getting near Dolphins running backs.

But it was on sweeps where Little became most notable to his foes, and to the rest of the NFL. Seeing him lead the way for the Miami runners along the outside of the field is a timeless memory in pro football history, and Little often made the most of it.

"Every football player has a little showman in him," Little admitted. "I knew when I got out there on a sweep and blocked someone in the open field, it was showtime for me. People would see me out in front leading the sweeps. . . people would see number sixty-six all the time on those plays. Also, I knew that the cameras would be on me, especially when we played in New York. That's the largest city in the country, and I knew that all the press was going to be there, and I would basically want to shine before all of the press."[12]

The Dolphins offense also delivered a shining show in their ninth game of the year, a 52-0 romp over visiting New England. It was Miami's best offensive output of the 1972 season, as virtually every player, including many backup players, contributed greatly to the victory.

Larry Little played a prominent role in Miami's next game versus the New York Jets. From the New York fourteen-yard line, Mercury Morris ran a sweep to his left, then cut up field. Little quickly realized that once Morris turned upfield, someone would need to block the one unaccounted-for member of the Jets' secondary—defensive back Steve Tannen. Little sprinted to Tannen's position and knocked him out of Morris's path to the end zone. Morris crossed the goal line, and Miami prevailed, 28-24.

"We had the attitude, that if we got the ball late in the game, we were going to score, no matter who we were playing," remembered Little. "It was because again, when our offensive line wasn't performing the way it should, Shula would come to me and say, 'You've got to get them going,' because he picked me as one of the captains. He knew that I was always an inspiration for the younger guys on the team. 'You've got to get them going,' he would say. Now I wasn't the kind of a guy that was a *rah rah* type of guy. But I would say to the guys, 'Hey. . . let's get it done.' Especially when you have the ball and when you consider that no team can stop us."[13]

Little's adeptness in swiftly recognizing what he needed to do on every play was vital to the success of the Dolphins rushing attack. Thanks to almost three full years of coaching by offensive line coach Monte Clark, and from working with the same teammates for the past few years, Little had also displayed to everyone that he had the mindset to excel at his position.

According to the man who played right next to him, offensive tackle Norm Evans, Little was able to do everything.

"Larry was a very strong individual," said Evans in a 2022 interview. "He was the perfect example of what it takes to play offensive guard. He had strength, and he could pull and lead sweeps. He was strong and he could blow out the middle nice and easy, and he was a great pass blocker too. He was just built to be a guard. He was stocky, and strong. . . and not too tall, so that makes it easier for the quarterback to see over him. He was the consummate offensive guard.

"He gave me a sense of security because he was lined up right beside me. I knew that with Larry, everything was going to be taken care of on the inside, and if I could do my job on the outside, everything was going to be great."[14]

Miami's greatness was going to be tested by seeming inferior teams during the final four games of the 1972 regular season. Today, we often call a contest between a superior team and a losing team a "trap game," meaning that the better team might be complacent or relaxed enough to overlook the poorer team, thus risking a possible upset defeat. There is a danger in this, because upsets happen all the time in sports. . . you just never know when it will happen. The Dolphins' perfect 10-0 record would now be on the line. To lose to the Cardinals, the Patriots, the Giants, or the Colts would be humiliating to the undefeated Miami team, and to Don Shula as well. The Dolphins dispatched those lesser teams, however, with few problems.

"Now we would feel that some teams might be a little bit tougher than other teams," Little said. "We weren't really worried about the Cardinals, or the Patriots, or the Giants down the stretch. But we still took it one game at a time."[15]

Yet what was not on any statistical sheet, at least not directly, was how well the Miami offensive line was playing regarding not committing errors on the field. They were so well versed through the numerous repetitions in practice each week from offensive line coach Monte Clark on how to get the job done, that they were like a well-oiled machine. The Dolphins would be the least penalized team in the entire NFL in 1972, and they took great pride in that.

"Our motto was, 'Don't ever beat ourselves,'" recalled Norm Evans. "And Monte drove that into us. We were not going to beat ourselves. In other words, we're not going to make blocking mistakes, we're not going to be getting offsides penalties, we're not going to be getting holding penalties. We're going to know our assignments, and we're going to execute them. We're not going to beat ourselves. So, I think that had a lot to do with our success back then."[16]

The success continued throughout the remainder of the year. In week thirteen in Yankee Stadium in the Bronx, the New York Giants tried to end Miami's twelve-game winning streak. By the final gun, however, that streak reached thirteen games. The Dolphins held on to a 23-13 victory over the Giants.

But a more memorable event for Larry Little occurred after the game with the Giants. Little participated in the filming of a national television commercial with a couple of his teammates. It was the old cycle of results. . . winning leads to fame, and fame leads to publicity. In the modern age, as the 1970s were rapidly becoming, publicity for professional athletes meant television commercials. The product that Little and his buddies were endorsing was none other than Vitalis hair products for men.

That commercial is somewhat comical, even by today's standards. An attractive female is seen walking among the Miami players in the locker room after a game, something that was unheard of and quite taboo back in 1972. The actress, while discussing the worth of the Vitalis products, pulls Larry Little's jersey off over his shoulder pads. Little's surprised and quizzical facial expression at her actions brings a memorable dose of humor to the commercial. The producers of the ad did not give Little any dialogue to recite, but neither did any other Dolphins players. The ending includes the actress giving quarterback Bob Griese a pat on his buttocks, as she tells him, 'Nice game, Bob.' Griese has the same kind of shocked look on his face after receiving her "greeting" as did Little. It was probably considered at that time a watershed commercial. The attempt was to sell Vitalis hair products, but having a female walking around an all-male locker room did raise some eyebrows back then. Yes, the 1970s saw a whole new bunch of provocative ideas on Madison Avenue.

"I forgot Bob Griese's agent's name at the time, but he was involved in the filming," Little expressed. "[Miami offensive tackle] Wayne Moore was in the commercial too. I believe that Vitalis commercial was the first national commercial that I was ever in. Now I did a local commercial here in Miami for MacArthur Milk. That was the milk that I grew up drinking. We all grew up on MacArthur Milk. But we got a few residuals from that Vitalis commercial too if I'm not mistaken."[17]

The residuals of the 1972 regular season for the Dolphins wore down to one game left on their ledger. One game to determine whether they could complete the first undefeated regular season since the 1942 Chicago Bears completed their regular season with an 11-0 record. But the 1942 Bears had lost the NFL Championship Game to the Washington Redskins, and that was a fate that Coach Shula and his players desperately wanted to avoid. The team that stood in the way of keeping the Dolphins from finishing their 1972 regular season undefeated was none other than their division rivals, the Baltimore Colts. Fortune—and prognosticators—favored Miami, mainly because Baltimore was having a dreadful year. They could only earn five wins in 1972, and by the end of the season, it appeared as if they were merely playing out the string.

Coach Shula continued to prepare his team strenuously for the meeting with Baltimore, however, just as much as he would whenever he went up against his old team. But this game in the final week of the 1972 regular season meant quite a bit more, and everyone knew it. The Dolphins were determined not to let anyone, especially the Colts, rain on their undefeated parade. The Miami defense led the way, as they forced the Colts to commit six turnovers. From there, the Dolphins offense relied on their balanced attack to register sixteen points. Baltimore scored none. It was Miami's third shutout of the season, and it provided the team with an excellent springboard with which to enter the playoffs.

When asked many years later how confident the team or its players felt about going undefeated, perhaps it was offensive tackle Norm Evans who explained things the best regarding his feelings on the matter.

"I felt that we might be able to go undefeated in about the last quarter of the last game that year," admitted Norm Evans. "We didn't take anything for granted, and Don Shula pounded it into us to never take anything for granted."[18]

One unique occurrence that no team or individual player took for granted was for a running back to gain 1,000 yards rushing in one season. In addition to their string of fourteen straight victories, the Dolphins in 1972 also became the first team in NFL history to have two running backs—Larry Csonka and Mercury Morris—gain over 1,000 yards rushing in one year. That was quite an accomplishment, but so was the new team rushing record that the Dolphins set in 1972 as well. Miami's ballcarriers set a new standard in league history with 2,960 total ground yards.

"That was a great feeling," recalled Little. "And also, Jim Kiick ran for 500 yards [521 actually] that year. We set the NFL team rushing record that year. Monte Clark instilled a lot of pride in us. And we felt that there was nobody that we couldn't beat or that we couldn't block. And he made us study film very hard. And with the other guys [on the offensive line], they all had a lot of pride too. There was no fear in any of us."[19]

The Dolphins certainly were not overconfident, mind you. Miami would face the Cleveland Browns in the AFC Divisional Playoffs on December 24, 1972. The Browns were coming off a ten-win regular season, and even though Miami was listed as slight favorites to win this game, Coach Shula expressed to his players that they were not to overlook Cleveland by any means.

"I have learned that you never take a playoff team lightly, no matter who they are," Shula affirmed. "If they reach the playoffs, they have to be good. I knew the Browns would give us all we could handle. They gave us one of our toughest games of the year."[20]

Larry Little had a tough game against Cleveland as well. His primary blocking opponent in this playoff struggle was none other than Walter Johnson, a six-foot-four, 265-pound defensive tackle, whose specialty was penetrating opposing offensive backfields and disrupting running plays. Johnson gained a special brand of notoriety by wrestling professionally during the off seasons. He even wrestled an actual 600-pound bear and beat him when he got the furry creature in a headlock! Johnson was also an efficient pass rusher, as evidenced by his sack of Miami quarterback Earl Morrall in the second quarter of the game. It was one of four sacks that the Browns registered on that day.

"The better my opponent played, the better I played," declared Little. "There was no doubt about it. Because I knew that they would bring out the best in me. I don't remember Walter Johnson getting a sack on me though, but he may have. He was good. He was good."[21]

While Johnson may have matched up well with Little, the Browns offense matched up well with the Dolphins defense, at least in the second half, when they came from behind to take a 14-13 lead over Miami late in the fourth quarter. Just as Shula had previously predicted, this playoff game versus Cleveland would turn out to be one tough contest for his players. The Browns would actually outgain the Dolphins in total yardage (283 to 272). But it was Shula's defense which kept the game close. They managed to intercept Cleveland quarterback Mike Phipps five times, which kept the Browns from adding to their point total.

Miami's point total desperately needed a boost in the final minutes of the game, and just as they had responded to pressure all year long, they did so again. The Dolphins went on a seven-play, eighty-yard drive to earn the winning score on an eight-yard run up the middle by Jim Kiick. Miami had prevailed, 20-14, for their fifteenth win in fifteen games. It was indeed an impressive accomplishment, but the pressure that the Dolphins felt against the Browns would be felt even in increasing volumes the following Sunday when they would face the Cinderella team of 1972, the Pittsburgh Steelers. The Steelers were in the process of having their greatest season ever [up to that time]. They had won the AFC Central Division with an impressive 11-3 record, and they were coming off a 13-7 victory over the Oakland Raiders, in a contest which featured running back Franco Harris' fabled "Immaculate Reception."

The man that Larry Little would be blocking in the upcoming AFC Championship Game would be none other than Joe Greene, who was known by his timeless nickname of "Mean" Joe Greene. The six-foot-four, 275-pound Greene dominated opposing blockers like few defensive tackles had ever done before in pro football history. Two blockers were regularly required to block Greene on many plays. On occasion, even three blockers were necessary to keep him from rushing opposing quarterbacks or making tackles in the offensive backfield. He was a verifiable beast on the football field, and everyone knew it.

Larry Little knew it also. He had faced Greene several times before the 1972 season, and he knew what a huge challenge it was to block that big number seventy-five in black and gold. On one previous occasion, Little got the best of Greene, and kept him out of Miami's offensive backfield. Greene was not used to being shutout and halted from making tackles, and his frustration level thereby grew increasingly with practically every play. Finally, near the end of the game, "Mean Joe" snapped.

"Now the first time that I played against Joe, that was in 1970," remembered Little. "We were playing Pittsburgh in the preseason, and Joe was saying that I was holding him, and he was a brash young guy, and he kicked at me. And I looked at him and I said 'Joe! Why? Why would you do that?' He didn't know what to say. He just dropped his head and walked back to his huddle. And no, he didn't kick at me again. Now that was in my fourth year in the league, and he was trying to make a name for himself, which he did."[22]

The two combatants are good friends today, and because both men are honored Hall of Famers, both greatly enjoy talking about the moments of their youth with each other when they see one another at the annual Hall of Fame gatherings. Greene defends his own side of the "kicking" story, however. Let's just say that Mr. Greene stands firm in his belief that he was being held by Mr. Little. In a 2022 interview, he expressed his memory of the event.

"I thought that Larry was holding me," Greene relates, "and some people think that I kicked him. But in reality, I kicked *at* him. And then he looked at me and said 'Joe. . . why? Why?' And I was quite embarrassed by that, and I just turned around and walked away. All I could do was just walk away."[23]

Neither lineman would be walking away from the intense challenge that stood before each of them in the 1972 AFC Championship Game, however. But just before that contest, the Pro Football Lineman of the Year award was announced. The winner of the award for that particular year was ironically Joe Greene of the Pittsburgh Steelers. The news that Greene won the award irked Little a bit, who even though he won the Pro Football Offensive Lineman of the Year award again in 1972, well, it is accurate to say that he felt at least somewhat slighted by not being chosen as the winner of the award that Greene had won. Little may have also read a few of Greene's public statements prior to the 1972 AFC Championship Game, which undoubtedly got him fired up to play against Greene that day. A few of Greene's comments went something like this:

"Playing against Miami and Larry Little is the kind of challenge that you like to have," said Joe Greene in the 1971 game [a 24-21 Miami win]. "I didn't get to the passer at all. Larry is a darn good offensive lineman, but it's really not that easy to compare him with some of the other guards in the game. Even though he's larger than the average guard, he's just as quick and he's definitely stronger.

"I'd have to say Larry has earned his reputation primarily as a pulling guard. He completely annihilates defensive backs and linebackers when he leads power sweeps for Csonka and Morris. Little is also an effective pass blocker, but it's on running plays where he really excels.[24] Now don't get me wrong, Little is a good guard. . . probably one of the best. But they [the Miami blockers] will have to double-team me. My thinking, in any such matchup, the best offensive lineman can never block a good defensive man one-on-one. . . at least not consistently."[25]

The sports media loves to search for a story. . . any story. Football teams are not immune from observing what their opponents are saying in the press, especially before a big game. Greene's gentle bravado was a slight example of what has been termed as "bulletin board material." Simply defined, "bulletin board material" in football terms are statements from a player (or players) from one team that their opponents will post on their team's bulletin boards. The idea is that their players will get a chance to read those statements prior to a big game, in the hopes that their foes' comments will "inspire" them when they go up against their opponents. . . who probably should not have voiced those statements to the media in the first place. An individual like Larry Little might be the subtle subject of Joe Greene's thoughts just prior to the 1972 AFC Championship Game, but a player's verbiage can sometimes backfire. Words can lead to actions, and one player's words might do a lot to stimulate his opponent to play the game of his life. For his part, Little was not taking Greene's bait on the eve of the conference title game at Pittsburgh, at least not publicly in the press. He preferred instead to heap some well-deserved praise on Greene.

"I don't think too many people have a good game against Joe Greene," asserted Little. "Right now, he is the premier defensive tackle in football. I'm trying not to look at this matchup between us from the standpoint of pressure, but rather from the fact that two good football players will be going full strength against each other. Yet I do know that if I don't do a good job against him tomorrow, I don't think that we can win the game. Greene is their iron man. . . the one they build their defensive efforts around."[26]

Little took Greene's aforementioned sentiments—and Greene's lofty reputation—as a personal challenge. He also decided to make amends for the snubbing of the "Best Lineman" honors that did not go in his favor.

"That was somewhat of a statement game for me," Little recalled in talking about the 1972 AFC Title Game. "I found out that morning that Joe Greene was voted as the best lineman in the league, and I was number two. And that gave me a lot of incentive going into that game."[27]

Incentive is vital in determining the results in the sport of football. Often in the pros, when two formidable competitors along the line of scrimmage go up against each other, it turns into a spectacular "game within a game," and it is worth watching all sixty minutes long. It was moments like Larry Little versus Joe Greene in the early 1970s which provided some of the most primal moments on the gridiron, and which certainly enhanced the legendary status of big games. Football is readily known as a team sport. But it is within these individual battles of player versus player that success or failure is often determined in each game of this team sport. Both Little and Greene were cognizant of this, as they took their stances and faced off against one another in what was the biggest game up to that time of the 1972 season for both Miami and Pittsburgh.

"It's unusual that the individual battle between a guard and a tackle will be the center of attraction like this one," admitted Little on the eve of that 1972 AFC Title Game, "and that certainly has to add to the pressure on both of us. Everybody who watches tomorrow will be studying our every move. I've got a lot of pride in how I play this game and I just can't see myself getting beat physically. Joe Greene's a good football player and I'm a good football player. As a result, somebody has got to lose some of the time. But, as far as it [losing his individual battle to Greene] being a continuous thing, well, I've got too much pride for that to happen."[28]

Little did all he could do to block Greene one-on-one. He was able to accomplish this goal, especially in the first half. The Steelers' defensive coaches realized by halftime that Greene was not penetrating the Miami offensive backfield as easily as he had done to many other teams throughout the season, thanks largely to the yeoman efforts of Larry Little. To counter this, Pittsburgh coaches had Greene line up in different locations along the line of scrimmage all throughout the second half of the game. Greene remained the focus of the Dolphins blockers despite the change in the Steelers' strategy. Only now, in the third and fourth quarters of the game, Greene would be double-teamed by the other Miami blockers. It was a situation of "darned if you do, and darned if you don't" for Greene. Little and his fellow linemen had succeeded in their mission.

"Larry played really well in that game," Greene recalled, "and the offensive line of the Dolphins played really well also. As I recall, quite a few of the times, I played over their offensive tackle [Norm Evans]. And there was a defense that we were using at that time, and Larry blocked me on pass protection, and then on running plays, he went through to block one of our linebackers after doubling up on me. So, Miami's offensive line was instrumental in their win, and Larry did his job. He did what they asked him to do."[29]

The Dolphins were asked to do quite a lot to emerge with a win in the 1972 AFC Championship Game. The Steelers grabbed an early lead, and Miami's offense was struggling. Late in the second quarter, Dolphins punter Larry Seiple was getting ready to punt the ball, when all of a sudden, he noticed that only one member of the Pittsburgh defense was half-heartedly going through the motions of rushing him. The rest of the Steelers players were running downfield to set up blocks for the return. Seiple's quick recognition and his survey of the scene was to be commended, because in an instant, he tucked the ball under his arm and ran thirty-seven yards downfield before he was noticed by Pittsburgh's defenders and driven out of bounds. A few plays later, Miami tied the game on a short touchdown pass from Earl

Morrall to Larry Csonka.

"No one knew it was coming but Seip," said Little of Seiple's daring run from punt formation. "Not even Shula knew. Seip saw that no one on the [Pittsburgh] defense was paying any attention to him. They turned their backs to him to block on their punt return team. So, when Seip saw that happen, he took off and started running. It was a risk, but it worked out."[30]

But it was ultimately a decision by Don Shula which pointed the way to a Dolphins' win in the championship game. Shula decided to replace Morrall, who had been struggling all during the first half, with Bob Griese, who last saw any action in week five against San Diego. Griese suffered an ankle injury in that game, and there were plenty of doubts that he would be able to play anymore in 1972. It was a bold and gutsy move by Shula. At least it appeared that way, but according to Griese, it was a move that the young quarterback was ready for.

"I knew what was going on," explained Griese. "I was healthy enough to run the second team at practice toward the end of the season. Earl was running the first team at practice. I was up to speed with what the team was doing. Coach Shula had said many times that one of the toughest decisions that he had to make was taking Earl out in that AFC Championship Game and installing me against the Steelers. I've been in there with those guys for years. When I came into the huddle, all I said was 'Okay, let's go.'"[31]

Miami did indeed go, and they traveled downfield with a good mixture of explosive Griese passes and a couple of clutch runs by their running backs. Jim Kiick took a pitchout from Griese and dove into the Pittsburgh end zone from two yards out for a third quarter touchdown. Later in the fourth quarter, Kiick followed Larry Little from three yards out and crossed the goal line once again, which extended Miami's lead to 21-10. Little walled off Steelers linebacker Henry Davis on the play. Davis was headed right toward making the tackle. . . until Little got to him first. Little's block enabled Kiick to find the hole that he needed to reach the end zone. The Dolphins then held on for a 21-17 victory. They had accomplished one of their main goals that they set following the end of the 1971 season. . . they were returning to the Super Bowl.

Both Little and Greene knew that they had given each other their best efforts. It was a struggle that both men knew was of the utmost importance, and both men knew that the entire football world would be focused in on how they both were performing along the line of scrimmage. Both men are pro football icons today, and both have expressed on numerous occasions their high regard for each other, focusing on their strengths and talents when it came to playing the game. Below is just a sampling of Greene's comments concerning Little's abilities.

"Larry was probably the quickest and most athletic of the guards that I played against," Greene said. "He had the most speed and strength of anybody who opposed me that I had to deal with. I was almost tens pounds heavier than Larry. Now I wasn't as strong as he was, and I couldn't out quick him, so I had a difficult time playing against Larry. He moved well. He ran well. He used his hands well. And he pass-protected pretty good.

"One of the things that I thought about Larry is that Larry was very quick off the ball in the initial snap of the ball. Once he got the jump on a defensive lineman, it was very difficult for that lineman to recover their balance against Larry. So, it was very important for me to beat Larry on my initial charge, because he was so quick. I had difficulty doing that, and I had a difficult time against Larry."[32]

There was a mutual respect between these two men. . . between these two gladiators. After the final gun sounded to the 1972 AFC Championship Game, and in a more reflective mood, Larry Little discussed with the press how he felt about his efforts on the day.

"I knew I had to be up for this game," admitted Little. "I concentrated all week long on nothing but how Joe Greene plays football. I think I had a pretty good day against him out there. Our offensive line did a hell of a job. We didn't allow any sacks. And we were able to run on them rather effectively. I'm deeply satisfied with the way we played as a team, because I felt all along that we could run on anyone."[33]

Larry Little had gone up against some of the greatest defensive tackles in pro football history during his years in San Diego and in Miami, and Joe Greene was at the top of that list. Each of those exceptional athletes had a heart and a drive for the sport that equaled that of the greatest linemen who have ever played the game. Anytime that Miami's best pulling guard went up against someone who was outstanding in his own right, the resulting clashes would clearly be spectacular. The one-on-one battle in the 1972 AFC Title Game between Larry Little and Joe Greene was proof of that.

"Probably, the best and the toughest defensive lineman that I ever had to face would go back to Joe Greene," confirmed Little. "With Joe, I was determined to try to out tough him. I knew that when I played the game against Joe, I had to have my 'A' game."[34]

The Washington Redskins were going to have to be on top of their game if they would have a chance to beat the Miami Dolphins in Super Bowl VII. The oddsmakers decided to make the Redskins the favorites, probably because they intensely believed that no team undefeated for an entire season, and that the Dolphins were due to lose sooner or later. That time was now at hand to see if those oddsmakers were correct. The 1972 season had boiled down to just one game. One more game to decide if Miami could accomplish their ultimate goal of being a world champion. . . or if they would lose their second straight Super Bowl.

The mindset of the Dolphins players ran the gamut from nervous to confident. Larry Csonka felt that the pressure was solely on Miami to rectify what they had failed to accomplish the year before in Super Bowl VI.

"No, there was no relief in knowing that there was only one game left to play," Csonka stated. "I think that it was exactly the opposite of it. I think there was more pressure, more concentration, and more strain than ever. You know it's easy to look back and skim over it now, but at the time, we learned that each week, someone was going to step forward. That's why it was such a great year for that team. Perhaps the greatest assembly of players that's ever happened. Well, I think that it's voted as that. It's the number one team in the history of the NFL. Because it's the only one that has achieved perfection."[35]

The ultimate chance for perfection was now just one game away. It would take applying all the lessons that the Dolphins had learned throughout the 1972 season to make this dream a reality. But it would take more than just the physical exertion that the players would commit to on the field.

"I think it all comes from the intelligence factor," surmised Csonka. "And the caring, the discipline that Shula installed in us that made us care, and everybody wanted to be the guy that made the play. And that stood out. . . that made us different. And that's what carried us through that season. No matter how thick or thin it got, someone stood up and led the charge. Someone stood up and made the difference. There's never been a more definable teamwork to take shape and take presence in the NFL than what our '72 team was."[36]

The Dolphins had another couple of factors going for them

as they prepared for Super Bowl VII: experience and confidence. They had gone through all the hoopla and extravagance that a Super Bowl brings in the previous year. They knew what to expect and judging from how they performed versus how the Redskins performed, Miami was more prepared for the distractions that are inevitable with any Super Bowl game. The Dolphins were certain as to what they needed to do and how to go about doing it.

Larry Little certainly knew what was expected of him. He never had any doubts regarding the game against Washington, or what the outcome would be. But he also acknowledged that the game represented different things to different people on the Miami team.

"Super Bowl VII was a game that Coach Shula had to win. . . no doubt about it," Little said, "because he had already got the reputation of not being able to win the big one. But he never brought that up to us. It was on his mind, but he never brought it up. We were very confident going into Super Bowl VII. We were a bunch of young guys, and we were playing against a bunch of old men who were known as 'The Over the Hill Gang.' [Washington head coach] George Allen had a lot of veteran players on his roster, but we were young and confident. We knew that they weren't going to beat us, and they knew that they weren't going to beat us."[37]

One Redskins player presented an air of confidence going into the game, however. His name was Manny Sistrunk, a reserve defensive lineman who saw an increased amount of playing time during the playoffs. Sistrunk ironically would be one of the Washington defensive linemen who would be facing Larry Little in Super Bowl VII. All during the 1972 post season, Sistrunk did more than his share of talking about his opponents, often in a derisive tone or message. He continued to do so when it came to describing Little.

"I had to block Bill Brundidge and Manny Sistrunk in Super Bowl VII," Little recalled. "Neither of them made a whole lot of tackles in that game. Manny had made some statements before that game that pissed me off. He said that I got my reputation by running over small cornerbacks, not against strong defensive tackles."[38]

Little did not require any extra reason (i.e., bulletin board material) to perform his best in Super Bowl VII, but the talkative Sistrunk inadvertently and unwisely gave him one. It stood to reason that if Little was not going to let an All-Pro like Joe Greene get the best of him in the 1972 AFC Title Game, he certainly was not going to let a backup defensive tackle like Manny Sistrunk show him up in Super Bowl VII.

Super Bowl VII was held on January 14, 1973, at the Los Angeles Memorial Coliseum. Dolphins tailback Mercury Morris adequately defended his reasons why he and his teammates would not come up short against the Redskins in that game. In true verbal fashion that has become Morris's trademark over the years, he hit his naysayers with equal doses of logic and reasoning.

"It didn't matter what our opponents' level was at the time that we were playing them," explained Morris. "It only mattered what our level was. For instance, we weren't actually dominating our playoff game against Cleveland, but we still had to take control of it, because we understood where we were the year before. So, we can't lose. We've got to get to the place where we could redeem ourselves, so whatever had to be necessary. . . it didn't matter what Cleveland's matter of play was. It only mattered what our level of play was.

"Against Pittsburgh in the AFC Championship Game, it was the same thing. We had to do whatever we could in the space and the time that we were in. Even when we played Washington in

Super Bowl VII. We go in there as the underdogs. Because they [the oddsmakers] say, 'Oh, they can't win seventeen games.' Well guess what? We already won sixteen. We only have to win one more. And it was the one that we came here for in the first place. We just happened to go unbeaten. Our goal was to get back to the Super Bowl and redeem ourselves in that one game."[39]

Redemption. That was the word that everyone involved with the Dolphins organization wanted to obtain the most, and only by beating the Redskins could that redemption be achieved. From team owner Joe Robbie all the way down to the youngest hanky-waving fan, Miami was ready for redemption in Super Bowl VII. Every player would attain this redemption through his own play on the field. Larry Little was certainly one of them.

"Of course, I was upset because we didn't win Super Bowl VI," said Little, "and I don't think that we played as well as we could have played in that game. Yeah, my attitude was that I was angry the way that we lost to Dallas in that game, and I wanted to prove the next year that we were a better football team than what we showed on that particular day. We didn't want to feel the way that we felt after we lost to Dallas in the Super Bowl. Therefore, we knew that we had to deliver another big effort."[40]

Little and his teammates were poised to deliver that "big effort." But did he or any of his teammates or coaches ever let some modicum of doubt or worry seep into the back of their minds prior to the game? Did they ever think about what their feelings would be if they won sixteen straight games, then somehow lost the seventeenth and final game?

"I have never in my pro career went into a game thinking that we may lose this game," affirmed Little. "My attitude was to win every game that we played. Losing never crossed my mind. It was never talked about what we would feel if we had lost a game. We were confident. I had felt that way in having a positive attitude because our coaching staff had a positive attitude."[41]

Miami's overall positive attitude weathered a trying first half against Washington. Both teams were evenly matched throughout a tough struggle in the first two quarters. The Dolphins drew first blood with a twenty-eight-yard touchdown toss from Bob Griese to wide receiver Howard Twilley. Then a key interception by Miami middle linebacker Nick Buoniconti led to another Dolphins' score. Miami was putting forth a great effort.

Larry Little's efforts in the game were proving to be a testament to his greatness. He managed to handle his blocking assignments with the success and professionalism that came from his unquenchable desire to become a world champion. Moreover, Little was also effective with his sidebar mission. . . that of giving Washington defensive tackle Manny Sistrunk something to think about. As it turned out, Little's key block against Sistrunk paved the way to what would eventually be the game's winning touchdown, a one-yard run by Jim Kiick.

"All I ever thought about during the game was my performance," said Little. "I just wanted to have a good game against who I was going up against. On Kiick's touchdown, Jim just ran right behind me. I knocked Sistrunk out of Kiick's way. Sistrunk didn't have a lot of moves. He was more like a road grater going straight ahead. I didn't say a word to Sistrunk. All I wanted to do was kick his butt."[42]

Miami's 14-0 lead was not truly an indication of kicking Washington's backside, but the Dolphins were in control of the game well into the second half. Even when the Redskins moved the ball into Miami territory, Washington's offense would commit a key mistake or error which halted their momentum and their drives. But just as it appeared as if the Dolphins were coasting toward a shutout victory, they made their only real miscue of the day as they lined up for what would be a game-clinching field goal attempt in the fourth quarter. On that play, Miami placekicker Garo Yepremian suffered the misfortune of watching his low kick thud against the back of the head of Bob Heinz, who was one of his own linemen. Yepremian picked up the bouncing ball and attempted to throw it. . . to no one in particular. Yepremian's hand was too small to grip the ball, and as he ran to his right, the pigskin slipped out of his hand. He then tried to grab it again, but he inadvertently hit the ball up in the air.

Washington defensive back Mike Bass was trailing the play, and he was in the fortunate position to grab the ball as it descended. Bass bolted for the uncluttered sideline, raced past a stunned Yepremian, and reached the Miami end zone for a forty-nine-yard score which gave the Redskins at least some small measure of hope as time in the fourth quarter was dwindling. Were the Dolphins players worried, or at least apprehensive upon seeing Bass score a touchdown? Larry Little was pragmatic in his response:

"Well, I don't think so, because we had the game in hand, all in all," expressed Little. "But there's always some uncertainty that might come up. . . when something else happens. But we were still up on the scoreboard, and the way our defense was playing that day also, was the reason why we were confident that we were going to win."[43]

Miami's lead was now down to 14-7. But the bottom-line fact is that they had come too far to see their dream get vanquished at this late stage of the game, and of the season. Their determination was evident from this moment on. The Dolphins defense choked off the last vestige of Washington resistance, and the final gun sounded.

Miami had prevailed by that 14-7 final score. An expansion team from the old AFL that was only seven years old had won a Super Bowl, and in doing so, had become the only team in NFL history to have achieved a perfect seventeen wins and zero losses record in one season. The 90,192 in attendance on that day in the Los Angeles Memorial Coliseum, and the millions across the United States and the world who watched the game on television, had witnessed a historic event. But what is most noteworthy all these years later is the fact that since that January afternoon in 1973, no team in the annals of the sport has been able to equal what the Dolphins were able to do. . . namely, obtain perfection in a single year.

Don Shula got his vindication in 1972, to be sure. As he rode triumphantly off the Coliseum's field on the shoulders of his players, he had laid to rest his previous label of not being able to win a world championship. Shula displayed a stoic appearance according to Little, and although he wore an ear-to-ear wide grin, he did not show any visible signs of relief following the triumph over the Redskins.

"I knew that he was elated," Little recalled. "But I didn't see him go 'shoo,' or give any one of those kinds of [victorious] facial expressions."[44]

Thanks in large part to winning Super Bowl VII and by going undefeated, Shula was named the NFL's Coach of the Year in 1972, the fourth and final time that he would be so honored during his esteemed coaching career. His previous three Coach of the Year awards all came when he was the head coach of the Baltimore Colts in 1964, 1967, and 1968. Following his team's victory in Super Bowl VII, Shula penned these lines, which summarized his thoughts about winning and about the sacrifices that his players in Miami had made since 1970:

"The ultimate goal is victory," wrote Shula, "and if you refuse to work as hard as you possibly can toward that aim, or if you do anything that keeps you from achieving that goal, then you are just cheating yourself. I feel that way about athletics, but more importantly I feel that way about life in general."[45]

Larry Little's life in general had changed dramatically on that victorious afternoon in Los Angeles. Many years after achieving the pinnacle of his profession with a Super Bowl championship, Little was asked whether he felt if another perfect season could be obtained by any pro football team in the future. He could not be completely certain, but he did know for sure what it took for his team to accomplish the feat in 1972.

"Well, it's hard for me to say," surmised Little regarding the question, "but deep down inside, I don't believe so. I believe that teams right now, if they went undefeated, would have to play their starters all the way through the season and the playoffs. And you want to keep guys from getting injured. If that does happen, they would just be joining us as a perfect team but not surpassing us."[46]

In the end, only time—and especially determination—will tell if any future team can wear the undefeated crown. Determination. Quite possibly, it is the most accurate word to describe Larry Little and the 1972 Miami Dolphins.

Miami Dolphins offensive guard Larry Little peers into the action on the field during a game from the 1972 season. Little was inducted into the Pro Football Hall of Fame in 1993. (David Durochik via AP)

Miami Dolphins offensive guard Larry Little (66) is seen in action during an NFL game against the New England Patriots, circa 1975. (Tony Tomsic via AP)

Miami Dolphins offensive guard Larry Little (#66) leads running back Jim Kiick (#21) on a sweep against the Baltimore Colts in a preseason game at the Orange Bowl in Miami on Aug. 31, 1970. (AP Photo/Toby Massey)

Miami Dolphins offensive guard Larry Little is all smiles in training camp as he prepares for his team's historic 1972 season. (AP Photo)

Larry Little is seen on July 31, 1993, holding his bronze bust with his presenter, Miami Dolphins Hall of Fame head coach Don Shula, on the afternoon of Little's enshrinement at the Pro Football Hall of Fame in Canton, Ohio. Photo courtesy of the Pro Football Hall of Fame.

The Pro Football Hall of Fame Parade! Larry Little and Don Shula participate in the traditional parade just prior to Little's enshrinement into the Pro Football Hall of Fame in Canton, Ohio. Photo courtesy of the Pro Football Hall of Fame.

Larry Little's bronze bust at the Pro Football Hall of Fame in Canton, Ohio.
Photo courtesy of the Pro Football Hall of Fame.

Each enshrinee at the Pro Football Hall of Fame receives a custom-made ring
to commemorate their honor and achievement. Here is Larry Little's Pro
Football Hall of Fame ring. Photo courtesy of the Pro Football Hall of Fame.

Larry Little and Don Shula pose for the cameras following Little's enshrinement speech at the Pro Football Hall of Fame in Canton, Ohio. Photo courtesy of the Pro Football Hall of Fame.

Miami Dolphins head coach Don Shula and his great offensive guard Larry Little pose for a photo on the afternoon of Little's enshrinement inside the Pro Football Hall of Fame in Canton, Ohio. Photo courtesy of the Pro Football Hall of Fame.

Pro Football Hall of Famer Larry Little enjoys returning to participate in the annual festivities at the Pro Football Hall of Fame in Canton, Ohio. Photo courtesy of the Pro Football Hall of Fame.

Larry Little relaxes while signing autographs at the Pro Football Hall of Fame in Canton, Ohio. Photo courtesy of the Pro Football Hall of Fame.

An artwork mural of Hall of Fame offensive guard Larry Little. Photo courtesy
of the Pro Football Hall of Fame.

CHAPTER 8

ENCORE FROM A POWERHOUSE

Repeating as a champion in any professional sport is difficult. It is probably most difficult in pro football, where one key injury, or one specific lost game, one missed field goal, one fumble or interception, or even one missed block, could be responsible for rupturing a team's chances to claim another title. Added to all of that was how a championship team was viewed by all the other teams in the league. They were the measuring stick, and as such, every one of their opponents planned and prepared to their full exertions to beat them. It would be a badge of honor to defeat a world champion. This was the situation that the Miami Dolphins found themselves in as soon as they began work in 1973 to defend their world championship.

No team had faced what the Dolphins had faced in 1973, namely, to try to win another Vince Lombardi Trophy immediately following an undefeated season. But they had a couple of important factors going for them in this quest. First, the players on their roster were mostly young athletes, and practically every one of them who suited up for the team in 1972 would also be wearing the aqua and orange Miami colors in 1973. Two, their head coach, Don Shula, was the ideal head coach to inspire them to return to the pinnacle of pro football in Super Bowl VIII. Shula's drive, determination, and motivation pushed his players like they had never been pushed before in 1972. It stood to reason that neither he—nor his players—were going to be satisfied with just one world championship under their belts.

"I didn't know what the odds were of going undefeated two straight seasons," admitted Larry Little. "We didn't do that, but we only lost two games all throughout the 1973 season. Then at one point in '73, we went on a ten-game winning streak. When we won the Super Bowl in '72, we wanted to have the same experience again by winning it again the next year. It was an exciting experience. Winning a Super Bowl was the greatest feeling that I ever had playing football, because I had never really been on any championship team before. Not in high school, and not in college. And I really enjoyed that moment, and I wanted to enjoy it again."[1]

The naysayers did not claim a spirit of enjoyment, in contrast. They had spent their time as the new pro football campaign approached scratching their heads and still wondering how the Dolphins managed to go undefeated in 1972. Still others were busy predicting that Miami would be hard pressed to defend their Super Bowl title. The Dolphins players, however, had it in their minds to just continue winning. They now owned the Shula blueprint, and they would follow it just as they had the previous year.

"I think it was the same tactic," commented fullback Larry Csonka, regarding Miami's approach to the 1973 season. "When you learned how to take it one game at a time, you start to repeat that."[2]

The Dolphins learned a lot about themselves throughout the 1972 season. They had been through a lot, and they had achieved a lot. They also knew that Don Shula had built them up to be a team that would not take anything for granted, regardless of the situation. But perhaps most importantly, Shula gave them a goal in 1972, which they completed. In 1973, they received a new goal from their head coach, and it stayed in the back of their minds all throughout that season.

"For one thing, the pressure was off our backs," assessed Little in speaking about the success of being a champion. "We had won a Super Bowl. . . we had done that. So, we went onto 1973, going on about our business, trying to win another Super Bowl. There was no complacency on our team. Winning two Super Bowls in a row had only been done once before [by Green Bay in 1966 and 1967]. To tie that record was our goal, and there was no doubt that we had a lot of confidence that we could do that in 1973. I thought that we would go undefeated again in 1973 before that season began. That was the level of confidence that I had with that team."[3]

Confidence among the team would be tried and tested right from the very first regular season game in 1973. The opening game versus San Francisco was held in the Orange Bowl. Just prior to that game, and indeed just prior to every Dolphins game at the Orange Bowl during the early 1970s, a religious invocation was given by a priest, a preacher, or a rabbi, just prior to the opening kickoff. It was thought to be a more publicly religious era during those years in America. Indeed, no other team managed to broadcast an opening prayer over the stadium's loudspeakers for the teams that would play that day more than the Dolphins. Why was Miami different in this respect? Was the city of Miami a more religious city than most cities in America?

"Yeah, I remember those pregame prayers," declared Little. "I seriously doubt that Miami was a more religious city than any of the others, because of the number of crimes that were occurring down in Miami. I believe that Miami had those prayers because [team owner] Joe Robbie was such a stanch Catholic. And they had a rabbi leading prayers on occasion too, because there was a big Jewish population down in Miami."[4]

Whatever prayers that may have been uttered for pleasant weather conditions on the opening day of the 1973 season certainly went unanswered. The weather on that September 16th day was ironically like the first game at Kansas City from the previous year. Both contests featured extremely hot and humid weather conditions, which considering how much Shula's team trained in the Florida heat all summer long, should be a checkmark in Miami's favor. The reasoning was also considering that the 49ers were not used to such hellish conditions, and that the strength-sapping heat in Miami would get the better of them.

But that is not exactly how the game played out, at least not in the first half. San Francisco kept drinking plenty of fluids, and wet towel compresses were distributed to their players liberally on the bench. The 49ers managed to take a 13-6 lead over the Dolphins entering the fourth quarter. Then suddenly, the Miami offense woke up. They drove the ball deep enough into San Francisco territory on several occasions to allow Dolphin's place kicker Garo Yepremian to connect on two of his four successful field goals. A big ten-yard pass from Bob Griese to wide receiver Paul Warfield on a quick slant pattern was Miami's only touchdown of the day, but combined with Yepremian's contribution, it was enough. The Dolphins prevailed, 21-13.

Still, the hot temperatures on the Orange Bowl's Poly-Turf field that day were what most of the players remember to this day. It also made for a somewhat humorous sight of one of Little's opponents along the line of scrimmage.

"Playing on that turf in Miami, it was like twenty degrees warmer than by playing on natural grass," Little affirmed. "I remember playing that game against the 49ers in the 1973 season opener. I was playing against a guy by the name of Charlie Krueger, and he liked to chew tobacco, and the tobacco juice was all over his face, and all over his uniform. And he didn't even realize it! It was coming out of his mouth automatically. And I didn't want any of that tobacco juice of his to get on me!

"The heat in Miami was the main difference in that game. They [the 49ers] were all worn out by the fourth quarter. Some of their guys refused to come out to play in the second half because of that heat. Now we were drinking fluids during the games, but you know we didn't start drinking water in our practices until 1975. There's no doubt that we were more used to that Miami heat than our opponents. That was our advantage when other teams came to Miami to play us."[5]

Dolphins halfback Mercury Morris explains—in his own uniquely cerebral way—the thoughts behind Coach Don Shula's summer camp procedures of straying away from distributing fluids to his players:

"The misconception back then was that water was not good for you when you were on the field. So, Shula was in that camp where he believed that water would make you have cramps. Only when they found out the necessity of Gatorade, did they wise up and realize that people needed to be hydrated. It wasn't like proving how tough you were if you didn't have water, but that's what we went through during those times. So, our training camps were always grueling."[6]

The grueling nature of trying to repeat as world champions would deal with a test that rivaled hot temperatures the following week, when the Dolphins played the Oakland Raiders in California.

Oakland was always competitive, and they were certainly aware of Miami's eighteen-game winning streak, dating back to the opening game of 1972. The Raiders' game plan on September 23, 1973, was to stop the prized Dolphins rushing attack. Their defense did so by permitting Miami's runners to just a combined 105 yards on twenty-four rushing carries. Added to that was the fact that Miami quarterback Bob Griese could only complete twelve of his twenty-five passes for a mere ninety yards. When the final gun sounded, the Raiders efficiently ended the Dolphins' prized winning streak by a score of 12-7. It was indeed a humbling loss.

"We didn't play the football game we were capable of against the Raiders," admitted Larry Little later during the 1973 season. "We gained 105 yards on the ground. I guess that tells you something about the way we blocked. Our defense played a hell of a game, but we didn't do anything on offense, and Shula let us know that after the game. He told us that we were better than what we showed in that game, and we knew that we were better offensively than what we showed against Oakland. I was sorry to see it [the winning streak] end. I wanted to keep it going. But we just played a bad game."[7]

Despite seeing their run of victories come to an end, the loss to the Raiders was a tonic that Miami's players needed at a beneficial time in the 1973 season. It was as if the Dolphins now had a chip on their shoulders, which often gave their players an ample reason to get back into the fight. Losing a game so early in the year only meant that they were going to have plenty of time in the future to restore their winning binge.

"We were becoming very much a target, and then Oakland knocked us off," said Miami fullback Larry Csonka. "And once we realized that we could be beaten, we started to get hungry again. I think that losing to Oakland, and having them break our winning streak, took some of the pressure off. Everyone was trying to beat us, and everyone was playing above their usual manner, because they were going up against a team that hadn't lost in over a season. And when you got that off your back, after that loss to Oakland happened, we lost only one more game later in the 1973 season."[8]

Larry Little's blocking assignments for the next game against the New England Patriots in late September at the Orange Bowl would involve opening holes in the interior of New England's defensive line. He and his mates on the offensive line did so in brilliant fashion. Mercury Morris gained a career-best 197 yards rushing against the Patriots, and by the final gun, Miami accrued an impressive 301 total rushing yards.

The Dolphins' 44-23 romp over the Patriots set the Floridians back on the winning side of things, and they would not be defeated again for many more weeks.

"Everybody wanted to be the team that knocked us off," affirmed Little. "We knew that we were a target going into the 1973 season. And that's why the Oakland Raiders were so elated after they knocked us off in the second game of the year."[9]

Although they did not know it at the time, Little and his teammates were at the beginning of one of the best winning streaks that they would experience during the 1970s compared to their previous season. The Dolphins would next be visited by the New York Jets following their rout of the Patriots. New York was a team that was in the process of having its worst season since 1970. Miami had no trouble with them, as they crushed the Jets, 31-3.

The next game would present a more difficult challenge for the Dolphins, however. It would be a repeat of the previous season's AFC Divisional Playoff game between Miami and Cleveland, and it would occur at Cleveland's Municipal Stadium on Monday Night Football. Once again, the Dolphins would feature their running game as their main method of coming from behind and dispatching the Browns, 17-9.

The members of the Miami defense would provide the elements of victory the following week to help the Dolphins to coast to a 27-6 triumph over Buffalo. The "No-Name Defense," as they were labeled, limited the Bills offense to a meager seventy-six total net yards. Shula's men now owned a 5-1 record, which represented the best mark in the conference. Having a great record was becoming common for this Miami squad, but it did not come about by accident. Coach Shula permitted no letup among his players, his assistant coaches, or himself. They just kept grinding.

"Our keys," said offensive line coach Monte Clark, "are two four-letter words. . . want and work. Want to be the best and work to be the best. It's just been a willingness to work. . . their desire to improve. . . that's what got them [the Dolphins offensive linemen] together."[10]

Larry Little possessed a deep desire to please Coach Clark. Little realized how much he had learned from his offensive line coach during his early years in Miami, and indeed how much all his teammates on the Dolphins offensive line had learned while Clark was teaching them. Rarely did a practice session go by where Clark did not offer at least some important token of knowledge to his players.

"Monte was a perfectionist," admitted Little. "And he was a very detail-oriented person. In blocking, he would want your hands in the right place. He would want your feet in the right place to maintain your leverage at all times. He had a term that he called 'Stick, wall, and climb.' Basically, it meant to stick or hit your opponent, then you wall him up, then you climb on top of him to get him out of the hole that your running back was intending to run through."[11]

Little continued his superlative sticking, walling, and climbing blocking efforts the following week at New England, where the Miami ground attack once again proved too tough for the Patriots to handle. Once again, it was Morris's sweeps to the right which accounted for the majority of the Dolphins rushing yardage in a 30-14 win. Miami then cruised to their sixth straight victory the next week by defeating the New York Jets, 24-14. They were now 7-1, and they were pulling away from the rest of the teams in the AFC Eastern Division standings.

The Dolphins' dominance over their divisional foes was even more pronounced during the following two weeks, both of which were shut-out victories. In week nine, Miami crushed the Baltimore Colts at the Orange Bowl by a score of 44-0. The Dolphins were succeeding in 1973 not just because of their running game, but also because of their passing game. Larry Little's contribution to the team's success in this, his seventh year in pro football, came about due to his growing intelligence in the strategic aspects of the game, and due to his undeniable physical strength and endurance.

"Chicken [Little] always asked questions," recalled Miami quarterback Bob Griese. "He wanted to know why we were doing this and why we were doing that. And he was as good in the fourth quarter as he was in the first quarter. He was good the whole game. You know now, they've got an electronic receiver in the quarterback's helmet where the coach just talks to them in their helmet. But back then, we didn't have that. Players ran the plays in from the sidelines. A lineman would rotate each play, or a back or a receiver would come in and give you the play. And then a receiver would run off the field, and then the next guy would come in with the next play. But I didn't have that. I just called my own plays.

"But there were different times, when I just needed some time to stay on the field and eat up some of the clock. So, there were times when I would ask the offensive line for their suggestions. Say that the previous play was a nine-yard gain. I might say something like, 'Alright. . . who's got a good play for second-and-one?' Chicken would always have a play. 'Run behind me Griese,' he would say. 'Run behind me.'"[12]

Griese and the rest of Miami's offense would continue to run behind Larry Little the following week when the Dolphins played their rematch with the Bills up in Buffalo. Csonka, Kiick, Morris, Griese, and reserve fullback Don Nottingham shared a total of forty-two carries to help Miami post a 17-0 victory over the Bills. As evidenced by the final score, the Dolphins defense once again performed superlatively. They surrendered 238 total rushing yards to Buffalo, but they kept their goal line from being crossed.

Miami's goal line was crossed by Dallas the following week, but only once. The Dolphins did just enough on offense to defeat the Cowboys by a score of 14-7. Once again just as in Super Bowl VI, Little was successful with his blocks on (Dallas defensive tackle) Jethro Pugh. This contest against the Cowboys was a struggle, however. Somewhat surprisingly though, Miami was not out for retribution, at least as far as Larry Little was concerned.

"It wasn't really a revenge game, because that [Super Bowl VI] was two years earlier," explained Little. "So, we had to go into Dallas, which was a tough place to play. I mean it was a hard-fought game against the Cowboys. The final score will tell you that. At that time, Dallas played what was called the Flex Defense. And that alignment had two [defensive] linemen up, and two linemen back off the ball. Well, that was just perfect for me, because when Jethro Pugh was back off the ball, I could surge forward and knock him back even further. And he was a good football player, mind you. But I thought that I was one step ahead of him in that game."[13]

Staying one step ahead of their next opponent was the next goal for Shula's team to achieve. On Monday evening, December 3, 1973, Miami played host to their foes from the previous year's AFC Championship Game, the Pittsburgh Steelers. This contest was a meeting with two distinct halves. The Dolphins, behind the extraordinary four interceptions from safety Dick Anderson (two of which he returned for touchdowns), took a 30-3 lead into the third quarter. Pittsburgh responded by scoring twenty-three second half points. It was not enough for the Steelers, however, as Miami prevailed, 30-26.

"That was like two separate games, with one in the first half and another one in the second half," said Little. "I mean we dominated them in the first half. One thing that helped us was all of those interceptions that we made. Our defense was so smart. Our defensive coordinator, Bill Arnsparger, was a genius. He had our defense ready to play in every game. But Pittsburgh was a good team, and they weren't going to lay down for us, especially after we beat them in the AFC Championship Game in 1972."[14]

Being unable to score even a single point in the second half against the Steelers proved that things were not right with the Miami offense, however. This fact was displayed beyond any doubt the following Sunday, as the Dolphins lost their first game since the second week of the season. The Baltimore Colts somehow sprung one of the league's biggest upsets of 1973 by beating Miami, 16-3. A total of five Dolphins starters on both offense and defense suffered injuries in that game, including Larry Little. It was true that by this time, Shula's team had already clinched their third straight AFC Eastern Division title and thus had no real incentive to play all its veteran starters in a relatively meaningless game at Baltimore. Nevertheless, it is always good to go into the playoffs carrying a winning streak. Those five injured Miami players would—for safety's sake—be kept from playing in their team's next game.

"I was taken out of some games in the fourth quarter so I wouldn't get injured," Little said. "We were getting beat up pretty bad up in Baltimore near the end of the '73 season, and they took me out of that game in the fourth quarter."[15]

Miami regained its winning edge in the final week of the 1973 regular season, when the Detroit Lions visited the Orange Bowl. Three more Dolphins starters were injured in this contest, which ended in a 34-7 Miami victory. It is never good to have any of your starting players go down just before the playoffs, but that is the dilemma that Shula's team was saddled with as the regular season ended.

Both of Miami's playoff games would take place at the Orange Bowl. The first contest had Miami facing the Cincinnati Bengals, the winners of the AFC Central Division title. On paper, it appeared as if the Dolphins had a much better team than Cincinnati, especially regarding overall playoff experience. And that is the way the game started, with Miami bolting out to a 21-3 lead. Everything that the Dolphins offense tried seemed to be working to near perfection. Csonka, Morris, and Kiick were all gaining good ground yardage, and just as their game plan dictated, they were eating up the clock and keeping Cincinnati's offense on the bench.

But despite taking an early command in the contest, Larry Little had his hands full. Little had to block All-Pro Mike Reid, a former All-American from Penn State University, and a multi-talented player who had enough moves to give practically every offensive lineman in the league a difficult time.

"The quickest defensive lineman that I ever played against was Mike Reid, with the Cincinnati Bengals," Little admitted. "He was extremely quick. . . as quick as a cat. Going up against Mike Reid, I learned from the films that I watched of him that I had to set up in my blocking stance really quick, in order to take his quick moves away from him. I was glad that he retired from pro football early so he could focus on his career as a concert piano player."[16]

Almost just as quickly as Reid set up to converge on Little, the Bengals managed to rapidly get back into the game just before halftime. Miami's offense inexplicably began to relax and make several mistakes, which never sat right with Don Shula. The Bengals' sudden surge drew them closer to Miami at 21-16.

Shula's diatribe and tongue-lashing directed at his players in the halftime locker room was one of the most volatile and profanity-laced of the head coach's career. Some players claimed that it was almost biblical in its proportions. Despite this, Larry Little was at this moment much more concerned with his issues with Mike Reid to focus on Shula's rants.

"I don't really remember it [Shula's tirade]," said Little. "I know that we did not play a really good first half, even though we had a lead at halftime. But we went out there in the second half with the intention of dominating them [the Bengals], and that's what we did. . . we dominated them."[17]

Shula's outburst had the desired effect. The Dolphins defense would not surrender a single point in the second half, and the Miami offense put together a couple of key scoring drives in the third and fourth quarters to produce a 34-16 victory. Next up would be the AFC Championship Game. The Oakland Raiders would be their opponent in that contest, and it would be a chance at revenge for Miami. For his part, Larry Little did not enjoy one of his better games in that earlier meeting against the Raiders in the second week of the 1973 season. He was determined, however, to get the better of Oakland in the rematch.

"In the 1973 AFC Championship Game, I pulled a Joe Namath," recalled Little. "I predicted and guaranteed a victory, just like Namath did prior to Super Bowl III. You know, in every game we played that year, we scored at least some points the first time that we had the ball. In the playoffs versus Cincinnati, we scored the first time that we had the ball. And then I guaranteed that in the next game, the Raiders were not going to beat us again. I told the reporters that they could print that in the newspapers."[18]

Little was still feeling the ill-effects of his knee injury—that he received earlier in the season—throughout the AFC Title Game, but he soldiered on, nonetheless. He also endured an injury to his left ankle on Miami's first scoring drive of the game against the Raiders in the Championship contest. On that particular injury, Little fell victim to a common occurrence along the line of scrimmage. . . having an opponent fall on top of you. In this case, a member of the Oakland defense fell on top of Little's ankle.

Despite the pain in his knee and his ankle, Little opened several key holes for Csonka during the game, and the bullish Miami fullback charged through them to rush for 117 yards. Csonka also scored three rushing touchdowns, two of which came in the first half which gave the Dolphins a commanding 14-0 halftime lead. On Csonka's first touchdown, Little blew Oakland linebacker Phil Villapiano so far out of the fullback's intended path, that there was no Raiders defender anywhere near Csonka as he crossed the goal line. On Csonka's second touchdown from two yards out, a big block by Little on Oakland linebacker Dan Conners proved to be the necessary action that was required to open a hole for Csonka to score. After the play was over, Csonka saw Little limping back to the huddle. He embraced his blocker and said something in Little's earhole.

"I've said a lot of things to Larry over the years," Csonka recalled. "Mostly, I would ask him if he was alright. I wanted to know how much pain he was in, and whether he could perform or if he needed help getting off the field. You know it's one thing to get an injury. It's another thing to risk your career, by not hearing the bell ringing in your head when it's ringing. I did not want a minor injury to turn into a major injury on any of my offensive linemen, because everyone was very important. I was concerned about him [Little]. Any running back. . . it doesn't matter. . . if he's worth his salt at all, is very interested in the health and welfare of his offensive linemen, because without them, you're just a target out there."[19]

When asked what Csonka said to him following his block that enabled the Miami fullback to score his second touchdown, Little was understandably blunt in his description.

"He [Csonka] told me, 'Thank you for burying Dan Conners,'" said a chuckling Little.[20] "But Larry Csonka personified toughness. He was one tough football player. He played in Super Bowl VIII with a broken nose, and he broke it many times before that. He had a winner's mentality. . . no doubt about that. That guy loved to be my teammate."[21]

Like many of his Dolphin teammates, Little knew that the requirement to play the game while enduring aches, pains, and various injuries, was accepted as a given part of the sport. As the 1973 season wound down, the stakes got higher, and the need for key players (like himself) to stay in the lineup grew as the Dolphins neared the end of their season.

"So far, I've had nothing but nagging injuries," said Little just prior to the AFC Title Game versus the Raiders. "You've got to play with those nagging injuries. It's been that way most of the year."[22]

While Little's effectiveness against the Oakland defenders was stellar despite his injuries, his guaranteed victory over the Raiders appeared to be in question somewhat, especially when Oakland pulled to within 17-10 on the scoreboard in the third quarter. Miami's defense dominated the fourth quarter, however, and Csonka scored another touchdown to lift the Dolphins to a 27-10 win, their twenty-fourth straight victory at the Orange Bowl. The Miami ground attack registered a superlative 266 total rushing yards versus Oakland.

Little and his teammates thus became the first team in pro football history to go to three straight Super Bowls. Moreover, they would get a chance to equal Green Bay's record of two straight Super Bowl triumphs. It was indeed a great time to be a Dolphins player and a Dolphins fan.

"Oh, there was no doubt that the city of Miami was excited during those years," exclaimed Little. "You know, during those days, the city was still working on integration. But you could feel the whole city coming together as one in '72 and '73. It was a special feeling."[23]

Miami would next face the Minnesota Vikings in Super Bowl VIII in Houston's Rice University Stadium. The Vikings had a similar 1973 season to the one that the Dolphins had just registered. Both teams earned a 12-2 record that year, and both had very strong defenses. But it would be the Miami offensive line which would prove to be the game's strongest element. Coach Monte Clark had put them in a position to play the game of their lives against Minnesota. Despite that fact, the tension and the anxiety in the Dolphins locker room just before the game had at least one Miami player in a state of consternation, and Larry Little could not help but notice it.

"Ed Newman was my backup with the Dolphins in '73," said Little, "and he was a very fine guard. He would go on to play in several Pro Bowls after I retired. He was a hell of a guard. He was strong, and he could run well. But when we were getting ready to play in Super Bowl VIII, his locker was right next to mine, and he had the pregame jitters. This went on for several minutes, and I finally told him, 'Darn man. . . stop your shaking! You're making me nervous!'"[24]

If Newman and Little were nervous playing in that game, it certainly did not show. Little would be slated to block Minnesota defensive tackle Gary Larsen in Super Bowl VIII. Larsen was considered to be the most muscular of the Vikings' famous front four on defense.

"You know playing a guard position meant that a lot of guys—like Larsen—would bull rush you to get to the quarterback," admitted Little. "But once we put our pads on, we pass blocked every day in practice. Also, our defense would help me out. For example, if I was going to face a guy who liked to bull rush me to get to the quarterback, our defensive linemen in practice would bull rush me in practice, so I could be prepared for it to happen in the actual games."[25]

Little was able to absorb whatever Larsen would try to dish out in Super Bowl VIII. Miami utilized cross blocking to keep the Minnesota front four off balance all game long. Once the Vikings' defense tried to adjust to the cross blocking, Miami offensive line coach Monte Clark had his linemen focus on straight ahead blocking, where the likes of Little, Langer, Moore, etc., just plowed straight into the Minnesota defensive linemen in a thundering rush. That tactic worked just as well as the cross blocking did, and the resulting accumulated ground yardage from Csonka and Morris was the visible result.

"One thing that I vividly recall that day was when Larsen tried to stare me down from across the field while we were standing for the national anthem," chortled Little. "All I could think of at that time was that he was going to be in for a long day. And he had a long day. The whole Viking defense did. We had a heck of a day rushing. He didn't make a lot of tackles in Super Bowl VIII. I think that we scored on them the first three times that we had the ball. We went into that game believing that we could move the ball against anybody. We ran the ball down their throats."[26]

Some Miami running plays were used with the concept of allowing the runners to determine their own paths downfield, based on the blocks that they were witnessing from their offensive linemen. Tailback Mercury Morris was extremely adept at adjusting his initial route to a more profitable one, once he saw a different hole open up.

"On sweeps, we had a play called Ride 38," recalled Morris, "and that play had a lot of success. But some of our best plays, and the most successful plays that we had, were with just Larry and me. There was a play in Super Bowl VIII where he took out [Minnesota defensive end] Jim Marshall, and it was called 37 Trap Outside. On that particular play, Jim Marshall came up the field and tried to force me back inside. I was going outside, however, and Larry knocked Marshall off of his feet. Now everybody couldn't do that, but Larry had the skills and the abilities as a big man to do exactly that right there. And that play right there is an example of how we would take the strength of a team and turn them into weaknesses."[27]

Miami's strength from their constant battering runs had the desired effect. The Dolphins built a 17-0 halftime lead based primarily on their ground game, and on Csonka's relentless efforts to gain yardage. On Csonka's first of his two rushing touchdowns, he ran directly behind Larry Little, who drove Gary Larsen several yards out of Csonka's way. Shula was determined to keep his foot on the gas pedal in the second half. In the third quarter, Csonka scored his second touchdown, with Little breaking past the line of scrimmage and blocking Minnesota middle linebacker Jeff Siemon from getting near Csonka. The Dolphins' lead thus grew to an insurmountable 24-0.

Larry Little adequately got his job done in Super Bowl VIII. He knew full well that he and his teammates on the offensive line simply had to be mistake-free, and by most accounts, they were. They knew that no play was going to be successful if they were not successful when beginning the play.

"We always prided ourselves in being a smart football team and a tough football team," declared Little. "We may not have won all of our games after our undefeated season in 1972, but we had a lot of pride. We would regularly register the fewest holding penalties in the league after almost every season. We played clean football."[28]

The Dolphins cleanly got their job done in Super Bowl VIII. The Vikings finally managed to score a touchdown in the game's fourth quarter, however, but it was not enough to stop the determined efforts of Shula's team on this day. Miami prevailed 24-7, and thus had won two straight Super Bowls, an accomplishment that only the legendary Green Bay Packers of 1966 and 1967 had previously achieved. Check off another goal that was attained. It was indeed one of the greatest events for the team, and for Larry Little as well. The future beckoned, but for Little, the celebrations and the accomplishments were utmost on his mind.

"I wasn't thinking about the next year coming off the field after Super Bowl VIII," admitted Little. "I was just elated to do what we just did, which was beat a very good Minnesota Vikings team. I don't think that Super Bowl VII in 1972 was a fluke, because of the way that we beat teams in '73. We dominated teams more in '73 than we did in '72."[29]

Next up for Miami would be a new year, and another opportunity to dominate their opponents. But such an endeavor would turn out to be quite a challenge. Indeed, the 1974 season would be one of the most difficult challenges that Larry Little and his teammates would ever face.

CHAPTER 9

COULD HAVE MADE HISTORY. . . AGAIN

N o team in pro football history has ever won three straight
Super Bowls. The Miami Dolphins were aware of that fact
as they prepared to enter the 1974 NFL season. They used that
point as a form of motivation. They had already accomplished
some very remarkable achievements in pro football history up
to that time. They were the first (and thus far only) team to ever
go undefeated in a season. They became the first team during the
decade of the 1970s to win back-to-back Super Bowls in 1972
and 1973. With those accomplishments in mind, was the goal
of attaining three straight world championships in the forefront
of their thoughts as the 1974 season approached?

"No, Shula did not bring up the subject of winning a third
straight Super Bowl in any of our meetings," remembered Little.
"But we players knew in the back of our minds that we could
do that. . . that we had the ability to win another Super Bowl."[1]

But before Little could contribute to helping the Dolphins
make NFL history again, he first had to address what was probably
the most eventful offseason of his pro career. The Larry Little
Gold Coast Summer Camp of his was still going strong. Thanks
to Little's fame as a star member of a world championship NFL
team—and a dynastic team at that—a growing number of kids
in and around the city of Miami wanted to attend the camp.

And a lot of influential people were regularly taking notice of Little's efforts. The North Miami Beach Jaycees lauded him for "services rendered to the community." And the Florida Jaycees named Little as one of the five outstanding young men in the state. Practically every youngster in South Florida was familiar with Little, and they all looked up to him.

"Our youth, both the teenage boys and the little kids, have established him as their idol," remarked Northwestern High School football coach Alkin Hepburn in 1973. "He has a tremendous impact. It's very rare to see Larry go through the community without stopping to talk to the kids."[2]

The attention that Little was receiving at this point in his life was understandable. He had a past as a child that was similar—and in some cases identical—to those kids who were participating in his summer camp. Those youngsters could relate to him better than they could to perhaps any other player on the Dolphins roster. Despite that, Little would often have to address the aspect of modesty in his life, due primarily to his noticeable popularity.

"That camp is just as much a part of me as football is," proclaimed Little in the 1970s. "I know a lot of younger people in the camp because I know a lot of their parents. I'm always around the community, and sometimes the kids notice the nameplate on my car. They'll wave and I'll stop, and we'll start talking. It isn't something that's planned. I do have my private life too, you know. It's an impromptu thing. They know that I don't want to be a phony with them. I just want to be like any normal human being. . . to get along with people, and to have them get along with me. We have been doing the camp for a decade, and I want to do it as long as we can keep being productive and doing things positively.[3]

"I am convinced that the important value of the camps is the opportunity it affords the kids to get away from the neighborhood.

To mix with other kids from other neighborhoods. They get a chance to learn the art of getting along. They learn to cope with issues. We stress discipline [at the camps] and expect everyone to live up to the rules. . . while having a good time. It works. We get letters from the parents. They report changes in their sons for the better. Evidently, we are making some impact."[4]

Little was encouraged by the positive results of his camp. But he became more introspective of the activities of his years as he aged. In a more contemplative mood, Little spoke more about how fame had affected his adult life and how he had to sacrifice privacy for his dreams that he had all during his youth. It was a tradeoff, to be sure. But at this moment as he grew older, he had to accept his fate. He was getting a taste of his own popularity. . . practically any time that he stepped outside of his home.

"I don't like to be recognized every time I go out," said Little following the 1973 season. "But it's inevitable. I'm from Miami, and I know a lot of people. I have no regrets, understand, but sometimes, it's a light hassle. I try to wear different types of hats, but people still recognize me. They want to talk about football. Heck, I'd rather talk about music, because I'm a music fanatic. But they want to talk about football, and the season and everything."[5]

Little's fans were not the only ones who wanted to talk about football, however. A new league, the World Football League (WFL), was looking to raid NFL rosters for quality players. Naturally, the world champion Dolphins were a major target for the new league's owners, and they focused on signing some of the biggest names in the sport. They succeeded in getting five Miami players, including Larry Csonka, Jim Kiick, and Paul Warfield, to put pen to paper, thanks to the enticement of a major pay raise for each of them. Joe Robbie could not—or would not—compete with the cash that a team like the Memphis Southmen of the WFL had in their satchel. As a result, a segment of the Dolphins would be leaving the team as soon as the 1974 season concluded. Many football historians point to that departure by those Miami players as the official end of the Dolphins' 1970s dynasty.

But Larry Little did not look disapprovingly at the move that Csonka, Kiick, and Warfield made. He understood the economics of the game. He also realized how short a typical career lasts for a pro football player, averaging four to five years, and that's without injuries plaguing their careers. Indeed, a player's loyalty to his team could only go so far when faced with the chance to fill up his wallet.

"No, I didn't feel any offense toward them leaving," opined Little. "I knew that they were going. I knew how things were down in Miami. I knew that [Dolphins owner] Joe Robbie was not into spending a lot of money. And those guys went to where they were going to make more money. But I felt good for a guy like Csonka, because he was going to a situation that was best for him. It is wise for the players to get the money while they still can."[6]

Getting that money seemed to be the mantra of all the NFL players during the summer of 1974. The NFL team owners and the NFLPA were at odds during that offseason, and it was due to the business side of the sport. All this at a time when the players' union contracts were due to be renewed, resigned, or renegotiated. Both the players' union and the twenty-six team owners at the time had plans on what they desired to achieve in the debates. And there was a recent template for the structure of these talks. Back in 1970, the players briefly went on strike to obtain a fairer monetary package from the owners. But the strike that occurred in 1974 would be much more contentious, and it was destined to be a difficult struggle that led to caustic disagreements and arguments. Moreover, it lasted several weeks longer than it did in the 1970 players' strike.

The players in the league felt that they deserved higher base salaries of up to $5,000 more for both veterans and rookies alike. The owners, on the other hand, stood firm in their belief that the players should not receive those pay increases. The NFLPA also wanted to obtain a more reasonable plan for free agency, should an athlete try to go to another team after the contract with his current team concluded. The owners once again disagreed with that notion. On and on it went. The players' demands grew in number, and the owners' response was commonly one word. . . no.

The players also had another dilemma to deal with during the strike: seeing some of their veteran teammates cross the picket lines and return to summer training camp. Miami's squad was not immune from this action. Larry Little was entrenched as a captain of the team, and his sturdy foundation as a team leader was adeptly required by his peers in this confrontation against the owners. But Little saw several of his veteran teammates put their picket signs down and pick up their shoulder pads and helmets. One such player who did not participate in the strike was starting halfback Mercury Morris.

"That turned out to be a tumultuous year for me," said Morris, referring to 1974. "I hurt my left knee, but before I did, Joe Robbie renegotiated my contract, and I became the second-highest paid player on the team next to Bob Griese. The catch was that even though I was not going to be practicing because of my injury, he wanted me to report to camp. That was the condition that Robbie used to effectively have me break the line of the strike. He just wanted the optic of Mercury Morris breaking the strike line.

"I remember some of my teammates had a Winnebago out in front of Biscayne College, where we held our summer training camp, and the guys were out there marching with their signs: 'No Freedom, No Football' read most of them, a quickly developing decree during the strike. When I came driving out there in my new Ferrari 365 Berlinetta, Larry Little called me a turncoat! I said, 'Yes, but I'm a rich turncoat!'"[7]

Morris's experiences were not unique. Practically every team had at least one veteran player who was on strike and who would eventually decide that they would return to training camp. Those players were often referred to by the veterans who stayed on strike as "scabs." The longer the strike continued, the tougher it was for the players who were not contracted to make any money to stay out on strike. The owners realized this and planned for this, and so they prepared for a strike of attrition, where increasing numbers of players would eventually cross the picket lines and go back to camp. It was just a matter of time.

The Dolphins certainly had their share of striking players who eventually got tired of pacing back and forth while carrying picket signs. Larry Little looked at the situation pragmatically, but unlike several of his teammates, he decided to stay true to the union's decision to strike.

"Tempers got a little strained to begin with," recalled Little when discussing the 1974 player's strike. "A couple of our pro-union guys should have realized that the guys who crossed the picket line and went back to [training] camp were guys that they would have to play with after the strike ended. We had thirty-four veterans report to training camp before the end of the strike."[8]

The 1974 NFL Players Association strike lasted a total of forty-two days, as it was finally called off by the NFLPA on August 10. A deal was eventually agreed to by the players and the owners a full three years after the strike began. The deal that was signed in 1977 gave the players (rookies and veterans) essentially a little raise in their basic salaries, reduced the pension vesting period from six to four years of service, improved medical and dental benefits for the players, and it permitted more freedom for the players to seek and obtain trades with other teams. To acquire all those items, the players agreed to no-strike, no-lawsuit clauses during the length of the new contract.

Most of the players around the league felt that the strike of 1974 enabled them to take at least some steps closer to the economic improvements that they were seeking. Larry Little's feelings toward the strike focused more on the team's individual personalities than the points and counterpoints of the players' union and the team owners. He also tried to get his mind back into playing football as quickly as possible. So too did his head coach.

"Nick Buoniconti may have been our player representative during that strike, but later on, I was our player rep," Little recalled. "When the '74 strike ended, Shula did not force us to go through those four-a-day practices like he did following the '70 strike. We were a veteran team by '74. We played for him for several years by that time. So, by '74, we knew him, and he knew us. He knew what our abilities were by '74.

"We had some guys who did cross the picket line and went back into camp before the strike was over, but we really didn't hold a grudge against them. I knew that I wasn't going to be one of the players who crossed the picket line. I didn't have a grudge against any of the guys who did, because they thought that they were doing the right thing for their own particular situation. Once we went to camp, that was it. We had a job to do, so let's do it."[9]

By this time in the summer, there were several preseason games remaining on the Dolphins schedule, and thus there was no time to waste in order to get back into solid playing shape. Shula's players may have felt as if their backs were to the wall in one aspect. They knew that this would be the last year that Csonka, Kiick, and Warfield would be suiting up for the team. As a result of that, they wanted to make the most of this swan song of an opportunity for the men who were leaving at the end of the year to play in the WFL.

"I still felt that we were good enough to win without those guys," deemed Little. "To lose two good running backs like Csonka and Kiick has to be a concern. But you know that we still played well, and we still won games, although we weren't as good as we were the year before. I know that right before he signed with the WFL, Csonka called me and told me that he was leaving. And then I mentioned to him to 'take me with you.' The WFL did contact me, but I stayed with the Dolphins. But by then, contacting me and showing at least some interest in signing me, it did help me to renegotiate my contract with Miami, because Miami knew that I had other offers, and they wanted to keep me."[10]

Little was smart in sticking with the Dolphins and staying in the NFL. The WFL folded two short years later due to insolvency and a lack of overall revenue. Other leagues had come and gone all through the years from the first pro player (1892) to the present day. Little knew that the NFL had a foundation that was rock solid and was beginning its fifty-fourth season in 1974. He knew that there was something to be said for the reliability and the consistency that the NFL provided to its players. Besides, Miami was his home, and he was a member of a world champion squad. He knew that winning another Super Bowl title was a distinct possibility if he stayed with the Dolphins.

Strategically, most of the Miami players had an advantage over their opponents, due largely to the amount of time that they had spent with each other during the past several seasons. The team's offensive linemen certainly knew the nuances of all that they considered for their specific positions.

"We've been together for three years now," said Little in an interview from 1972, "and every year we improve. Now we all know the system, and it doesn't just mean all I have to do is throw a block, and my responsibility is over. I know where the running back is all the time. I know what the guy next to me is doing all the time. I'm totally prepared on every play we run. It's a lot more scientific than it may look."[11]

The scientific look that Miami presented was certainly considered by many so-called experts to be intimidating to the other teams in the league. The Dolphins began the 1974 season as two-time world champions. That fact would catch the attention of every one of their foes. It did not take long for the Dolphins to realize that because of their reputation as being the champions, they had an identifiable target on their backs.

Miami would begin their fifth year with Don Shula as their head coach up in New England to play a team that was comprised of even younger players than those who formed Shula's roster. The Patriots were primed to spring an upset on the sluggish Dolphins, and they did so with a dynamic offense and an opportunistic defense. Miami's offensive line permitted four quarterback sacks of Bob Griese. Larry Little was not responsible for allowing any of them, but that did not matter. Miami was beaten by a better team on September 15, 1974, by a score of 34-24. It was a shaky start to a season that would test the Dolphins' resolve to achieve whatever goals that they might set for themselves.

"The scores in those games in 1974 were tighter and more competitive, no doubt about it," Little expressed. "Because you know that when you win championships like we did, things got tougher every year. All the other teams wanted to be the team that beat you. And we didn't play our 'A' game in every game. In that game at New England to start the '74 season, I was playing against [Ray] 'Sugar Bear' Hamilton. I don't remember him beating me for any sacks."[12]

Fortunately for Miami, they did play better the following week, as they rebounded to post a key 24-16 victory over the Buffalo Bills. That was a very important win, because it quickly got the players' minds off the loss to the Patriots, and it realigned and refocused their minds on the rest of their season.

"We never believed that Buffalo could beat us," said Little, "and they never did during the 1970s. We always found a way to win against Buffalo."[13]

The Dolphins would then play their third straight away game in week three at San Diego. The Chargers would claim a 21-7 lead going into the fourth quarter. But Miami was not going to go down without a fight. They scratched and clawed back with three unanswered touchdowns to post a 28-21 win. It was the kind of triumph that proved that they had the sterner stuff needed to come back in a contest that looked like it was going to be a demoralizing loss.

The visit to San Diego would be a pleasant trip for Larry Little, who got a chance to visit his old stomping grounds when he played for the Chargers from 1967 to 1968.

"I didn't really talk to any of my friends on the Chargers until after the game," said Larry Little. "Tommy Prothro was the head coach of the Chargers by then. I do remember a funny story about Mercury Morris and the Chargers though. When Mercury was traded by the Dolphins in the summer of 1976, he told Shula that he could trade him to any team, except San Diego. He told Shula that 'San Diego was terrible.' And that's where Shula traded him to."[14]

Larry Little's time with the Chargers was only a distant memory by 1974, however. He was a fixture in Miami's offensive line by this time, and their offensive line would be challenged by a division rival in the following game. The New York Jets would visit the Orange Bowl on Monday Night Football in week four, and seemingly like most of their games that year, it was a competitive contest. Every time that the Dolphins would take what appeared to be a comfortable lead, the Jets would strike back behind several big plays from their popular and famous quarterback, Joe Namath. In the end, the last few minutes decided the winner, as the Miami defense managed to make enough big plays of their own to put a timely halt to Namath's success on that evening. The Dolphins prevailed, 21-17.

"Although Joe Namath was a great quarterback for the Jets, we would always seem to find a way to win against them," said Little. "But the Jets always played us tough though, like they did on that night."[15]

The tough games would continue as the 1974 season went on. Just as Little and his teammates were coasting toward another AFC Eastern Division title, they ran into a team that was in dire need of a victory. The Washington Redskins would play host to the Dolphins at RFK Stadium on October 13, 1974. A thirteen-yard touchdown pass from Bob Griese to Howard Twilley gave the Dolphins a 17-13 lead with less than two minutes left in the game. This time, however, it was the Miami defense which surprisingly surrendered a winning scoring drive to the Redskins with just seconds remaining.

The 20-17 loss to Washington was a dismal and demoralizing loss for the Dolphins. Keep in mind that Washington's roster was filled with older and slower veteran players, many of whom were holdovers from Super Bowl VII, and many of whom were well past their prime. The Redskins certainly got their revenge in this meeting.

"That was a close game all the way through," admitted Little in a 2022 interview. "The Redskins found a way to win that game, and we didn't. But actually, we didn't lose a lot of games in 1974, and when we did, we didn't blame each other for any of our losses. Keep in mind that we also didn't have Bill Arnsparger as our defensive coordinator that year, and that affected our defense. He went to the Giants before that season started to become their head coach.

"But I don't think that we ever got complacent, and I don't think that we ever overlooked a team. Because in the NFL, we believed that any team could beat you on any given day."[16]

The unexpected loss at Washington proved that Miami was vulnerable in 1974, much more so than in previous seasons. The Dolphins knew that the time had come for an internal gut-check. Fortunately for Miami, they had the mental framework, the desire, the right players, the determined coaching staff, and perhaps most importantly, the intensity to get back on the winning track.

The Dolphins' next opponent would be the Kansas City Chiefs on October 20, 1974. This struggle in South Florida was exactly that. . . a struggle. It took a determined drive late in the fourth quarter for Miami to sneak out a 9-3 win.

The Dolphins' victory over the Chiefs signaled the beginning of their best winning streak of the 1974 season. It would last for five games, and it would provide the team with the confidence that they needed to eventually fulfill their desire to earn another playoff berth. Miami defeated their division rivals, the Baltimore Colts, by a score of 17-7 in the week after their win over Kansas City.

Miami relied on their substitute running backs, Benny Malone and Don Nottingham, both of whom would run for over 100 yards against the Colts. Larry Csonka sustained an injury which led to Shula replacing him with Malone and Nottingham. Regardless of who was carrying the pigskin, the Miami rushing attack would account for an impressive 252 total yards in the win over the Colts.

Csonka still played when he could, despite his various nagging injuries, and he relied even more on the work of his All-Pro guard, Larry Little. Csonka was just not as fast as he used to be prior to his leg injuries. Little continued to open holes for the rugged fullback as he had always done, and the Miami offense continued to succeed. Both men realized that this was a time for resiliency to be the main ingredient to producing victory.

"I think that Larry Little was a guy you could count on, play in, and play out," Csonka assessed. "He never had moments of doubt. You know that he was gung ho, and he was going to be the first one up the hill. And you know, we're going to take that hill, come hell or high water. And when he came to us [from San Diego], he had that attitude. . . that attitude that said that if you have a big gun, you shoot it. And that's what we did.

"You had to read the language. . . the language of emotion. And once you get that and your offensive linemen have that, then you have tremendous confidence in them. And when you look in the huddle and they're looking back at you, and staring straight into your eyes, and looking at you with an unspoken message of 'Run Behind Me,' that extols a confidence. Well, I think it's a rare thing. I doubt very much that it exists in maybe two or three places in the NFL today."[17]

Miami's winning streak continued the following week with a 42-7 romp over the Atlanta Falcons. Then came a 21-0 victory over the New Orleans Saints. Csonka saw more action in that contest and carried the ball eight times, despite his knees and ankles still giving him problems. Shula hinted after the game that even with his team's numerous injuries, however, his defense was playing solidly.

"Our defense was outstanding," summarized Shula after the game. "We looked upon this game with the Saints as an important one. We were just coming off a big win, we had injuries, and we were favored against the Saints."[18]

That favored status would fortunately continue with the same results for one more week. The final game of the Dolphins' five-game winning streak occurred on November 17 at the Orange Bowl. Their opponent on that date was the Buffalo Bills, and this matchup turned out to be one of the most competitive games of the 1974 season. Miami came through with a vital scoring drive with less than a minute remaining in the game to pull out a vital 35-28 victory. The win boosted Miami to an 8-2 record, which was good enough to give them a one-game lead over Buffalo in the AFC East.

"We were still a very confident team at this point," declared Little. "We realized that the games were more competitive in '74 than in '72 and '73, but we still felt that we could win those tighter games."[19]

Those tighter games would include their next one. Miami had earned their victories during the 1974 season mostly by making the big plays when they really needed them at critical moments of their games. But that trend failed to materialize in their eleventh game of the year at New York's Shea Stadium. Instead, it was the Jets who made the big plays which led them to a 17-14 upset victory over the Dolphins. Clearly, Miami's undefeated season of 1972 was far away in their rearview mirror. The loss to New York was a sobering reminder to the Dolphins that they could not overlook any of their opponents if they expected to get back into the playoffs.

"That might have been the type of game that we overlooked," acknowledged Little. "We would go up to New York and regularly dominate them in previous seasons. We always looked forward to going up there and playing them. In '74, we just didn't play well enough up there to win."[20]

The Dolphins could not afford to overlook anyone else on their schedule. They had three more games remaining at this point of the 1974 season. Miami knew that if they won all three of those contests, they would once again secure the championship of the AFC East. This they did with victories over the Cincinnati Bengals, the Baltimore Colts, and the New England Patriots.

"We expected to win our division," exclaimed Little. "We had the feeling as the 1974 season wore on that we were going to win the division. Let me put it this way: It wasn't a shock for us that we won the division again. We were that good."[21]

Little and his teammates would be making their fifth straight trip to the NFL's postseason tournament in 1974. Their divisional playoff game on December 21 against the Raiders at Oakland was destined to become one of the greatest postseason games in NFL history. It was chock-filled with dramatic and exciting plays from both teams, and it also featured a thrilling ending. The Raiders and the Dolphins were considered by many to be the two best teams in the league by this time in 1974, and they would certainly play like it in this playoff tilt. Both teams were as prepared as they could be for each other, but one team had a strange and unique opportunity to be even more prepared for their opponents. . . if they took advantage of it.

"I can tell you something that happened before that game," related Little. "We practiced the day before the game at the Oakland Coliseum. And somebody from the Raiders mistakenly left the Oakland game plan there. Someone on our team or on our staff found it, and they gave the game plan to Shula. And Shula said to that person, 'No. . . we don't do that. We deal with our own game plan. We don't look at their stuff.' And that just showed the kind of integrity that our coach had."[22]

Could that Oakland game plan been a phony one to see if the Miami team would take the bait. . . a ruse, so to speak? That is impossible to say. But what is easy to say with all honesty was that Don Shula was a stand-up guy, and he proved it with that example. Many coaches would have jumped at the chance to see their opponent's game plan prior to the game, and it is documented to have happened more than once in the NFL's storied history. But Shula taught his team a valuable lesson with his decision.

He wanted them to play the game fairly and win the game on their own merits, and not by any possible dishonest means. To him and to his players, honesty was one of the most important factors in the makeup of the Miami Dolphins.

An honest assessment of this playoff game would be that it was a contest of two evenly matched teams. It turned out to be a see-saw affair, where each squad answered the other with a score of their own after being scored upon, and where no team dominated their opponent throughout the contest.

"Well in most games, and in a game like that, we knew that we were playing against a good football team," explained Little. "We had the kind of an attitude of becoming familiar with Oakland. We knew that the Raiders had a lot of very good football players on their team."[23]

The very good Miami football players took an early lead. . . a really early lead. Rookie reserve wide receiver Nat Moore, who would eventually become Larry Little's roommate when the Dolphins played games on the road, returned the opening kickoff eighty-nine yards for a touchdown. That start gave the fans an idea as to what they could expect in the drama department. Miami safety Jake Scott then suffered a knee injury which would keep him out of the rest of the game. Oakland took advantage of Scott's absence in the second quarter on a thirty-one-yard pass down the middle of the field from Ken Stabler to setback Charlie Smith. Dolphins place kicker Garo Yepremian then booted a thirty-three-yard field goal just before halftime to give Miami a 10-7 advantage at intermission.

"We were still very confident going into halftime of that game," recalled Little. "Yes, we had some of our defensive players suffer injuries, but that was just part of the game. The replacements had to step up and fill in. We still felt confident, but we knew that the second half would still be a fight, no doubt about that."[24]

Oakland quickly fought back early in the third quarter to take a 14-10 lead on another Stabler touchdown pass. It was now time for the Dolphins offense to get back in gear and reclaim the lead. This they did on a scoring pass from Griese to his All-Pro wide receiver, Paul Warfield. But despite their renewed advantage on the scoreboard, the Dolphins were wise enough to know that this was not a time to relax on the field.

"No, we never relaxed in that game," said Little. "We always knew that it was a sixty-minute game, and that anything could happen. We were determined to keep our foot on the gas pedal as they say."[25]

As the see-saw nature of this affair continued, Miami began the fourth quarter with more points, thanks to a forty-six-yard field goal off the foot of Garo Yepremian. The Dolphins now owned a 19-14 advantage. They knew, however, that a five-point cushion would not be enough against Oakland, especially with practically a full quarter left to play. That thought was proven true a few minutes later, when Oakland scored again to take a 21-19 lead, midway through the fourth quarter.

The back-and-forth character of this game was both exciting and nerve-wracking. Miami eventually marched down the field again and reserve tailback Benny Malone ran a sweep to his right. Leading that sweep was none other than Larry Little, who knocked the Raiders' cornerback Skip Thomas away from Malone's path toward paydirt. Malone then broke a couple of attempted arm tackles by Oakland safeties Jack Tatum and George Atkinson with second and third efforts. Malone's incredible scoring run put the Dolphins back in front, 26-21, with just two minutes left in this playoff struggle. Many people commented in the aftermath of that game on the irony that Miami's offense had scored too quickly, and that they had left too much time on the clock for Ken Stabler to pass his Raiders downfield.

"Before Benny Malone's touchdown, we were confident that we were going to score," admitted Little. "I didn't know that we were going to score the way that we did. . . because of a great run by Benny. The play that he scored on was called Flow 38. Now Benny did not have the speed nor the quickness that Mercury [Morris] had. But he was still a really good running back. In that game where we scored on that sweep. . . where Benny scored on that sweep. . . I don't believe that he scored too soon. You score when you can score. I don't believe in that scoring too soon stuff. After Benny scored though, I thought the game was over. I thought that we had won the game on that Flow 38 play."[26]

The team that scored last would likely be the team that would win this battle of wills. As it turned out, Stabler did have enough time to drive his offense through the Dolphins zone defensive coverage. The completions added up for Stabler on this final Raiders drive of the game, and he soon positioned Oakland's offense to be just eight yards away from Miami's end zone. The Raiders scored what turned out to be the winning touchdown when Stabler was chased out of his passing pocket and lofted a pass to the end zone, where Raiders' setback Clarence Davis snared it amongst a crowd of several Dolphin defenders. Miami lost this dramatic struggle, 28-26.

"It just so happened that Oakland came back and made a great, great play," said Little. "It was in a crucial situation, with Stabler falling down and throwing the ball up for grabs, and Clarence Davis was able to catch the ball. What I remember about that play was that I was standing on the sidelines, and when Davis scored that touchdown, my head dropped to my chest. And I thought, 'Oh my goodness.' It just wasn't meant to be.

"Now another thing about that game that I remember, was that they. . . the Raiders' players. . . carried John Madden off the field. And they still had the Steelers to play. I mean they beat us, and we were the defending champs, but they acted like they had just won the darn Super Bowl. They were so excited because they were able to beat us."[27]

This loss was devastating to Little and his teammates. They had been to the mountaintop in pro football for two straight seasons, but they were unable to make it three straight. They were not alone in this pursuit, however. To this day, no NFL team has ever won three straight Super Bowls.

"Coach Shula did not really say too much to us after that playoff game at Oakland," remembered Little. "He felt. . . we all felt. . . that it was a big disappointment to us. Because we felt that we should have won that game. If it wasn't for that fluke play. . . Clarence Davis's touchdown catch. . . we would have won that game. That was a tough loss. Because watching Stabler, we all thought that he was going to be sacked on his winning touchdown throw. It looked like he was going down, but he managed to throw the ball before his body hit the ground."[28]

The 1974 season thus ended for the Dolphins. A premature ending to be sure, considering how close they had come to making pro football history again. They were just one score away from advancing to what would have been their fourth straight AFC Championship Game. Despite that failure, they had to look back at a season where in the spite of so many injuries to key players, they had played well enough to win their fourth straight AFC Eastern Division title. Yes, it was a year which had plenty of could haves and would haves, but that was not how Coach Shula developed and prepared his players. Larry Little knew full well that the emphasis now was on the job ahead, not on what was in their rearview mirror.

"We knew that things were changing on the team, and we knew that we would have some new players coming in the following season," said Little. "But we still had a core of good players on our team. We still had some players who knew how to win. But after winning two straight Super Bowls, it was tough to end the year on a losing note."[29]

The team that Larry Little gave his sweat and his strength to had lost a postseason game for the first time since Super Bowl VI in January of 1972. The Dolphins were now faced with a scene of regrouping and reestablishing their dynasty. It was a chore that would prove to be easier said than done.

CHAPTER 10

WHERE DID THE GOOD TIMES GO?

The winds of change would be blowing amidst Larry Little's pro football career during the mid-1970s. They would also be blowing for his team. Miami's fortunes as a consistent winner would be challenged repeatedly during the second half of the decade.

Defensive coordinator Bill Arnsparger's departure left Miami defenseless following Super Bowl VIII, and his absence was detrimental to the team.

Miami offensive line coach Monte Clark also left the team a couple of years later. Losing those two men created a negative void in knowledge and leadership for the Dolphins, and it was a void which Coach Shula was never adequately able to fill with comparable talent and abilities. The Miami defense gave up just 150 points with Arnsparger as their defensive coordinator in 1973. In 1974 without Arnsparger, their defense surrendered 216 points. Their offense recorded similar numbers when Clark left the team. The Dolphins scored 357 points in 1975 with Clark on the coaching staff. Without him in 1976, Miami scored only 263 points.

The loss of Clark would naturally have more to do with Larry Little, because Clark was the team's offensive line coach. But the loss of Arnsparger included a somewhat strange occurrence in the summer of 1974. Don Shula had developed a very strong friendship with Arnsparger while they were both in Miami, and after his former defensive coordinator became the head coach of the Giants, Shula wanted to help him to get off to a good start in New York. Shula asked some of his players, Little among them, for a favor. Little adamantly declined Shula's request.

"I was in summer camp," recalled Little, "and before a preseason game against the Giants, the Dolphins staff wanted us to go and talk to the Giants' players about. . . truthfully, I don't know what it was that they wanted us to tell the Giants' players maybe just more of a pep talk, because I know that it was Arnsparger's first year with the Giants. But I refused to do that. To me, that was a conflict of interest."[1]

The variety of conflicts would continue for Miami throughout the 1975 season. The most visible difficulty that the Dolphins would experience was an incredible number of injuries. No less than eleven starting players suffered injuries during the 1975 season. Some of them never played one single down all year long. But despite their losses of nine defensive regulars by season's end, Miami's defense still managed to give up only nine touchdown passes, which ranked as the fewest in the entire NFL.

Losing so much in the form of overall game and strategy experience would have detrimental effects on the Dolphins' fortunes in 1975. But Don Shula did not get the reputation as being one of the greatest head coaches in NFL history by accident. He installed several quality replacement players to fill in the voids left from his injured men, and those new players did an admirable job.

"Despite whomever we had on our roster, the desire to win was easy to keep going," admitted Larry Little. "Because we had endured some heart-breaking games, and we wanted to go back and rectify those losses. That loss to Oakland in the 1974 playoffs is a perfect example. We all looked forward to playing in 1975 after that loss to Oakland in the 1974 playoffs, because we still thought that we were a very good football team. Now we lost some guys after that game to the World Football League, but we still felt that we had a lot of talent coming back, and we were still a very confident football team."[2]

Miami's confidence would be tested right from the get-go. The 1975 season began on an ominous note, when the league's schedule makers wanted to see what they thought would be a revenge game between Miami and Oakland at the Orange Bowl on Monday Night Football. But Oakland did not adhere to the script as they struck for several big touchdowns to post a 31-21 triumph over Miami. It was not the start to a new season that an All-Pro star like Larry Little wanted to see happen. But the momentum to beat Oakland—at least as far as Larry Little was concerned—did not come from any amount of retribution from the previous year's playoff loss.

"When I went up against them [the Raiders]," explained Little. "I never thought of it as playing it as a revenge game. I just thought about doing my job. . . and about us doing our job. . . and winning the football game."[3]

Miami immediately went back to practice, stressing the basics and the fundamentals. That meant running the ball more effectively, and that was something that both blockers and running backs took to heart. One big key to the success of the Dolphins rushing attack involved overall speed, a God-given gift that both offensive guard Larry Little and halfback Mercury Morris had in abundance. Not everyone on the squad could perform the plays swiftly enough, however.

"Once in practice, I can't remember who the quarterback was, he was turning around and making the move to hand the ball off quick enough, coming out from underneath the center," Morris remembered. "So, Shula tells me to 'Beat the quarterback across.' And so, when he turned around to give me the ball, I was already on the other side of him. He was a quarterback, and Shula wanted to let him know that you can't just mosey out of that stance.

"Because I used to shade the normal places [in between the tackle and the guard] where the halfback would line up, I instead lined up shading the outside of the tackle. So that extra step and a half would give me the ability to be running full speed in four steps."[4]

Running at full speed. If there was anything that Shula preached to his players during practice, it was that adherence to going full speed on everything. Much was expected from the players in 1975, and at times, it may have seemed to some observers that the players were jogging more than sprinting. It was indeed a time for introspection, and for challenging each other to deliver stronger efforts.

It was also a time for changes to occur in pro football. The players on most teams in the era of the "Me" generation, otherwise known as the 1970s, saw quite a few alterations in the sport. One of those changes involved the addition of foreign substances that pervaded the NFL. There was no shortage of stories going around the league during the mid-1970s regarding the aspect of performance enhancing drugs, which were somehow available for every team. Drugs such as anabolic steroids were being introduced to many players. Those drugs, and many similar drugs, were not outlawed by the NFL rules like they are today. As a result, some marginal players during those years, who were finding themselves listed on some possibly expendable lists on their team's roster, were not opposed to doing whatever it took to remain an active player in the league. Taking drugs such as steroids to build up their muscle mass, and to give them higher levels of physical strength, served as the avenue that some of those players took to continue playing pro football. With competition serving as the key to making a player better and more formidable, taking those drugs were not out of the question for some players.

Larry Little observed the use of those foreign substances by some of his teammates during his pro career. Amphetamines (speed) such as Dexedrine and Benzedrine were otherwise called "pep pills," and they were given to many players to get them hyped up prior to a game. The distribution of those drugs quickly got out of hand. In 1973, Dr. Arnold Mandel, who was a team doctor in San Diego, admitted to handing out 1,700 amphetamines to various Chargers players. Former San Diego Pro Bowl guard Walt Sweeney once acknowledged that taking speed was as much a part of his pregame preparation as putting on his shoulder pads.

"We had steroids back then when I played," remembered Little in a 2022 interview. "We had bennies. They were often called uppers. We didn't have any bennies in Miami. I saw them in San Diego. I was a rookie in San Diego when I took some of them, and for me, the only reason why I took them, was because I saw some of the veteran players take them. They didn't really have a marked effect on me, except at night. I couldn't sleep at night. I would come home and talk to my mom for hours, and not really realize that I was talking that long. We had a guy on the Chargers who would give the rookies bennies. But there was a veteran player on the team—and he is deceased now—who sat me down and said, 'Look, I'll do it this time, but I don't want you doing this. I'll give you one now, but I don't want you doing this.' He was someone who I trusted and who I respected. In the end, I was offered about five bennies during my time in San Diego, but I didn't take them regularly. . . only once in a while. I didn't see them or take them in Miami."

"Some guys on the Chargers took bennies to get up for a game. Mostly, it was the trainer who gave them to the players. I never saw any of my teammates in Miami take any drugs. But I saw players take them in San Diego. I would say maybe right around fifteen to twenty players in San Diego took them at least once during their pro careers."[5]

It is important to note that many of the players who took drugs in the 1970s were not giving much—if any—thought about the possible future detriments to their health from taking those substances. The information about those potential detriments just was not available to the players during those years. Sadly, many players who did take anabolic steroids and other drugs in the 1970s have died prematurely, which culminated their many years of numerous health problems that could have resulted from taking those substances. The here and now was the only time frame that entered the minds of those players who took drugs during the 1970s, as they tried to get an edge in practice and in the games.

The here and now for the 1975 Miami Dolphins, however, involved staying on top of the AFC East. Following their unexpected loss to the Raiders in their first game, Miami made a statement with victories over New England, Green Bay, Philadelphia, the New York Jets (twice), Buffalo, and Chicago. Little and his teammates built a 7-1 record and churned out five straight 200-yard rushing games. Everything looked fine once again.

But everything was not fine in the second half of the 1975 season. Miami suffered an injury-filled and mistake-filled 20-19 loss to Houston in the Astrodome in week nine. Following the loss to the Oilers, Larry Little sought out one of his old coaches with the San Diego Chargers. Bum Phillips was serving his first year as the new head coach of Houston, and even though the two men did not have much time to reminisce, they both shared a special smile with each other that was rooted in each of their pasts.

"Well, you know Bum was a defensive line coach in San Diego when I was with the Chargers," Little mentioned. "After that game, he told me that 'you're having a great career.' And we shook hands."[6]

As amiable as things were between Little and Coach Phillips, such cordial feelings would not be visible the following week. The youthful Baltimore Colts came into the Orange Bowl on November 23, 1975, and with inspired vigor upset Miami, 33-17. Even worse than the loss was the fact that Bob Griese injured the tendon in his big toe while he was trying to avoid a spirited Baltimore pass rush, and as a result, he would be sidelined for the remainder of the year.

"Well, Bob was a scrambling quarterback," explained Little. "You didn't know which way he would run. He would sometimes run to his right, and sometimes to his left. He would also circle around the pocket to avoid the pass rush. But that was his game, and he was very efficient at it. It just so happened that his scrambling caught up to him in that first game in '75 with the Colts."[7]

Griese's injury was just the most prominent of many that befell the Dolphins starters in 1975. Between all the injuries and the unexpected defeats, the second half of that season was quickly turning into an unfamiliar one for a juggernaut team like Miami. . . a team that was used to winning. Suffering defeats had a detrimental effect on the Dolphins. The loss to the Baltimore Colts and their formidable defensive linemen gave Little and his mates all that they could handle.

Little had to readjust his blocking technique somewhat by the mid-1970s. He was nearing a full decade of playing pro ball, and that amount of time was taking a toll on his physicality. It was not too discernible of a toll, particularly among his opponents. But it was evident, at least to Little himself.

"My very best years were 1970 and 1971," explained Little in the mid-1970s, "because I was still playing with brute strength, and I was all out, gung ho. At that time, I was blocking defensive linemen ten yards downfield and putting them on their backs. Now I'm going to get more finesse. I'm getting older, trying to preserve myself. It's a natural thing for an offensive lineman. I might not be as aggressive now as I was, but I know more [now] than I did [then]."[8]

The league-wide competition that Little and the Dolphins faced by the time that 1975 rolled around proved to be upgraded. The rivalries between the teams in the AFC East could occasionally be individualistic in nature. Sometimes, amid losing, a player will allow his anger to get the best of him, and sometimes as a result, he will voice his frustrations. There are stories in football where players from opposing teams who line up just a few feet from each other along the line of scrimmage express their displeasure with each other. Such discontent would sometimes result in taking out one's dissatisfactions with their foes in the form of voicing insults about their ancestry or their family members. Most of that is Hollywood's version of the sport, however. In reality, incessant mouthing was something that Coach Shula did not tolerate.

"That did not really happen as much as people think it does," admitted Little. "I know that a lot of times when I played, we didn't do it. But what they're saying while they are in a three-point stance. . . you don't know what they are saying to each other. You couldn't really hear them. I know that our [offensive] line didn't do any of that."[9]

What the Miami offensive line did do during the latter stages of the 1975 season was refocus their attention on the job that lay ahead. Their efforts proved to be beneficial, as the Dolphins resumed playing solid, fundamentally sound football. Miami limited the visiting New England Patriots to just one touchdown in a 20-7 victory. They then built a big lead against Buffalo, then held on for a 31-21 triumph.

Those two victories over New England and Buffalo boosted Miami's record to 9-3, with just two games remaining in the 1975 regular season. The Baltimore Colts were breathing down the Dolphins' neck in second place, however, with a record of 8-4. They would welcome Miami to Memorial Stadium in the thirteenth week of the 1975 season to determine which team would win the AFC Eastern Division.

That contest turned out to be a defensive fight. The Dolphins were playing with many of their best players on the bench in street clothes and leaning on pairs of crutches. The Colts were in a much healthier condition in comparison.

Baltimore proved their desire to be worthy of the division championship with a clutch fourth quarter six-yard touchdown run by Lydell Mitchell, and a game-winning thirty-one-yard field goal in overtime by Toni Linhart. Larry Little would not be going to the playoffs for the first time since 1969.

"I never thought that we would miss the playoffs as long as we had Don Shula as our head coach," Larry Little said bluntly. "But Baltimore had a very good team that year. They were building a strong nucleus of talent on their team, and that year [1975], they had a great year. You have to give them credit. They beat us twice that year."[10]

But if the Dolphins players and their coaches and even their fans thought that 1975 ended up badly with a 10-4 record, they were ill-prepared for what awaited them in 1976. That Bicentennial year of 1976 began on a positive note, however, as the Orange Bowl's Poly-Turf field surface was ripped up and replaced by a natural grass field. Many of the injuries that occurred there during the past six seasons were now just a bitter and distant memory. Unfortunately for Shula and his team, the changing of the turf in the Orange Bowl was perhaps the only good thing that would happen in 1976.

Another change indirectly involved Larry Little. His former offensive line coach, Monte Clark, accepted the vacant head coaching job in San Francisco. Replacing Clark was another veteran coach, John Sandusky.

"Considering both of those guys, I would say that John was not as much of a technician and a teacher as Monte was," explained Little. "John may have had more experience than Monte, because he [Sandusky] had been around the league much longer than Monte. But as far as teaching offensive blocking technique was concerned, Monte could out-coach anybody."[11]

The 1976 season was one of the two worst in Don Shula's coaching career, as the Dolphins could win only six games and lost eight. For the second straight year, they missed the playoffs. It was not as if Miami was outclassed, however. The Dolphins suffered four losses by a combined total of just eleven points. And just as in 1975, the 1976 Miami team once again suffered a myriad of injuries. Coach Shula repeatedly was forced to place different players in different positions all year long, which tested the flexibility of his healthy players—or at least his semi-healthy players.

"Going into that 1976 season, I felt that we had a pretty good football team," admitted Little. "But our injuries kept mounting up and mounting up. Nobody can predict who is going to get injured and when those injuries will occur. No doubt about that."[12]

Don Shula would see twenty-two of his players go down to one injury or another in 1976, the most common of which were knee injuries. That would equate to 144 total games lost in overall playing time. Losing so many players for so many games had a detrimental effect on the team, as well as in the won-loss column.

"You know, when you're not used to losing. . . that may be why things got so disappointing that year [1976]," explained Little. "And you know that we lost a lot of close games that year to go along with all of the number of injuries that we had. We just had to try and play it out. It wasn't like the guys were thinking that it was normal to have a losing season. And it wasn't that guys were overpaid, or that guys had their cars revving up in the parking lot, ready to go home. Although we lost a lot that year, we still continued to play hard."[13]

Regardless of how hard Miami played in the first few games, there would be an event in Little's life outside of the football season that would affect his life significantly. This was the first meeting with his future wife, Rosie. The two began dating in Miami after Little had already established himself as one of the best offensive guards in pro football. That fact did not really hold a lot of interest with Rosie, however. . . at least not at first.

"I met my wife in a doctor's office," recalled Little. "She was working for a doctor, and a friend of mine told me that he saw a lady that he thought I would like. And I went to meet her. And you know when I first started talking to her, she acted really stuck up. So, I said to myself, 'Well the hell with you too then,' and I left the office where she worked at. But I gave her my address before I left, and then one day to my surprise, she was ringing my doorbell!" Larry chuckles at the disbelieving memory. "Now keep in mind, I was a bachelor at the time and the middle of my 1976 season. There was just something about that woman, and we started things up right then and there."[14]

It did not take too long for Rosie DeJesus to develop an interest in Larry Little. It would eventually become a match made in Heaven, as both discovered over time their mutual interests in each other. It may not have begun that way, but over time, the two have become as strong of a husband-wife team that anyone could find.

"He was very sweet," said Rosie of Larry. "At the beginning when we first met, however, we weren't really into each other. But later on, as we got to know each other, that all changed. And he was just like a big old teddy bear. I also got along very well with Larry's mother. I could see the same qualities in Larry as I could in his mother. I knew that he was a football player when I first met him. My parents certainly thought very highly of him."[15]

This meeting and the culmination of a growing and fonder relationship would create the backbone of what Larry would continue to fight for every time he entered the field. He not only was looking out for himself, but he was also now thinking of Rosie, and eventually his children when he entered the gridiron in the years to follow.

While back on the field in 1976, the Dolphins would exhibit a lackluster effort in an equal number of contests throughout the rest of the season. They would suffer two separate three-game losing streaks during the year, something that was shocking to the team, the coaches, and to the Dolphins fans. Perhaps the most humiliating "victory" came about on October 24, when Miami barely held on to beat the expansion Tampa Bay Buccaneers, 23-20. The Bucs were on their way to a historic 0-14 record in 1976.

Things were not too much better for the Dolphins. By the final month of the 1976 season, Miami would end up losing four of their final five games. It was indeed a degrading scenario, and it led to rank frustration among many of the veteran players. . . including Larry Little. After a particular game versus the New York Jets, some media writers attacked the Dolphins' efforts on the field—and especially their faltering rushing attack. Little, being the newspaper reader that he was, took the criticism personally, and he responded.

"I've been bad rapped," exclaimed Little after reading the writer's critique in 1976. "He said some things about me that were very unjustified. I want to take him in here and show him the films of the Jets game. I was angry.

"From the early years, I learned that Miami is the city of the front runner. When we win, there are 75,000 people in the stands. When we lose one game and there are only 50,000 people there. Look, it's going to get better. The [running] backs we have known what they're trying to do, but we have to get everything a little more coordinated between the line and the running backs. It's not that we [the offensive line] are not doing the job upfront, like some people might think. There are a lot of things that I can attribute it to [the lack of Miami's rushing yardage in 1976]. It's going to take some time. We do have some new young people in the game here. . . and we haven't coordinated with them yet. So, we may not look as smooth as we have in the past."[16]

There is a lot of pressure to win when it comes to pro football, for all the coaches and the players involved. Perhaps it was more of a situation where it was a response to a culture shock. Larry Little and his teammates were simply not used to losing, and they were not immune from or opposed to showing their displeasure.

"I couldn't help getting a little uptight" expressed Little in a 1977 interview. "I got fed up by everything. . . the losing, the injuries, the embarrassment of looking like a bunch of schoolyard kids at times. It just got to me. I was very disappointed at what happened to the club.[17] Man, I hate to lose. I feel if you accept losing, you're a loser. I'm not a loser."[18]

Every pro football team eventually undergoes a series of ebbs and flows. . . a cycle of wins and losses wherein you eventually start losing games that you almost always won in the past. Larry Little and his teammates were at that stage in 1976. And the Miami offense knew that there was always room for improvement, even if it came just a little bit at a time. The Dolphins' only real tangible hope as 1976 came to an end, however, was that things would somehow improve in 1977.

"I was pretty optimistic going into the 1977 season," recalled Little. "You know every year at the beginning of the year, we had a few new guys who were coming to the team. And I was trying to be a leader and be a team captain, which I was. I just had to become familiar with our new offensive linemen coming in, and trying to give them encouragement, and letting them know that we can still be a good football team. I especially tried to help the young African American linemen who were trying to make it in the NFL. I tried to advise them and help their progressive development so they could make it in the league."[19]

The progression on the Miami defensive line was not improving, however. Two of their younger defensive linemen, Don Reese and Randy Crowder, were both arrested on federal drug charges in 1977. In a sense, it was the sign of the times in the city of Miami, where the scourge of drugs was an ongoing dilemma that touched many individuals and families in the South Florida community.

"They were both arrested for selling cocaine," remembered Little. "Well, I didn't know what they were doing at that time. But all the young black players who came into the league. . . or at least with the Dolphins I would say. . . we, the veterans on the team, tried to lead and guide them the right way. And Reese and Crowder. . . let's just say that I was shocked when what happened [their arrest] happened to them. They were both very good people, and thankfully, they both got their lives straight and back in order. Randy was a super player for the Dolphins, and he went on to play for the Tampa Bay Buccaneers. And Reese went on and played for the New Orleans Saints. They didn't have to do the drug thing, but they did turn their lives around."[20]

There was really nowhere to go but up for Miami following the debacle that was 1976. All the players and coaches held strong to the belief that they would improve at least somewhat in 1977. They just had too much veteran leadership to fail. Furthermore, the Dolphins were "due" for a healthier season in 1977. But for an older veteran like Larry Little, Father Time was slowly creeping up on him.

"If you're asking me, Larry was slowing down," admitted Little's former teammate in Miami, Larry Csonka. "But as you become more mature in the NFL, and become perhaps combat fatigued a bit, you also learn a lot of things. You're a much smarter player. So, he was just as much of a force at the end of his career as he was at the beginning of his career. Intelligence and experience had a lot to do with that."[21]

The experience that the 1977 season presented was a unique one for the Dolphins. They just barely missed the playoffs with an exemplary 10-4 record, which was four more wins than they earned in 1976. Little and his cohorts on the offensive line once again contributed strong run-blocking efforts all year. They ran for 143 first downs, which was second-best in the entire league. Little was once again pulling and blocking on sweeps like it was second nature to him, and even if his speed was slowed by a step, his strength certainly was not. That type of upper body strength of his enabled him to move almost every opposing defensive lineman that he faced from penetrating into the intended direction of Miami's runs.

Miami would need Little's strength in 1977. That was because the rest of the AFC East division was improving rapidly. Competition was strengthened in both Baltimore and New England, as those two rivals vied with the Dolphins for the division title. It was a struggle that was not decided until the final week of the season. Larry Little, however, did not harbor much worry regarding his team's competition.

"I didn't really think too much about how competitive the division was at that time," expressed Little. "I always believed that our football team could beat any other football team that we went up against. I never thought that if we had been in another division, things would be different. I also didn't think about the other teams in our division, as far as being better than us. We knew that we were the team to beat in our division. All the other teams in the AFC East. . . we knew where their focus was. They wanted to beat the Miami Dolphins, because of our past reputation."[22]

Miami's reputation as a perennial contender was bolstered by losing only two games within their division in 1977. However, it was those two defeats—one to Baltimore and one to New England—which kept them from reaching the playoffs. Nevertheless, improvements abounded for Shula's team. They won both of their games against NFC teams. One of those contests was on Thanksgiving, and it was indeed a very distinctive meeting with the St. Louis Cardinals on November 24, 1977. Quarterback Bob Griese made headlines by throwing for a career-best six touchdown passes against the better-than-average St. Louis defense.

Larry Little once again performed admirably. The Miami offensive line permitted only one sack in the game, and the offense recorded a season-best 503 total yards. Practically every play that Griese called in the huddle ended up gaining yardage. The Dolphins romped over the Cardinals, 55-14. But there was more to see in this contest than just the scoring, however. While many people were observing Griese's efforts and the big numbers tabulated by the Miami offense, several others preferred to remember another element from this one-sided affair. . . the fistfights.

Pro football teams have their pride, to be sure. And when a team is getting humiliated by their opponent on the scoreboard, they sometimes take umbrage at surrendering so many points. Running up the score on their opponents—whether it is planned or not—is a transgression that is often not easily forgivable. St. Louis was in that very situation as darkness descended over Busch Memorial Stadium. The Dolphins were once again driving the ball downfield in the fourth quarter, when the television cameras focused on several players pushing, shoving, and then punching each other after a play was over. Although he did not expect to be involved in any such extra-curricular activities, Larry Little found himself right in the middle of the scuffle.

"Yes, I remember the fights," said Little in a 2023 interview. "I got fined by the league office for it. What happened. . . you know, Cardinals offensive guard, Conrad Dobler, had that reputation at the time of getting in fights. I think that the guys on our defense. . . I think that Miami linebacker, Bob Matheson, if I'm not mistaken, spit on him. And Dobler went berserk. All throughout the game, a fight would break out here, and a fight would break out there. And I was on the sidelines because the game was so lopsided. I was already out of the game, and I had my cape on, because it was cold. Now I didn't actually leave the sidelines when the fight began. A guy from the Cardinals hit me along the sideline. Charlie Cornelius was a graduate of Bethune-Cookman just like me, and he was one of my teammates on the Dolphins. He also got hit by somebody on the Cardinals. That's what made me leave the sidelines. I had to stick up for Charlie.

"I ran on the field, and I joined in on the fight, and that's how I got fined. I admit to hitting one guy, but I don't remember who it was. I have no idea who it was, even to this day. Now when all of this happened, the game was almost over at that point. If I'm not mistaken, Conrad Dobler was thrown out of the game. In the letter that I got from the league, Commissioner Pete Rozelle said something to the effect that he 'didn't expect me to do something like that on a football field, because of my previous reputation.' Coach Shula didn't seem to mind, though. He didn't say anything about the fights after the game, even though some of us got penalized. You know that he knew that we were out there for each other, so he didn't come down on anyone for the fights. I think he enjoyed it as a matter of fact."[23]

The Dolphins greatly enjoyed their romp over St. Louis. But it would be their last real hurrah for the 1977 season. They managed to win two of their final three contests, but that was not enough to secure another playoff berth.

The pivotal game occurred on the season's final Sunday, when Miami's main adversaries in the division, the Patriots and the Colts, faced off against each other to determine which of the top three teams in the AFC East (Miami, New England, or Baltimore) would make the playoffs. It was a convoluted mess, with tie-breaker procedures emanating from the dirt field at Baltimore's Memorial Stadium. A late fourth quarter comeback decided the affair.

"The thing about that game was that New England jumped out to a big lead," remembered Little. "At that point, I really thought that they would beat the Colts, and we would be in the playoffs. But as what happened, the Colts came back with their quarterback, Bert Jones. They came back to win that game, and that's what put them in the playoffs instead of us. If New England would have held on and beaten Baltimore, we would have been in the playoffs."[24]

As a result of New England's loss to Baltimore, the 1977 season ended in Miami's third straight year without a ticket to the postseason tournament. The following year, a bunch of changes were in store for the league. The NFL schedule would be modified somewhat in 1978, as the league declared that there would now be sixteen regular season games (instead of the previous fourteen regular season games) for each team. There would also be an extra team that would make the playoffs each year, increasing the number of playoff teams at each of the two conferences to five.

"We didn't think about those extra two games," admitted Little. "We just didn't think about the amount of games on our schedule. We just went out and played whoever the league put in front of us."[25]

But there were more changes than just the number of games to be injected into the sport. Larry Little would indirectly become a beneficiary of one of those new modifications that year. As he entered his eleventh season in pro football in 1978, he and the rest of the offensive linemen in the league would now be allowed to extend their arms while blocking. Little would now also be allowed to grasp the jersey of the man whom he was blocking, so long as his hands and arms did not reach beyond the shoulders of the defenders. These two new rules represented a radical shift in how blocking was taught for many decades. One man who surprisingly had a say in this new change to the rules was ironically Little's own head coach, Don Shula, who was an outspoken member of the NFL's Competition Committee. Shula was for many years against making too many changes to the rules of the sport. But in 1978, he finally relented to public pressure.

"I'm a defensive coach with a defensive background," Shula explained, "but I was willing to compromise. The owners wanted to do something to produce more offense, and the fans indicated that they wanted more scoring. To me, it was great the way we had it. But I had to look at the entire picture and I was willing to compromise as long as the integrity of the game was not violated."[26]

Larry Little's integrity was of stellar variety, driven in part by years of sacrifice and hard work. He had by 1978 become one of the NFL's elder statesmen, and a leader in every aspect to his teammates. He was naturally looked up to by the younger players in Miami, in part for his age, but in a larger sense because of his success all throughout his career on the field. He simply performed like a leader should. There was a seriousness to his level of play, and to his performance on both gameday and at the Dolphins' daily practices. He regularly stressed to the younger

Miami players about what was expected from them.

"I've got too much pride to give up on myself," exclaimed Little back in 1977. "We can be a great team again if everyone goes to the wall for the club. Hopefully the kids we got now can mature naturally. I hope for their sake they do."[27]

Little would get to view his teammates' maturation and experience a renewal of sorts with the 1978 Dolphins. The team continued its trend of improvement that they began displaying in 1977. Their defense recorded three shutout victories in 1978, and their offense scored 372 points, which stood out as the most in the AFC, and the second-most in the entire NFL. Miami also had three separate three-game winning streaks in 1978.

To get to the postseason, however, Don Shula knew that he had to improve his team's running game. Yes, he had the blockers. But what he needed was a quality tailback who had both the strength to run inside up the gut and the speed to run outside on sweeps. The trade for Delvin Williams answered that need. By the end of the 1978 season, Williams accumulated 1,258 yards rushing, at that time the most of any Miami runner in one year.

"Delvin was a hell of a football player," exclaimed Little. "Anytime that you run for over 1,000 yards in a season, you have done well. He got over 1,200 yards in his very first year with us."[28]

The addition of Williams was vital for Miami's hopes to return to the playoffs. The Dolphins managed to put together enough big wins to earn a strong 11-5 record. They did not win their division, but they did claim a wild card berth to get into the 1978 postseason tournament. The veterans on the team were glad to be back playing for another opportunity to win a championship.

"It definitely felt good to get back into the playoffs again in 1978," expressed Larry Little. "That's what you play for every year. It's always good to have another opportunity to go to another Super Bowl. After we had gone to the Super Bowl in 1973, we all thought that we would get back to another Super Bowl.[29]

"[But] the '78 Dolphins were not the same kind of team as in the Super Bowl years. We had much more strategy back in those days, plus we had depth. . . a lot of veterans. The '78 team was more emotional, especially with so many young players fresh out of college. We had more *rah rah* that season. A lot of the young players came up to me and wanted to know the ins and outs of [pro] football. As the year went along, they sure asked their share of questions."[30]

Despite the infusion of youthful spirit in Miami, the next trip to another Super Bowl would not occur in 1978. They succumbed to the surging Houston Oilers in the first round of the 1978 playoffs, 17-9. It was a sobering end to what, up to that time, had been a promising year for the Dolphins. Despite what appeared to be a very strong performance, Miami suffered the fate that many teams eventually must deal with. . . that of their more experienced players getting older and slower, and that of their younger players still lacking enough experience and/or talent to come through in the clutch when it mattered most. But there was another good reason why the Dolphins failed to beat the Oilers in the 1978 playoffs. Houston was simply just a better football team than Miami, especially when it counted in the fourth quarter.

"We were going up against one hell of a football team in the Houston Oilers," confirmed Little. "I don't remember too much about that game, but I do remember that Earl Campbell had a great game. And to no surprise, considering he was a Future Pro Football Hall of Famer. Earl Campbell, who was a rookie in 1978, led the league that year with 1,450 yards rushing. He was a helluva competitor. He would dish it out whenever he hit his intended running lane. He was so hard-nosed. He played hard. . . very hard." Larry sighs, his eyes dropping. "Unfortunately, his legs took such a beating when he was playing, and he still feels the effects of all of those hard hits today."[31]

The effects of all the hard hits were also something to consider for a former. . . but soon to be non-former. . . member of the Miami team. In 1979, a prodigal son returned to wear the aqua and orange. Larry Csonka would play one last year of pro football, and in what could have been considered as the last step in his sentimental journey, he signed on to play with his old coach and his Miami buddies. But Csonka was not just signing on in South Florida to give Dolphins fans another chance to cheer for him. Rather, he was determined to play as well as he did when he was younger, and lo and behold, he did. Csonka would gain 837 yards in his swan song from the sport. Moreover, he would also score thirteen touchdowns in 1979. The culmination of his final season in pro football came when he was named the NFL's Comeback Player of the Year.

For his part, Larry Little would do his best to see that his old friend went out as a success. Both Little's and Csonka's bodies had been through a lot during the past decade. But both men still had the innate desire to deliver the best of themselves to each other and to the game that they both loved. Little once again plowed into opposing defensive linemen to open holes for Csonka to smash into, and when he was not carrying the ball, Csonka would once again do his best to block opposing defenders. In a sense, it was just like old times for the two future Hall of Famers.

"I was happy to hear that [Csonka] was coming back to play again in Miami," proclaimed Little, the smile taking over his entire face. "That's because I knew that when he was done with the World Football League, he went to play for the New York Giants. And he got beat up pretty bad up there, because his offensive line up there in New York was not as good at the offensive line that he had when he was in Miami. He knew that he was better off with our offensive line in Miami than what he had to deal with in New York with the Giants. When Csonka was teamed up with Delvin Williams in our backfield in '79, we had a pretty good running game. Also, our offensive linemen were still good." Larry chuckled at his sly back patting.[32]

Larry Csonka, Delvin Williams, and the Dolphins offensive line were probably one of the most unheralded and underrated rushing attacks in the decade of the 1970s in the NFL. The total ground output of the 1979 Miami team was a respectable 2,187 yards. Even in his final pro season, Csonka still considered his offensive line as not just his protectors, but as his main enabling ingredient to achieving yardage, touchdowns, and awards. And of those men on the Miami offensive line, he was sure to point out the abilities and the importance of Larry Little.

"He and I were going to go all the way through the undefeated season and the championship years," said Csonka when discussing Little's contributions to the team. "So, with Little came the basic foundation for our power running game. It started to fall into place when we got Larry Little. It started to pay off. To have the kind of knowledge that Larry had, and the kind of confidence that we had in each other was truly special. We knew each other's movements, and we were able to read each other's body movements at the point of impact. We had that kind of unity in each other because we had been through so much together. We had that kind of confidence in each other."[33]

The confidence that the 1979 version of the Miami Dolphins would see in each other would resemble—to some degree—what the team accomplished in the early part of the decade. Miami would make the playoffs once again in 1979, and even though they did not advance any further than the divisional round of the postseason, it nevertheless was still a successful season for Don Shula and his players. For the final time in his pro football career, Larry Little would be a member of a division-winning team in 1979.

"It's always great to go to the playoffs." said Little. "It's a statement that by going to the playoffs, you must be doing something right on the football field."[34]

Miami recorded a 10-6 regular season record in 1979. Their first-round playoff game would be in Pittsburgh, and for the second to the last time in their pro careers, Larry Little would get a chance to see his old adversary, Joe Greene. It was a time for the two men to reminisce about their early days and the Dolphins-Steelers rivalry from the first few years of the 1970s. Both men were honest in recent interviews when discussing each other's (and their own) abilities at the latter stages of their playing days.

"He wasn't getting older, he was getting better," assessed Greene of Little's blocking skills. "He was better at his technique than he was earlier in his career. And I think that I got better also. We were still playing the game, and we were still learning new ways to beat our opposition. Overall, defenses across the league had to be better in 1979, because offenses kept getting better by that time."[35]

According to Little, Joe Greene was still regarded as the toughest player that he ever played against, even in 1979. He knew that he would be receiving a full gamut of moves and strategies from Greene whenever he was faced with the task of blocking big number seventy-five in black and gold. But both men also probably recognized that their physical strength at this point in their playing careers was about the same as that of each other. As always in the sport of football, strategic measures had to be addressed to get the better of your opponent. . . or to show improvement on the gridiron in some way.

"Joe talks about my technique getting better as I played

longer," explained Little in a 2023 interview. "It probably did, because as you got older, you had to change some of the things that you had been doing earlier in your career."[36]

The Steelers built an impressive 20-0 first quarter lead, and they never looked back. Larry Little's final visit to the NFL's postseason tournament ended in defeat, 34-14.

"Now in that 1979 playoff game at Pittsburgh where they beat us," recalled Little, "we didn't even challenge them. I played offensive tackle in that game instead of my usual offensive guard position. I could play tackle, and I wouldn't feel uncomfortable doing it. There's a difference in technique at tackle, but the basics are about the same as at guard.

"I didn't have to block Joe Greene in that game. But I did see a lot of [Pittsburgh defensive end] L.C. Greenwood. L.C. had those long arms of his, and he sure used them. That was like going from the frying pan into the fire."[37]

There would be one more not-so-fiery season as a pro player for Larry Little in 1980. By that time, he decided that he had accomplished whatever he could in the league. His body of work in the NFL with the Chargers and the Dolphins was filled with as many awards and honors as an offensive guard could possibly earn. Most importantly, he was a member of two winning Super Bowl teams, including one as an undefeated world champion. But the 1980 season for Little would be a rather nondescript one, void of accolades and achievements. He did not make any All-Pro teams that year. Moreover, his team was unable to reach the playoffs, as the Dolphins could record just an 8-8 record in 1980. His knee injury in the sixth week of that season at New England effectively ended his playing career in the NFL.

But in retrospect, Larry Little could not look back at his experiences and his accomplishments as a player in the NFL in a critical way. He got as much out of his abilities as he possibly could. Moreover, he developed quickly as a player. It did not take him too long to go from an untested rookie to a steady starter to an All-Pro performer. As a veteran player, Little was looked upon as a strong and reliable team leader and captain. Finally, he was a champion. . . an honor that no one could ever take away from him. Larry Little indeed had many good times playing his favorite sport, ever since he was a kid on the streets of Miami. . . indeed every time that he buckled up his chinstrap.

CHAPTER 11

SAYING GOODBYE TO THE GAME

When do you reach a point in your life when you know that it is time to retire from your chosen profession? It is a question that Larry had to answer sooner or later. Some people want to avoid retirement for as long as possible, perhaps because they need to make more money during a period with a struggling national economy. Or maybe it is because they know that their jobs are too important or provide them with too much enjoyment to just give up participating in them. There could be dozens of reasons why anyone decides to sidestep retirement.

The world of a professional athlete is a little bit different, however. The physical health of their bodies will typically give them clues as to when they should retire. But there are some similarities here too. Some athletes try to keep playing for as long as they can, for some of the same reasons why average wage earners continue to stay in their jobs. The need and the desire to make more money is always a factor for athletes and non-athletes alike. But for pro football players, the hope that the team that they play for just might win a championship in the upcoming season, or the season after that, is a big incentive to remain on a team's roster.

For Larry Little, the time had come for him to recognize and to realize that his playing career in pro football had reached its end. Most players in the sport of pro football never get to play in the playoffs, much less the Super Bowl. Fewer still ever get to be on a team that wins a world championship. So, in that respect, Larry Little was more fortunate than a lot of NFL players, and lasted longer than most. He had tasted the joy of winning all that a player can win in the game of pro football. By the end of the 1980 season, his last year as an NFL player, he was the proud owner of two Super Bowl rings and numerous trophies and plaques, each of which honored him as one of the best offensive guards to ever play the game.

So, Little could look back at his recent past to reminisce about his accomplishments. But what were his thought processes when it came to retiring from the game? What were the steps that he went through to make his decision to retire? In fact, his decision to finally call it quits did not happen abruptly or in haste. It took some time to contemplate the whole issue. Were there any exterior elements or other opinions from his friends or family members that added some facts to aid his choice to retire? In Little's case, not really.

There were times in his veteran athletic career where Larry felt he was closer to the realization that he was nearing the end of his journey as an active player. There were times in the latter part of the 1970s, however, where he casually felt that he still had something more to give to his team and to his profession.

"You always feel [that] you can improve," admitted Little in the mid-1970s. "I feel I'm improving with age, [and] getting a better knowledge of my position. Before a season, you try to do the things you did the year before a little bit better."[1]

Little undoubtedly heard from his friends and his teammates as he advanced in his pro career the old adage, "You're not getting older, you're getting better." But even he could not deny that Father Time had a say in the actions of everyone who ever played pro football. Indeed, there were moments in Little's career when he felt somewhat burdened by the game, most noticeably while enduring Miami's losing season of 1976. Yes, playing pro football was his greatest dream. He certainly was living his dream. But even dreams that are fulfilled do not always go the way that we had hoped. Sometimes, there are occasional speed bumps or road barricades in the way. Larry Little would have to deal with some of those "alterations" to his earliest dream from time to time. He did not say a whole lot about the bitter feelings that he sometimes felt during his playing career. But when he did, his remarks were an eye-opening look into how even a solemn warrior must deal with their own thoughts about how the game can wear you down.

"I know I'm tired of football," admitted Little later in the 1970s. "The reason I'm still in it is the money. Let's face it. I don't have anything to accomplish in football anymore. I've played in three Super Bowls, the Pro Bowl, and been voted the league's best offensive lineman. Now money is making me go on."[2]

The money issue. Invariably, it is one of the most important factors in a pro athlete's decision to play their sport. . . and to continue playing their sport. It indeed can become a contentious issue as well, especially when a performer feels that he is being undervalued by his team. A player and his agent during the era of the 1970s went into meetings and contract negotiations with the team owner and general manager much in the same way that an Army goes into battle. The agent wants what is best for his client [the player], and the general manager wants what is best for the owner and for the team. These two diametrically opposed sides will each present their cases and will each ask the other side to make compromises. Sometimes, compromises are not to be found on either side. Sometimes, neither side wants to budge an inch on their position. That is when disagreement can turn into harsh feelings toward the other side. In most cases, however, as time wears on, cooler heads will eventually prevail, and an agreement is reached, and a contract is signed. There are instances, however, where no deal can be reached, and the agent will sometimes advise the player not to report to training camp until a deal can be reached. This has happened to many pro athletes over the years. Such an occurrence happened to Larry Little in 1980. He made a conscious decision not to report to training camp.

The situation for any player who does not attend training camp on the prescribed date that he is expected to be in the team's training facility usually involves one reason: money. Or rather, the lack of it. The player who does hold out does so because he feels that he is making less money than he deserves. His agent goes into discussions with the team's front office, and after much give and take with dollar amounts, the player eventually returns to camp with a new contract, or he returns to camp with an understanding—and perhaps with a promise—that his financial situation with the team will soon be settled. During the time that a player stays out of camp, he inevitably does some soul searching about his situation. He tries to think about what would be best for him at this stage of his pro football career. Larry Little did that in the summer of 1980. He eventually settled for a few thousand dollars less than what he had hoped to obtain through his agent's renegotiations with the Dolphins management.

"It [his holdout] was over money," Little admitted. "But I didn't want to see all of my offseason conditioning go to waste," Little expressed. "That's the main reason I came to camp. I put so much into getting ready for this season, I didn't want to see it all go down the drain. I felt very uncomfortable being at home knowing that practice was going on."[3]

Little had to address some specific issues when he returned to the training camps during his later years with the Dolphins. One was his physical health. How was it? Was the sweat and strain of a decade of pro football wearing him down too much? Another factor that he had to think about was his role on the team. Would he still be a starting offensive guard, or would some new and younger guards replace him in the starting lineup? Also, would he be required to fill in at offensive tackle, especially if the team was beset with more injuries at that position? He had done a good job of playing the position of offensive tackle, particularly in the 1979 AFC Divisional Playoff game at Pittsburgh. Indeed, Little would have a lot on his mind as he suited up to play in his final year of pro football. It was a situation where his mind had an equal say as his body.

"It's not any tougher to get psyched up [to play]," admitted Little in 1980, "but I feel different from four or five years ago. Sometimes I tend to feel [that] I'm getting older when I'm really not that much older.[4] There's no doubt that aches and pains were a part of what I was going through. Back when I was younger, the aches and pains would last for a couple of days. But as I got older, they lasted for a few days. Plus, as I got older, the toll of the two-a-day practices during the preseason started to get to me."[5]

Coach Shula's priority when dealing with his older veteran players (like Little) was to put the welfare of his team first. To do that in Little's case, Shula would have to be willing to bring in younger offensive guards and help them get their bearings, as it were. He wanted to ease them into a position where they would eventually take over for a guy like Larry Little, and then excel at their position, just as Little had done. But a former All-Pro performer like Little had a lot of pride, and even though he was willing to help and give advice to his youthful proteges, that did not necessarily mean that he wanted them to take over his starting role on the team. . . at least not all at once and at least not right away.

"I'm not going to lie down and accept being a substitute, because that's something I haven't been accustomed to," commented Little in the latter part of his pro career. "But it's something I can deal with if I have to at this stage of my career. Two years ago, I don't know if I could have dealt with it. But now I'm thirty-four years old, and I will be thirty-five in November, and I know that I can't play forever.

"Right now, I don't consider myself a substitute. When the [1980] season starts, if I am in a backup role, I still wouldn't consider myself as a substitute. I'd just be playing behind two good guards. I know there's a hell of a lot of guards in the league that I am better than right now, at my age. It's a matter of being in a place where you might not be needed versus being in a place where you are needed."[6]

Riding the bench. Being a benchwarmer. Those are terms that no player ever really admits to wanting to hear or do, all the way back to the very first time that they began participating in sports as youngsters. But there are only eleven players who can be on the football field for each team at the snap of the ball. Most of the other players are thus standing along the sidelines, awaiting their opportunity to get in on the action. Every player on a team has a role, and every player accepts that fact. Larry Little, by the 1980 season, had come to accept that he would not be a starting player in every game anymore. He was a "team player" first and foremost, and that fact was something that he took pride in all throughout his career. He was not a "selfish" athlete by any stretch of the imagination. Few are the pro football players who remain in the sport.

But no player plays the game forever. Sometimes, a player's coaching, or his team's coaching staff, can "help" a player to decide to retire. Sometimes, being cut from a team, and then not being picked up by another team, will give a player an undeniable hint that their career in the sport is over, whether they wanted to believe it or not, or whether they accepted that result or not. That did not happen to Larry Little. Had he been cut by the Miami Dolphins, he almost certainly would have been snatched up on the same day by another pro team in need of veteran leadership, or in need of a quality offensive guard to fill in their ranks.

One factor that Little would not have to consider regarding his retirement would be something that can occur in the back of many players' minds. Most NFL players ply their trade for losing or mediocre teams. That is just an accepted fact. The feeling that a player may never become a part of a contending squad, or have a chance to experience a winning season, can sometimes push a player into retirement. Little never experienced that type of mindset with the Dolphins, especially with Don Shula as the head coach of the team. Little knew that Shula would never tolerate coaching for an average team or a team which sat at or near the bottom of the league's standings. So, Miami was in good hands, whether Little remained on their roster or not.

The 1980 season would be Larry Little's final year as an active player in the NFL, but he did not know that for absolute certainty when the season began. He did know that he was beginning his fourteenth season in pro football at that time, and by playing for over a decade, he was presumably testing the odds with each succeeding season. Time was indeed taking its toll on his frame of mind.

"I know that during my final year as a pro football player in 1980," Little recalled, "I would just sit at my locker and ask myself, 'Why in the hell am I still doing this?' I was about thirty-five years old. I was ready to retire. I was ready to get out. I didn't want to play much that year, but because of injuries to some other players, I had to go in and play. I owed it to myself to play, because I was getting paid to play."[7]

Little was not naive when it came to his overall physical health. By playing the sport of football, he knew that his body was going to take abuse every time that he stepped on the field.

He was a survivor at this point in his career. He was not getting more brittle, mind you. Rather, like any veteran player, whenever he suffered an injury, it just took more time for that injury to heal. That is something that is an expected occurrence for any pro athlete as he ages in his sport.

"I didn't really feel like I was bucking the odds of the matter of the health issue," Little said. "Because fortunately, I was pretty healthy. I had a few injuries over the years, but I was pretty healthy.[8] I know that I was at least kind of healthy, overall, going into the 1980 season. I know that my body had begun to start breaking down a little. I played for thirteen years at that point. I gave it everything that I had, and I knew that my career had to be coming to an end sometime soon."[9]

Leaving it all on the field. That is a term that athletes are very familiar with. It means giving every ounce of your strength, your physical abilities, and your cognitive mind to your teammates, to your coaches, and to your sport. . . on every play. It is not an easy thing to do, but for an athlete like Larry Little, leaving it all on the field became a way of life. The same went for the other veteran players, many of whom were suffering from various injuries during the past few years.

When discussing the aspect of injuries, Larry Little was always pragmatic in his responses.

"It could be that I can't ever feel like a kid anymore," Little expressed just before the beginning of the 1980 season. "And neither can the other veterans. Maybe that was the trouble. Maybe everybody grew up too fast around here."[10]

Little's lament as to the condition of the older Dolphins players was certainly heard throughout the league, as every NFL team had to deal with the problems of injuries and aging veterans. Little was cognizant of the fact that, despite his best efforts at being a strong example of endurance for his teammates, he still could not stop the effects that time had delivered to his body. But when his body needed some encouragement, only more aches and pains were seemingly having a voice.

"What happened was that I had ankle surgery just before the 1979 season," explained Little, "and my ankle was never the same again after that surgery that I had. But I thought that I could still play."[11]

Despite his problematic ankle, Little buckled up his chinstrap for the Dolphins for another year. But he was not in the same frame of mind as he was in any of his previous pro seasons.

"My last year, when I came back in 1980, I wasn't looking to start for the team, to tell you the truth," Little confirmed. "I was looking forward to standing on the sidelines with a baseball cap on my head. But with so many other players getting injured at that time, I needed to play."[12]

Larry Little's final season as a professional football player (1980) began at Buffalo. He did not see any action in this game, as his former backup, Ed Newman, started in his place. Newman was almost six years younger than Little, and by this time, Coach Shula wanted to infuse more youth in as many positions as possible in the lineup.

"Ed was ready to play by 1980," admitted Little. "I knew that he was ready to play. He had paid his dues by being a backup for both guard positions. . . for [Bob] Kuechenberg and myself. He came to our team back in 1973 as a rookie. So, I knew that Ed was ready to play. And I'm quite certain that our offensive line coach John Sandusky wanted Ed to play too. I think that they wanted me to get the hell out of there."[13]

The whole Miami team wanted to get the hell out of Buffalo at the conclusion of their opening game of 1980. Buffalo was a place where neither Shula nor Little ever saw the Dolphins lose during the 1970s, yet they lost this time. The game featured many mistakes by both teams, but the Bills rode a wave of momentum that never seemed to diminish in the second half, as they posted a 17-7 upset win over Miami. The Dolphins were outgained 357 yards to 200 in their loss to Buffalo, and quarterbacks Bob Griese and Don Strock threw two interceptions each. It was not the way that Little or his teammates wanted to see the 1980 season begin.

"Buffalo hadn't beaten us in so many years," declared Little. "I remember after that game as we were leaving on the team bus, their fans were so excited and so happy about beating us on that day, they started pulling their pants down and mooning us as we were leaving."[14]

Despite that planetary parting shot from the Bills fans, the opening loss at Buffalo was immediately followed by a rededication and a rejuvenation among the Miami players, many of whom were still in high school when both Larry Little and Don Shula first came to the team. The Dolphins quickly posted a come from behind 17-16 victory over the Cincinnati Bengals in the Orange Bowl, and then another couple of clutch wins, 20-17 over the Atlanta Falcons, and then 21-16 over the New Orleans Saints. Miami was now 3-1, and things were looking good. Fortune was not on their side, however. The injuries to key personnel started to mount up. So did the losses.

Thanks to more injuries on the team's offensive line, Little was back in his starting position at offensive guard by the time that the Baltimore Colts came down to Florida on October 5th to play the Dolphins. Little faired rather well in the game, but Miami's offense was unable to accumulate enough scoring drives to be competitive, and Baltimore won, 30-17. A 34-0 shutout loss to New England followed, and that game proved to be most detrimental to any hopes that the Dolphins might have had to compete for a division title. Larry Little went down with a knee injury in that game, and that effectively knocked him out for the season.

"Bob Griese's career and my career ended on the same day, in that game at New England," remembered Little. "We were both injured in that game."[15]

The Dolphins did their best to lick their wounds following their embarrassing loss to the division rival Patriots. Coach Shula knew that the rest of their slate of games in 1980 would not be easy, however, and the results proved it. Miami followed up their debilitating defeat at New England with losses in two of their next three games, giving them a record of 4-5, and essentially ending their chances for a division title. The team could never build on any slight momentum that they may have had. The Dolphins failed to win some tight ball games in the second half of the year, and the verdict was foreseeable. The 1980 season would become one of a failure to live up to their previous standards, which were established in the early years of the 1970s.

Miami's final game of the 1980 season was in the Orange Bowl against the New York Jets, a team that had only won three games up to that point. By the contest's final gun, they would make it four wins, as they defeated the Dolphins, 24-17. Also, with that game's final gun, Larry Little would walk off the football field for the final time as an active player. It had to have been at least somewhat debilitating to end his playing career on a losing note, but in reality, there are only a few tokens of athletes who ever go out on top as champions.

It was also a reflective time for Larry Little. He would certainly not be blamed for going back briefly in his mind and reminiscing on the many memories that he had of all his years playing the sport. Little reasoned with his situation in a pragmatic way, as he weighed all the pros and cons. He knew, as does anyone who faces a change in their lives in one aspect or another, that he could not change his past. His future? Well, that was still up in the air. He was not 100 percent sure of what would be his plight in his upcoming years, and in the decade of the 1980s. Nevertheless, he pondered his situation thoroughly at this time in his life.

"You know I was thirty-five years old at that time," Little laughed at himself in a 2023 interview, "and I had just finished playing pro ball for fourteen years." Little threw his hands, the idea that his career had outlasted all the odds was astonishing, "By that time, I had enough. I hated training camp, and Coach Shula still continued to run the toughest training camp of any team in the league, and my body just didn't want to do it anymore. I think that after fourteen years, even Coach Shula was ready to see me go," Larry quibbled. "After fourteen years, that was enough for me and him."[16]

In a contemplative moment when discussing his retirement from playing pro football, Little had similar opinions that most former players mentioned upon their retirement from the game.

"The hardest thing about retiring is missing the camaraderie among the guys," Little expressed back in 1981. "I'm going to miss the good times, but a lot of us are still around town and we get together every now and then and talk about the old memories. I had already made up my mind that I was going to retire, so it wasn't anything that I agonized over or dwelled on. I gave pro football fourteen years, and now it's time to move on to something else."[17]

It was an accepting and satisfied Larry Little who would go up to Don Shula following the Dolphins' 1980 season to inform him of his career intentions. He had given his heart, his mind, and his body to the team for fourteen years. Now it was time to make his plans known, and he would do so in February of 1981.

"I don't recall the actual date that I announced my retirement," said Little, "but I remember when I told Coach Shula that I was retiring. He set up a press conference for me to announce my retirement. It was at the Dolphins office, and I remember that I wore a rust-colored sports jacket.

"Joe Robbie [the Dolphins owner] was there also. Joe made a statement at the press conference that stuck out to me. He said that I had a job with the Dolphins organization as long as I wanted it. But that was just to find out that Joe didn't mean that I was going to be paid by the Dolphins organization. Instead, he wanted me to get involved with the Miami Parks and Recreation Department."[18]

Joe Robbie did not get to the upper echelon of millionaires by just being lucky. He had plenty of business savvy to go along with whatever good fortune he may have had. His comments at Little's retirement announcement was exactly what one might expect. He sounded magnanimous. He evoked praise for his newest retiree. And he probably wished that in retrospect and in reality that he meant every word that he spoke.

"We're only saying good luck to Larry," expressed Robbie, "not goodbye. He's going to be around a long time with the Miami Dolphins family."[19]

Despite his kind sentiments, what Robbie displayed to Little was the old bait and switch maneuver, where he offered Little one thing, then removed it, and replaced it with something completely different without fully disclosing his real intentions or ideas during Little's retirement press conference. Such moves have been going on in business environments for thousands of years. Larry Little was just the latest person to see it happen firsthand.

"That's what he [Robbie] meant when he said that I would continue to have a job with the Dolphins organization," said

Little. "He wanted me to meet with the city commissioner, Miller Dawkins, to talk about doing things for the city's parks. But to me. . . to say that I was going to have a job with the Dolphins organization as long as I wanted it, and then for him [Robbie] to not really mean it. . . that was kind of insulting to me. The city's Parks and Recreation Department doesn't have a whole lot to do with the Dolphins organization."[20]

Little did not accept Joe Robbie's offer to work with Miami's Parks and Recreations Department. If Robbie had offered Little a job as a technical adviser with the team, that might have been different. But Little had reached a set of crossroads in his life, and he knew it. His new turning point would involve his own business ventures. He had just finished doing all he ever wanted to do as an active player of his favorite sport. Now he would cut bait with his old team as he ventured out onto a different path for his life. With the certified announcement of his retirement following the 1980 NFL season, the days of Larry Little's involvement in the game of football were officially over. Or were they?

CHAPTER 12

IT'S IN THE BLOOD

The sport of football is indeed an enticing sport. It draws people to it. . . for the action, for the excitement, for the pressure of performing well. There are numerous reasons why both fans and players fall in love with the game. Football is a proving ground for many men. It gives them a chance to display—perhaps even to just themselves—how strong they are, both mentally and physically. Football gives a man an opportunity to become a part of a group of other men who are like himself. The team concept of participating in the sport of football is indeed very appealing. Everyone during their lives feels the need to belong to a group or an organization that is stronger than just one person. The need to belong to a group is one of the driving forces for every young man to wants to participate in any team sport.

Football is probably the best "team" sport in America. A typical high school, college, or professional team consists of at least forty players. Regardless of the level of play, however, the players in football must accept the idea of putting the team first above their own individual goals. A player receives that initial lesson into the game soon after they put on their very first uniform as a kid. That youthful curiosity to do what your football heroes do on television each weekend is a great lure for kids to explore the sport. That is what happened to Larry Little when he saw his first football game on television, then got a chance to emulate what those players did when he was out on the streets of Miami. Like many youngsters, Little got hooked on the game. It was a feeling that never left him, and it probably never will. You do not spend most of your formative years enjoying something like the sport of football, only to abandon it in an instant.

But Larry Little did not really have any specific plans to continue exploring any possible avenues within the game of football following the end of his pro playing days. He instead remained busy with several different enterprises and jobs, and they took up much of his time.

"I didn't feel any worry or anxiety when I finally announced my retirement from pro football," Little recalled. "I had some other endeavors that I was involved in that were taking up my time. I had a roller-skating business with my teammate Nat Moore, and that's what I had my focus on. And then I also became an athletic director and a teacher at a high school here in Miami. . . at Miami Thomas Edison High School. I started teaching right after I retired from the Dolphins. I taught two or three civics classes for a couple of years. It all came down to the fact that football-wise, I was old. But I was still me. And mind-wise, I was still young, insofar as getting into something else that I could do besides football."[1]

The sport of football would not relent, however. It had a strong grip on Larry Little, and it did not take too long before football once again showed up in his life. An important inroad was made into Little's life on a non-assuming day when forces beyond his knowledge were already at work. The former offensive guard for the San Diego Chargers and the Miami Dolphins was about to be contacted by someone from his past.

"Well, what happened, once I retired, Bethune-Cookman University had some problems," Little recalled. "I was in Miami, minding my own business, and Lloyd 'Tank' Johnson, the athletic director at Bethune-Cookman, who happened to be one of my coaches when I played there. . . he called me one day. He said, 'Larry, we're getting ready to make a change here, and we are ready to make a move. I want you to come back and become the head football coach at Bethune-Cookman.' I never expected to hear those words. I don't have any coaching experience. He said, 'Yeah, but we need you.' He basically said that he needed somebody to save the football program at the college."[2]

Small colleges did not have a lot of financial wealth to draw upon when it came to budgeting their athletic programs in the early 1980s. If the revenue that was raised for the sports programs at small colleges did not offset the costs to run those programs, some schools would—over time—end up trimming or outright cutting some of the sports. Bethune-Cookman was nearing just such a situation when Lloyd Johnson telephoned Larry Little in the spring of 1983.

"I think that what he was really saying was that influential people were talking about the school dropping football," explained Little. "And he wanted me to be the one to try to come in and save the program."[3]

Larry Little would be a good choice to become the new head football coach at Bethune-Cookman University. He had the requisite pedigree, meaning simply that he was a loyal alumnus of the school. That had to count for something. But perhaps most importantly, Little was both popular and indeed famous in Daytona Beach (where Bethune-Cookman University was located) and also throughout the State of Florida. Thanks to his Gold Coast Summer Sports Camp, which at this time was well over a decade old, the word of the success of the camp had spread far and wide throughout the Sunshine State. Little's fame? Easy. A two-time Super Bowl champion, a player in several Pro Bowls, and a former All-Pro. Indeed, Little's professional accolades were certainly not lacking.

Johnson knew that Little's achievements would be a drawing card of sorts to keep Bethune-Cookman's sports popularity viable and in the public eye in a positive way. He had good reason to feel this way. I mean, how many Super Bowl champions became college head coaches at the college in which they attended? The answer was not many. Quite simply, Johnson's decision was what we call today as a "no-brainer."

"I gave it a lot of thought," said Little in assessing Johnson's request. "I'm thinking that it [being their head coach] would be a lot of pressure. I knew that I would only have a part-time coaching staff. But after a little while, I decided to give it a try. And it worked out. The year of 2023 marked the school's 100th year of playing football. The school's football program survived."[4]

Larry Little was back in football in the fall of 1983. The sport was just too important to him to not return to it. The game of football wanted more from Little. It was as if football had a mind of its own. It knew that Little had more to offer than just what he gave to the sport as a player.

But a football coach? How would Larry learn how to be a coach? Sure, he had played the game for many years and would inevitably remember different practice drills that he performed for his position and would invariably recall certain statements that his past coaches said that you could reiterate to his players. But he thought of other sources he could derive such coaching skills. Today, there are coaching clinics for new coaches held all throughout the nation. Similar clinics were also around when Little first came back to Bethune-Cookman to be their new head coach, but he never attended them.

"I never went to any of the coaching clinics," explained Little, "because we didn't have a budget at Bethune-Cookman that would allow it. Neither my assistant coaches nor myself. . . we just couldn't afford to go to any of them. Now if memory serves, I think that I went to a coaches' convention once in San Diego. So, I did go to one coaching convention."[5]

Little's decision to put on a coach's cap and don a whistle would, in effect, be representative of a natural transition for him. Yes, as is sometimes the case, a retired player who loves the sport of football will often seek out a path to stay in the game, at least at some level or in some way. An older player with leadership qualities who wants to continue working in the game will often seek out coaching opportunities. The country is filled with former pro football players who have landed jobs as coaches in high school, college, and in the pros. If a former player continues being employed for several years as a coach, chances are good that he will move around the country every few years, going from team to team. It is an endeavor that can be trying, especially if a player has a family that he must uproot from time to time.

But as Little mentioned, such was not his case. He did not actively seek out coaching positions. . . at least not at first. But when he decided to accept his new role at his alma mater, he went into it with the same determination and resolve as he did that made him an All-Pro performer in the NFL. Nobody wants to start a new job and be labeled as mediocre (or worse). Little wanted to see his new team of young student athletes win, and he would do whatever he could to ensure that success would be obtained at Bethune-Cookman.

Little had to start at coaching from the ground up, however. He knew that there was a lot more to it than what meets the eye. He did, however, have at least some foundation of knowledge to draw upon when dealing with young men who were a generation younger than himself.

"By me having my boy's camp with my partners for fifteen years, that kind of prepared me to get into coaching," Little surmised. "That was an unseen benefit that I got from holding that camp each summer."[6]

One major factor in Little's new occupation as the head football coach of Bethune-Cookman University would be recruiting players. College football greatly differs from pro football in that distinct reality. The pro players are either drafted or signed as free agents. The college players must be recruited, and many schools compete off the field with each other to lure the best high school seniors into accepting scholarships at their school and playing for their team. The whole recruiting process is very competitive across the nation.

A school requires funding to compete in the recruiting battles. As much money as possible in fact. Coach Little knew that the Bethune-Cookman budget was small. Whatever he was going to do in this situation, he was going to have to do it economically. He was going to have to be conservative with the dollars that the college offered him. His plan was an efficient one, and it was one that made the most sense. Many of his college coaching duties involved scouting and recruiting. In those areas, Little had to be savvy with his choices and decisions.

"Well, we didn't have any scouts at Bethune at that time," admitted a chuckling Little. "I would do whatever scouting and recruiting with my assistant coaches. You see we didn't have the money to stay in hotels like they do today. So, what I would do was both logical and economical. We did most of our scouting and recruiting in Miami, so we could stay at home, and so we wouldn't have to pay for hotels. But mostly, we did our recruiting by telephone. We had to do it that way. We didn't have the budget that the bigger colleges had.

"The university would rent a car for us. . . or mainly for me. And when I recruited in Miami, I would stay at my mom's house. And when the other coaches would go somewhere to recruit players, they would stay with their families, instead of staying at hotels. But we still managed to recruit some good football players. And we even had some guys who were drafted and who went on to play pro football."[7]

Little at least had some name recognition to help him influence high school athletes to consider playing for him at Bethune-Cookman. Quite a lot of those young men knew all about Little's summer sports camp, so they were familiar with him and with his past exploits. Little could not promise any of those kids that they would one day become pro football players. But he could promise them something that would—in the end—become much more valuable to them.

"My sales pitch to those young men was that they would get an education," Little declared. "I talked to them about football, but I [also] talked to them more about getting an education and being successful in life. You see when I was playing, I only had to consider me. But when I was coaching, I had to consider seventy-five or eighty different personalities that I had to deal with."[8]*

Many of Little's players at Bethune-Cookman did not receive much attention from most of the bigger or more familiar colleges during their senior year of high school. Some of those young men were destined to enlist in the various branches of the United States military. Others either did not possess a high enough grade point average or did not possess the athleticism to earn a college scholarship at a larger school. Despite those facts,

---

* Author's Note: There were no set number of players that were defined in college football during Little's time as head coach at Bethune-Cookman, hence the large number of players who made the team.

many of those players received at least some amount of attention from the recruiters.

"Oh yeah, there was no doubt that there was competition in recruiting between the schools," Little affirmed. "I knew right from the start that I probably wasn't going to be getting a blue chipper. But I would always try to get a red chipper. That's what I would call the athletes who were just below the blue chip-level athletes.

"One player that we got was Michael Floyd. Florida A&M was going after him very hard also. But I got him to play for Bethune because they [Florida A&M] were only talking to him about football, but I was talking to him about football and education. Looking back, we did manage to get some pretty doggone good football players, and they helped us win two conference championships at Bethune."[9]

The hard work of actual on-field coaching for Little and his coaching staff was now ready to commence once he had his roster of players set. At his first training camp as the new Bethune-Cookman head coach in 1983, Little had surrounded himself with assistant coaches who were familiar to him in one way or another, and at one time or another.

"Rick Stockstill was a graduate assistant at Florida State," recalled Little. "Willie Blackmon was there too. He heard that I was getting the job as Bethune's head coach, and he called me. He wanted to be on my staff. He wanted to coach our offensive line. I wanted to bring him on board, because if I didn't, I would have to coach the offensive line *and* be the head coach. Jimmy Warren was one of my former teammates who played with the Dolphins and who also played with the Oakland Raiders. The other coaches who were already on the coaching staff stayed at Bethune.

"Alvin Wyatt was also there. He was my teammate way back when I was a player at Bethune. And Willie 'Foots' Lee. . . he played at Bethune. He was another guy who was already there when I got hired. At that time [in 1983], I was willing to give almost anyone a chance at coaching, but I wanted someone with experience too. Coach Jack McClairen had experience. He was my head coach when I was playing at Bethune Cookman. He had been coaching for a long time, and he was also on my staff."[10]

The time for Little to prepare his coaches and his new team, however, was rather short. Yes, it was a small number of assistant coaches on his staff to be sure, but as previously stated this was a bare-bones operation, and everyone knew it. But that fact was not going to stop Larry Little from demanding the best of himself and his coaches.

At this time, Little looked to obtain some coaching wisdom from the wisest coach that he knew, Don Shula. He knew that Shula did not rise to become one of the winningest head coaches in pro football history by accident.* He sat down with his former boss just before the start of his first training camp at Bethune-Cookman to gain some quality tidbits of knowledge.

"You know the thing to being a coach. . . in particular a head coach. . . is to surround yourself with good assistant coaches," Little declared. "One piece of good advice which Don Shula gave me when I got into head coaching, was to let my assistant coaches. . . coach. He told me not to overcoach. You know what I mean? I was an offensive lineman, so of course, I spent most of my time with the offensive line. Now I had an offensive line coach, but I wanted to make sure that they [the players] were being taught the right way. Coach Shula also gave me some more advice. He told me to 'listen to your players, because you don't know everything.'"[11]

Little gained a lot of football education from Don Shula over the years. You don't spend eleven seasons in the NFL playing for

* Author's Note: As of this date, Shula still has the most victories as a head coach in NFL history with 347.

the same head coach without picking up at least some tokens of knowledge. Just prior to beginning with his own head coaching duties at Bethune-Cookman, Little also picked up something else from Coach Shula, and it was indeed a beneficial piece of tangible help.

"What happened was that Coach Shula allowed me to have a Dolphins playbook, which I took with me to Bethune-Cookman," said Little. NFL playbooks are held in the highest regard. A player can get fined quite a bit of money if he loses his playbook. When a player leaves his team to retire or to play for another team, his playbook must be returned to the team's possession. The fact that Don Shula allowed Larry Little to take a Dolphins playbook with him to Bethune-Cookman showed the high level of respect and appreciation that Shula had for Little. "I don't know if he ever gave the playbook to anyone else." continued Little. "If they didn't go into coaching after they were done playing, there was no need for it. But with that playbook, I had familiarity with the plays."[12]

Little's first season in 1983 as the head coach at his alma mater was somewhat of an uneventful one. The Wildcats had struggled through a 4-4-1 campaign, which was probably expected by many observers. Few are the rookie head coaches who can come into a faltering program and turn it into a winner overnight. But there was at least some hope. Their four victories in Little's inaugural year as the team's head coach were over the likes of the District of Columbia, Alabama State, North Carolina A&T, and Central Florida. Bethune-Cookman's offense racked up 224 points in 1983, and their defense did an even better job, as they limited their opponents to just 144 points all year long.

But losing games was difficult to deal with, regardless of whether they occurred in the pros or in the colleges. Little had spent most of his years as a player with the Dolphins with the annual expectation of winning an average of ten games each year.

Now as Bethune-Cookman's head coach, he would be forced to deal with winning less often. How did he adjust to such a change in outcomes?

"I did feel positive after my first year in coaching there, because we lost some games that we could have won, and that we should have won," Little expressed. "And then the core of that team was coming back again the next year. But in a way it [the lack of regularly expected victories at Bethune-Cookman] did affect my psyche somewhat. But I felt that when I played the game, I might have to go up against a player or a team that might be better than me. But I knew that every time a team played us, they would be in for a battle, win or lose. And that's how I wanted our players to approach their opponents when I was coaching."[13]

In all the years that Little was the coach of the Wildcats, both he and the team saw a mixture of ups and downs, good games and bad games in the Mid-Eastern Athletic Conference (MEAC). But to Little's credit, Bethune-Cookman improved their win-loss record in his second season as their head coach. His 1984 team produced a strong 7-3 mark. That represented the best record that Little would achieve in his tenure as the Wildcats' head coach. From that moment on, his teams began the downward slide to mediocrity. His 1985 team produced a respectable 6-4 mark. Then the bottom fell out, as Bethune-Cookman could earn only an average of four wins per year.

Despite that fact, Larry Little managed to keep the school's football program above water. They may not have survived in victorious fashion every year, but they did survive. That fact was a commendable result of his efforts at being a coach at any level. The 1991 season would be the last for Larry Little as the head coach at his alma mater. Even though his team only produced two winning seasons in the nine years in which he was their head coach, Little nevertheless saved the program from distinction.

Thanks to Little and his name recognition, the Bethune-Cookman football program continued to endure.

"Well, I was able to oversee the program," said a modest Little. "I was able to give the program a little bit of recognition. We won two MEAC championships there [in 1984 and 1985]. I think that they would have found someone to coach if I didn't say yes to coaching. I think that they would have found a way."[14]

Little would have probably preferred to have found a way to remain as the head coach of Bethune-Cookman. . . if things had remained the same when he first got hired for the job. But things rarely stay the same in any sort of business or sport. An internal shift in the direction in the school's hierarchy caused changes to occur in the athletic department and in the football program. Larry Little would have to personally deal with what he saw happening at his alma mater.

"Well, I didn't decide to leave Bethune," explained Little. "They [the college] decided for me to leave. I'll put it this way: When Lloyd 'Tank' Johnson, who was the athletic director who brought me in there to be the head football coach. . . when they pulled him from being the athletic director, and gave him some bogus job instead, and they knew how close I was to him and he was to me. . . I knew then that my job was on the line. I would have left anyway, but it didn't have to come to that. But despite the way that I left Bethune, I did leave with a sense of pride. I left there knowing that I, my coaches, and my players were able to save the football program there."[15]

That sense of pride was evident for Larry Little, in that he was able to help so many young African American men to obtain a college degree while he was their head coach. But one factor still lacked equal representation in the category of organized football. The coaching ranks across many pro and college teams during that era had a noticeable lack of African American coaches. If a prospective African American went into one of the historically black colleges of the South to obtain a coaching position, his chances would be better than at many other universities.

Today, the coaching opportunities for African American men has increased at every level of play. But several decades ago, such was not the case. The ugly specters of prejudice and ignorance were still prevalent among the various coaching communities. Some people still felt that African American coaches could not do a quality job at the role of coaching the sport of football. A guy like Larry Little no doubt heard stories about opportunities for African American coaches that were given to Caucasian coaches, based on skin color alone as the mitigating factor for selection.

"At that particular time in the early 1980s, I didn't think about it," said Little regarding the lack of African American coaches in pro and college football. "But once I thought back on it, it was. And it's still happening today. You know there are more teams today, and when you sometimes have twenty-eight to thirty coaches on some staffs, you've got to have some black coaches in there somewhere."[16]

Little was, as he said, not really thinking too much about the numbers of African American coaches throughout America when he first took the reins at Bethune-Cookman. At that time, he had too many other pressing issues that all head coaches must deal with to put a respectable product out on the field. As soon as he ended his tenure of time as the Wildcats' head coach, Little was in a state of limbo. He certainly knew by that time that he wanted to continue coaching. When asked if he was ever interested in doing football broadcasting, he shrugged and respectfully declined.

"The reason why I didn't want to get into broadcasting," explained Little, "was because once I got into coaching, I discovered that I enjoyed it."[17]

Little also enjoyed his times as a player for the Miami Dolphins.

One day in 1992, he suddenly discovered that the Dolphins were looking for a new offensive line coach. It was welcome news, and the timing could not have been more perfect. Little felt that he had as good of a chance as anyone to obtain the position. His reasoning seemed sound. He had built up a solid resume of outstanding work for over a decade as an All-Pro offensive guard for the Dolphins. He had coached in the college ranks for the previous nine years, and he knew how to relate to the young players on his team. And perhaps even most importantly, he had a strong desire to stay in coaching. He just seemed like the natural candidate. . . the perfect fit. . . to go back to Miami and begin work as their new offensive line coach.

But we cannot always predict what decision makers will do. Larry Little discovered this firsthand, and the news did not sit well with him. He lost a job to someone whom he felt (or perceived) was not as experienced, or perhaps not as qualified, as he was. That was the situation that Little found himself in during the spring of 1992. In effect, Don Shula may have been trying to change the culture of his team in some way. Little was now left to try to figure out how to deal with the bad news, and what future decisions he was going to have to make.

"I didn't get depressed when I was told that I wouldn't be getting hired by the Dolphins," Little recalled. "But I was pretty upset that I didn't get the job. Dwight Stephenson [former Miami offensive lineman and assistant Dolphins offensive line coach] called me, and he told me that he was giving it [his coaching job at Miami] up. He decided that he was going to go into a private business instead. They [the Dolphins] didn't think that one coach could coach the offensive line. Shula never really told me why he didn't hire me for that job, but he told me that he wanted to go another direction. I would have loved to coach in Miami, but it wasn't meant to be. At that time, I was bitter. But I moved on."[18]

To his credit, he did not let Shula's decision linger on his mind for too long. At that time in the early 1990s, the NFL executives had been engaged in developing and operating a new league which would help to give young players who were previously unable to make pro rosters a chance to improve their skills, and a chance to show scouts that they could play the game. It was called the World League of American Football. It consisted of seven teams in North America, and three teams in Europe. Another main reason for the formation of such a league by the NFL brain trust was to increase fan support for American football in foreign countries. To that extent, the World League of American Football was at least moderately successful. When he heard about the opportunities that this new league might present coaches as well as players, Larry Little jumped at the chance to become involved.

"What happened was John Wooten [Little's former agent and a longtime offensive lineman with the Cleveland Browns] called me up one day and told me that they were starting up a new league called the World League of American Football," Little said. "It was a league that was owned by the NFL. The teams in that league were going to be more like minor league teams. Their goal was to get the players in that league prepared to play in the next level. . . the NFL.

"When I expressed my interest in participating in the league, a man by the name of Pete Hadhazy, who was the general manager of the Ohio Glory team, contacted Coach Shula for a recommendation. Shula gave it to him. Without his recommendation, I probably wouldn't have gotten that job."[19]

Shula's recommendation certainly carried a lot of influence, and it helped to keep Larry Little on the coaching sidelines. Even though he had to move his family out of Florida and to Columbus, Ohio, it was a welcome opportunity. Little's assistant coaches for the only professional team that he ever coached included the likes of Barry Pettyjohn (Little's offensive line coach), Joe Viadella (the running backs and tight ends coach), Dennis Thurman (a former defensive back for the Dallas Cowboys) was Little's defensive coordinator, and Wally Chambers (a former defensive end for the Chicago Bears and the Tampa Bay Buccaneers) served as Little's assistant head coach, and Mike Dunleavy (the linebackers and special teams coach). But they were not the only coaches that made their way up to Ohio.

"One of my assistant coaches at North Carolina Central, J.D. Hall, played quarterback for me at Bethune-Cookman," added Little. "Sam Washington was another assistant coach of mine who was previously coaching at Johnson C. Smith University in North Carolina. All of those guys were guys that I brought in, but a couple of them were already there. My linebackers coach was Robert 'Stonewall' Jackson. He was a legendary coach at North Carolina because he had been around for so long. He was also one of the first African Americans to come from an HBCU school to play in the NFL. Damon Frenchers was my defensive line coach. I never had a full-time coaching staff there. They all had other duties besides just coaching."[20]

Despite the motivated coaching that occurred in Columbus, the Glory unfortunately struggled all year. They only managed to produce one victory in ten games, a 20-17 win over the Frankfort Galaxy. It was a tough year for the team, as their win-loss record indicated. But their strained efforts had as much to do with the uncertainty of the league as anything else.

"The year before I took over the team," Little explained, "they were in Raleigh, North Carolina. Roman Gabriel was the head coach of the team that year.* That team became the Ohio Glory

---

* Roman Gabriel was a former pro quarterback with the Los Angeles Rams and the Philadelphia Eagles.

team the next year. We were in the same league with the Barcelona team. The league also had teams in Germany, Montreal, London, Barcelona, the Netherlands, Scotland, Spain, Hamburg, and New Jersey. We also had a team in Alabama [the Birmingham Fire]. Now the team that I had in Ohio, we played at the Horseshoe, a nickname of the football stadium on the campus. It was the largest stadium in the league."[21]

Despite the potential for large crowds at their home games, and further large crowds at their games in Barcelona and Montreal, the World League of American Football was not founded on a firm financial base. The NFL tried it primarily to see if it could succeed on its own. Many members of the NFL's brain trust also were frankly not exactly sure what they wanted to do to promote pro football in Europe. Some wanted an actual NFL team placed somewhere in Europe, but most did not. In the end, they decided to discontinue the league after two seasons (1991 and 1992) and focus instead on allowing NFL teams to play a few games each year in Europe. The emphasis had evolved to just promoting the popularity of the NFL overseas, and European fans were just going to have to accept that fact.

Larry Little would have to accept the fact that his tenure as the head coach of the Ohio Glory was over almost as soon as it had begun. The team—and the entire league—folded in 1993.

"I was disappointed when I heard that the league folded," said Little. "Part of my disappointment was because a lot of guys who were on that team had told me that they wanted to come back the next year and play for the team again. But unfortunately, they shut down the team. . . and the whole league too. I felt bad for those players."[22]

Little did not feel too bad for himself at this point in his life, however. He had been bitten by the coaching bug, and he knew that he possessed enough experience to continue coaching at one level or another. He just had to resume his search for a team that needed a new coach. Out went the resumes. Little applied to more than a dozen pro teams in his attempt to obtain another coaching job. His efforts did not meet with success, however. Some teams communicated with him and spoke to Little about their plans. But many did not, and that was indeed unfortunate.

"They knew I was unemployed," said Little back in 1993. "I was insulted by the people who I sent resumes to that didn't contact me one way or another. They said that I didn't have enough experience, but I was a head coach for nine years in college. I was a head coach for one year in the World League, and I played the game for fourteen years.

"I did contact New England and [head coach Bill] Parcells wrote me a letter and I respected that. I contacted Kansas City and [head coach] Marty Schottenheimer called me and told me what he was going to do, and I respected that. But the ones I sent resumes to and didn't hear from, I looked at it as an insult. I don't think they knew what they were missing."[23]

It seemed he had played all his cards, and yet he was unsuccessful. He took time to contemplate. He could probably sit down and sulk about his predicament. Or he could look to obtain more cards to play, and eventually that was the decision Little made. He decided to broaden his search for coaching positions, primarily in the college ranks. He did not care what division or conference wherein any of those teams belonged. After a short amount of time and a large amount of diligence, he finally found a team that was willing to give him a chance.

"I had heard that there was an opening at North Carolina Central University," recalled Little. "Their head coach at the time, a guy by the name of Bishop Harris. . . he was leaving to become an assistant coach in the NFL. And I knew somebody in the MEAC by the name of Ed 'Pee Wee' Boyd. I gave him a telephone call one day. He knew about my work at Bethune-Cookman. I told him that I needed a job. He then told me that if I was hired as the new head coach, I might have to 'line the field myself.' But I told him to pass the word around, and I soon got an interview. It all fell into play from there."[24]

The big man was now back in the football coaching business. But moving from one location to another is indeed difficult, especially if you must move to another state. Larry Little would find himself uprooting his family three times in the span of just three years, from Daytona Beach, Florida, to Columbus, Ohio, and then finally to Durham, North Carolina (where North Carolina Central University is located).

Little had to start at coaching from the ground up at North Carolina Central. Like Bethune-Cookman, North Carolina Central's football program was also in a "bare-bones" condition back in 1993. Moreover, the student athletes who would be playing for Little were too far removed in years from whatever memories they might have had as kids of the Miami Dolphins of the 1970s. As a result, Little had to "start from scratch" as it were, when it came to introducing himself to his new players. Fortunately for Little, however, he owned an item that brought him instant credibility.

"When I first got there in the spring of 1993," expressed Little, "those guys [his new players] were so young, they didn't know too much about me. But when they saw the Super Bowl ring on my finger, and when I told them a little bit about myself, they started to know more about me. But I didn't talk too much to them about me being a former player in the NFL. Instead, I talked to them more about being their new head football coach."[25]

The North Carolina Central Eagles had a good first two years under Little's leadership. They finished with a 6-5 overall record in both 1993 and 1994. On September 24, 1994, Little's new team managed to defeat his old team, Bethune-Cookman, 24-5. It turned out to be a memorable day for Little. As you recall, his previous departure from coaching Bethune-Cookman did not go all that smoothly.

"Bethune-Cookman was a Division 1-AA program at that time," recalled Little. "North Carolina Central was a Division II school at that time. Just before we played them [in 1994], Bethune gave us $25,000 to come down to their stadium to play them. Well, wouldn't you know? We beat them! I looked up into the press box on the Bethune side of the field with five minutes left to go in the game. When I looked up there, it was empty. That was my validation."[26]

Little's humorous feelings dissipated somewhat the following season, as his team regressed in 1995, dropping to a 5-6 record. But they rebounded the following year in a big way by achieving their best record ever during Little's tenure as their head coach. In 1996, the Eagles earned a highly impressive 8-3 record, which included a string of seven straight wins, and five victories in the Central Intercollegiate Athletic Association (CIAA), the conference in which North Carolina Central University was a member. Their offense gained a remarkable 4,188 yards that year, while their defense only surrendered 2,502 yards. The Eagles' defense was especially spectacular in not permitting opposing offenses to score, as they shut out three straight opponents during the middle of the season.

But despite putting up the best statistics and the most victories in his history of being a head coach, Larry Little would rapidly come back down to earth. North Carolina Central would fall to 4-7 in 1997 and 4-6 in 1998. He finished his career as that school's head football coach with an overall record of 33-32.

"I had a winning record there at North Carolina Central," exclaimed Little. "I didn't have a *great* winning record, but it was a winning record overall. When I was there, we were competitive, too. And we beat three Division I-AA teams during my time there too."[27]

The 1998 season would sadly be the final year that Little would be a head football coach at Durham, North Carolina. It would also mark his last year as a head coach at any level. But that was not his fault. External problems from other sources caused his opportunities for success to suffer greatly.

"I had a bad experience near the end of my time at North Carolina Central," Little remembered. "I wasn't tired of coaching. But when you have an annual recruiting budget of $8,000, which was low anyway, and then see that it gets cut down to just $3,000. . . that was a big cut. That made it difficult to succeed in recruiting. That made it difficult to succeed."[28]

Despite whatever ups and downs that he experienced as a head coach in his two stints leading young men at Bethune-Cookman University and at North Carolina Central University, as well as his year spent in pro football with the Ohio Glory of the World League of American Football (WLAF), Larry Little remained the same "thumbs up" guy. He stayed positive throughout all his days working with his teams. It was one of the secrets to his success.

"I never wanted to say anything negative to any of my players," Little expressed. "I never wanted to tell them how bad they were. I always tried to tell them how good they were, in order to help us beat our opponents. I tried to emphasize to them that they will be given many chances to quit something in life, but when the going gets tough, the tough get going. That was my motto. At times I felt myself saying some of the things that Don Shula told us when I played for the Dolphins. Like Shula, I would address the offense, the defense, and the special teams. I would tell all three of those units before every game to play physical and play hard."[29]

When it was over, it was time to reflect upon the past. Larry Little's coaching career was not a bad one. He had done what some coaches never seem to accomplish. He had managed to save one college football program from extinction, and he had molded and aided many young men who played for him into becoming good and great older men themselves as the years went by. By any standards, those accomplishments were indeed exemplary. But in the middle of his football coaching career, Larry Little received an equally exemplary and unexpected telephone call that would change his life significantly.

CHAPTER 13

A VIEW FROM THE PENTHOUSE

It had been a long journey in the sport of football for Larry Little. Back when he first started watching and playing the game as a kid, he dreamed of one day suiting up in the pros and playing pro football. He saw that dream come true, through his own hard work, his own desire, and his own willingness to never quit. He had risen from the lowest level of football—playing the game with his buddies on the streets of Miami—to the highest level of football. He was indeed proud of his accomplishments as an offensive lineman in the NFL. He earned All-Pro recognition six times during his fourteen-year pro career. He was named the league's Lineman of the Year three times, and he was a vital member of two world championship teams, including the only undefeated team in league history.

As he neared the end of his playing days, however, Little had to give some thought to the possibility of making it into the Pro Football Hall of Fame. The shrine, which is in Canton, Ohio, honors the greats of the game who have reached the highest level of achievement. Most players never even dare to dream about one day becoming a member of the Hall of Fame. Little was different, however. He looked at who was already in the Hall of Fame, and then he looked at his own accomplishments. He concluded that he stacked up well with the players who played offensive guard who already had a bust in Canton's hallowed halls. He also candidly felt that becoming a member of the Hall of Fame was on his "bucket list" of goals.

"I don't know what it takes," admitted Little, "and I don't know how many guards are in there, but my ultimate personal goal is to get into the Pro Football Hall of Fame. I'd really like to go to Canton someday. And not just for a visit."[1]

The Hall of Fame's bylaws stated that all former players had to wait for a full five years after retirement before they could be considered for enshrinement. Little had been a finalist several times for the honor prior to 1993. In his first year of eligibility in 1986, he was one of the last fifteen men to be considered for enshrinement. Two of those men in addition to Little were his former teammates in Miami, Bob Griese and Larry Csonka. None of the three were selected for enshrinement that year. Nevertheless, the feelings upon most knowledgeable pro football commentators admitted that eventually, all three of those Dolphins standouts would one day don the coveted gold Hall of Fame jacket.

The people who select who's chosen for the Hall of Fame—the Hall of Fame voters—consist of one pro football writer from a major newspaper covering every team, and then one vote goes to a selected member of the PFWA. Several other voters are at-large designates from the league office. This panel of under forty voters sit down in a guarded room to discuss each candidate's worth, and what they accomplished during their playing careers. It can sometimes get heated, or so we are told. Those voters rarely discuss out in the open what they talk about behind closed doors. A bond of secrecy guards their opinions on each of the candidates. Larry Little, like all potential nominees for enshrinement, was pragmatic toward the whole situation, knowing that there was nothing else that he could do to enhance his standing with the voters.

"I learned a long time ago I can't worry about things I can't control," said Little back in 1988. "Why they [the Hall of Fame voters] haven't gotten to me, I don't know, but it isn't anything I'm bitter about. I'm not the only deserving person who hasn't been inducted yet. I still feel it will come. I just hope it isn't forty years from now when my son would have to go and accept it for me."[2]

It was during the years after Little announced his retirement that accolades and positive comments were voiced by many of his former teammates on his behalf, in their effort to sway voters into electing him for Hall of Fame enshrinement. By 1992, both Csonka and Griese had been voted in. So too was former Miami wide receiver Paul Warfield and center Jim Langer. It was only a matter of time before Larry Little would also take his rightful place in Canton.

"He's destined to be in Canton someday," admitted Langer upon hearing of Little's retirement from pro football. "It was an honor to play with him. He was a blood-and-guts player on Sunday. He played for a great team and had a lot of success as an individual."[3]

Langer knew what he was talking about. He played right alongside Little on the Miami offensive line for ten seasons, and he had seen how well Little blocked. Moreover, all of the films of Little's efforts would back up Langer's claims. Those films should also be enough to sway the minds and hearts of those Hall of Fame voters.

But those voters were dealing with a lot of issues when it came to selecting a player for enshrinement. They were confined by the fact that by 1993, only seven men per class were allowed to be enshrined per year. That is not a lot of former players and coaches who were certainly worthy of the honor by the time that they reached the final stage of potential selection. Deciding who was more worthy than others, when comparing their achievements in the game, often took many hours and quite a few voting sessions until an agreement was finally reached. It could be, and indeed still is, a long and arduous process.

So, a former player like Larry Little was in the same boat, as it were, with all the other finalists who were awaiting a "Call from the Hall." He had to be patient and bide his time. He was best advised not to worry about the whole affair too much. Then one day in January of 1993, everything changed.

"I was in Ohio at the time," remembered Little, "and it was during the offseason for the Ohio Glory team. The guys in Columbus, Ohio, had a group to go out to the Super Bowl, and they wanted me to go out there and be with the fans. Well, there was a stopover in Las Vegas, and then from Las Vegas, we would fly to Los Angeles. I went to the hotel in Las Vegas, where I got a phone call. I forgot the name of the guy who called me, but he called me at that hotel and told me that I was going to be inducted into the Pro Football Hall of Fame."[4]

A flood of emotional thoughts undoubtedly went through Little's mind at this moment. His heart was probably beating faster too. Maybe not as much as it had when he lined up to play in a Super Bowl game, but darn close to it.

"I acted really cool when he told me the news," recalled Little. "I told him, 'Thank you very much. . . I appreciate the phone call.' You know. . . in a low tone of voice. Then right after I hung up the phone, I just yelled 'Hell yeah!' I knew that the phone call was legit. Now I knew that I was finally in the Pro Football Hall of Fame. They didn't play practical jokes [over the phone] back then like they do today."[5]

Larry Little's mind immediately went back in time at this moment. He remembered all the things that he went through to reach the pinnacle of his profession. He—that late bloomer who grew up in the downtrodden sections of downtown Miami—was going to receive the greatest individual honor that a pro football player can receive. Now to be honest, there was some measure of doubt that entered his mind by the time that 1993 rolled around. But as they say, anything good that you can receive is better late than never.

"Well, when I got to thirteen years of waiting," Little admitted, "I was getting to the point where I won't even get there. But after some people went in who I thought I was on the same level with. . . I don't want to say that I was better than, but I was on the same level with. . . it was at that time that I never doubted that I wouldn't be in the Hall of Fame someday, because I knew the kind of career that I had.[6]

"I was a finalist four other times, so I tried to remain on an even keel. I had been waiting a long time for this [enshrinement] and when it finally came, I guess you could say that I was ecstatic."[7]

Once it was announced in the media that Larry Little had been selected for enshrinement in the Pro Football Hall of Fame, he received numerous calls of congratulations from many people, family, and friends alike. He also received plenty of public statements from his former teammates, coaches, and opponents, all of which congratulated him, and all of which sang his praises. Below is just a brief sampling of some of their statements:

"I'm happy and proud that Larry Little was elected to the Pro Football Hall of Fame," declared Don Shula. "One of the joys of coaching is seeing your players honored for their accomplishments and the Hall of Fame is the ultimate honor. Larry was one of the dominant players at his position in the NFL and a key part of our success with three straight Super Bowl appearances and the only undefeated season in NFL history."[8]

Others, like Miami quarterback and fellow Hall of Famer Bob Griese, echoed his coach's sentiments regarding Little. Griese's health on the gridiron was partially due to Little's blocking abilities for more than a decade.

"Larry was a dominant offensive lineman for many years," Griese expressed, "and [he was] one of the best pulling guards to ever play the game. He certainly deserves to be in the Hall of Fame. He was the first offensive lineman that could [really] run. He was [also] a straight-ahead power blocker. He had the feet and the agility to pull in front of a sweep and run fast. He was faster than [running backs] Csonka and Kiick. He had a quickness for a big man that you didn't see back then."[9]

Next in line to offer praise to Little was a running back who saw plenty of daylight thanks to Little's efforts, the great Larry Csonka. When asked to define Little's legacy to the game of football, Csonka summed it up in one word. Then he described Little and the undefeated 1972 Dolphins in more words.

"Perfection," said Csonka. "That perfection was achieved by all of the members on that 1972 team. Perhaps that was the highest pinnacle of Larry Little's career. He was one of the strongest parts of our team. We were lucky to have him play for us."[10]

A couple of Miami linemen also chimed in with praise for their former teammate. Backup offensive guard Ed Newman learned how to play the position in the pros thanks to watching in person and on film how well Little performed. Manny Fernandez, a stalwart Dolphins defensive tackle, had to go up against Little every day in practice and in doing so, made himself a great player in his own right.

"I am so happy that Larry was elected to the Hall of Fame," expressed Newman upon hearing the good news. "I remember sitting on the bench in my early years as I was a reserve player behind Larry and that was like fanning a flame. I was going crazy, but no matter what I did I wasn't going to play, because Larry was the best. He made me reach for greater heights. I think the world of him. And I know he deserves to be in the Hall of Fame."[11]

"Larry Little has been deserving to enter the Hall of Fame for many years now," admitted Fernandez back in 1993. "A lot of the success that the Miami Dolphins enjoyed was due to the presence of Larry. He was a team leader and a great football player. Larry was not only an important part of our offense, but he also made our defense better, because we had to practice against him every day. He was one of the all-time great players."[12]

As happy as Little's opponents were when he announced his retirement, they were also equally happy for him when his Hall of Fame election was announced. One of those defensive players who had to deal with Little on more than one occasion was former Buffalo Bills and Washington Redskins defensive tackle Ron McDole.

"Larry Little was one of the great offensive linemen of all time," admitted McDole. "Trying to get past Larry was like trying to throw a paper airplane through a mountain. Larry was a mountain of a player."[13]

Naturally, Joe Greene of the Pittsburgh Steelers was quick to comment on Little's induction into the Hall of Fame. The battles that he had with Little were legendary in pro football lore, and they gave rise to the nationwide interest in the struggles that occur on every play along the line of scrimmage.

"Larry and I battled several times," said Greene, "and I came away with more respect for him from each of our games. Whatever he did during a game, I just couldn't seem to ever shake him. He just became a part of me. He was one of the best guards of all time. I just wonder why it took so long for him to be enshrined into the Hall of Fame. If I was allowed to vote for the Hall, he would have been in Canton years ago."[14]

Regardless of how long Larry Little had to wait to receive the honor of Hall of Fame enshrinement, he was finally in the building. He had done it. His dreams of playing pro football as a child had come full circle with the announcement of his Hall of Fame selection. As the days and weeks got closer to enshrinement day, more former players, opponents, teammates, and coaches continued to express their memories of Little, and to sing his praises.

"Larry and I had some pretty good battles, especially on passing downs," remembered former New England Patriots nose tackle Ray "Sugar Bear" Hamilton. "He let me get to the quarterback a couple of times. Overall, he probably won."[15]

Little heaped a lot of praise and thanks over the years to his former offensive line coach, Monte Clark. Once Clark heard of his former pupil's election into the Pro Football Hall of Fame, he stated his opinions in just a few blunt remarks, focusing on one of Little's signature plays.

"Larry was one of the best I ever saw at leading the sweep," Clark confirmed. "He took a lot of pride in putting his man [his opponent] on the ground."[16]

This listing of glowing statements and personal memories would not be complete without the sentiments of Little's fellow offensive guard for many years, the great Bob Kuechenberg.

"Larry Little has done as much to build the legacy the Dolphins have posted as anyone," remarked Kuechenberg. "He's as blue chip as they come. He was always one of the foundations, the cornerstone. There was an era of five or six years where we pretty much did what we wanted to do as an offensive line. We had great talent in the middle, and we took great pride in being the best middle section in the business."[17]

The best in the business. That was the mantra that the Dolphins offensive line proclaimed throughout the 1970s. Shortly after hearing the news of being selected for the Pro Football Hall of Fame, the NFL sent Little and the other members who would be enshrined alongside him to Honolulu, Hawaii, to present them to the fans at the league's annual Pro Bowl game at Aloha Stadium. In being questioned about what his years in Miami meant to him, Little was both appreciative and honest in his response.

"I want to say that these have been the best twelve years of my life," proclaimed Little. "I'm very proud of my achievements in Miami. The Miami Dolphins have always been good to me, and I hope that I've been good and fair to them over the years."[18]

It was important to note that by the day of his enshrinement, he was in between jobs. He began work as the new head football coach of North Carolina Central University right after he left Canton, Ohio. Little took several moments during his traveling to reflect upon the great honor that would be his in Canton, Ohio, in the summer of 1993. He also at this time let his mind drift back to those moments when he was younger, and to those memories of his when he and his father managed to get together to talk, and perhaps to reconcile their differences.

"Actually, he [Little's father] lived long enough to see me play pro football," Little said. "He passed away on the day that I retired. He never went to see me play any games in person because he was an alcoholic. But he bragged on me all the time, all around the place where he lived. He didn't live with my mom. He lived on the floor above a bar. And he would always tell people, 'Yeah, Larry Little is my son.' And he would also say, 'and Floyd Little, the former Denver Broncos Hall of Fame running back, is my nephew,'" Larry chuckled. "And I used to tell that man, 'Daddy, stop saying that. Floyd Little is not your nephew.'"

"My dad stayed in the Miami area. I didn't have a lot of contact with my father when I was in college, because I was away from Miami. But when I was in the pros, yeah, I would go over to the bar where he would hang out, and I would hang out with him sometimes, and we would talk. You know, I didn't understand nor care for how he lived his life, but he was still my father. That's the attitude that I had regarding him."[19]

Larry Little could easily have allowed the notoriety of the moment of his enshrinement to take over his mind or at least overshadow how he felt about his pro football career, and about his importance to everyone in society. To his credit, he refrained from doing that.

"I never let who I was consume me," said Little in a 2022 interview. "You know, I'm Larry Little, I'm great, I did this and that. . . no. I never let anything like that consume me. I just wanted to be a normal person and have a good football career."[20]

A good football career indeed. A player does not even get nominated for the Pro Football Hall of Fame without having what most onlookers would consider a great gridiron career, regardless of his position. Little accomplished all of that, with every snap of the ball. His legend grew over time, but it is important to note that he did not receive a description of "legendary" by most of those who saw him play as a youngster.

"Many people told me that I couldn't play this game when I was a kid," recalled Little. "There was no doubt about it. I was called all kinds of things when I first started playing football. I was called timid. I was called soft. I was told that I wasn't hard enough or tough enough to play the game of football. And I had to really carry that with me all throughout high school until I got to college. And like I said earlier, I wasn't one who got a whole lot of scholarship offers."[21]

What was it about Little's desire that kept him striving toward his goal in the face of such negativity? Mostly, it was his intensely strong need to prove the naysayers wrong, all the while staying focused on his goal to succeed at his sport. It was almost as if the comments that he heard from those who derided him did not matter too much to him. He kept those critics to the periphery of his vision and his thoughts. He was going to play pro football one day. That is what he spent his focus on, and that farsightedness remained at the forefront of his desires. In short, Larry Little was not going to be denied.

As the date of his Hall of Fame enshrinement neared, Little—who was forty-seven years old—would have to prepare his speech. His memories of his years playing the sport would naturally serve as the backbone of his remarks. He would also have to select someone to introduce him at his enshrinement. He chose Don Shula, the head coach who did much to bring out the best in him. Thanks at least in part to Shula, Little went from being a good player to an outstanding player in a very short amount of time. And thanks to Little (among others), Shula owned a pair of Super Bowl rings. Shula was honored to accept Little's request to be his Hall of Fame presenter, and both men went to the task of writing down their thoughts on paper.

Finally, the big day of July 31, 1993, arrived. Over 5,000 fans were crammed along the grassy hillside in front of the steps of the Pro Football Hall of Fame in Canton, Ohio. When the time came for Little's enshrinement, Don Shula arose and spoke highly of his former offensive guard. Not surprisingly, Miami's head coach was sure to mention what Larry Little meant to the team. . . as much off the field as he did on the field. That brand of excellence to Shula was what made his former player so great.

"Larry was a local product who made good," expressed Shula in his presentation speech. "But there was more to Larry Little than his great athletic ability. As big as Larry was physically, his heart was even bigger. Larry was a winner who didn't know what it meant to get out or get beat. He helped define that sense of pride that surrounded those great Dolphins teams. He was willing to do whatever was necessary to help the team win. There was a presence about him that was unmistakable. When Larry Little spoke, both his teammates and his coaches alike made sure to listen to what he had to say. He has given our team a special leadership from within, which is so important. That can only come from the strength of a player."[22]

Little's strength originally came from his family, many of whom were in attendance on that hot and humid Saturday afternoon in Northeast Ohio. Many of them were there to celebrate the accomplishments of one of their own, for all time. The Little clan had the foresight to turn this weekend into a summer family event.

"Oh, it was one of the greatest days of my life," recalled Little, now over thirty years removed from his Hall of Fame induction. "What made it so special was that we have a family reunion every year, and we were going to be somewhere else that year. I have a very large family on my mom's side. But we changed the location of the family reunion that year [1993] to be in Canton, Ohio, for my induction into the Hall of Fame. The Haynes family was on my grandmother's side, and the Shipman family was on my grandfather's side. We just combined the two to be at the Haynes/Shipman reunion."[23]

It was now time for Larry Little to step up to the podium, admire his bronze bust, and make his speech. Trying to summarize a life that revolved around the sport of football can be easy for some, and not so easy for others. Practically every Hall of Famer spends most of their enshrinement speech thanking the people who have had a great deal with their successes throughout their lives. Little was no different in that respect. He reserved his first mention of thanks to God. Then he also acknowledged those other great men who would join him on this day as his fellow honorees.

"I'm now part of an elite and extraordinary group," said Little. "I used to sit home on Saturdays, watching the Hall of Fame speeches in the summer and visualizing what kind of speech I would give.[24] This is by far the highest honor a player can achieve. When I look at the class I'm going in with, these people are top-notch. Chuck Noll and Bill Walsh, Dan Fouts and Walter Payton. They don't come any better."[25]

Back in 1993, the men who were entering the Hall of Fame were generally allowed to speak for a half-hour, should they choose to do so. But most of the speeches during those years lasted for around fifteen minutes on average. Larry Little was not a big talker when he was a player, and it only followed suit that he would not spend too much time pontificating on the front steps of the Hall of Fame on this day. His speech was just around three pages long.

"I accept this honor for my former players at Bethune-Cookman," expressed Little, "my former players and administrators of the Ohio Glory in the World Football League, and my present players of North Carolina Central University in Durham, North Carolina. I want to thank my college coaches Jack McClairen and Lloyd 'Tank' Johnson, who recruited me out of high school and gave me a chance to continue my education and gave me an opportunity to reach my goal. I can't say enough about 'Tank' Johnson. He was there for me as a player, and he has been a good friend to me all my life, and he is the one who has gotten me into the coaching profession I am in today. I want to thank my first professional head coach, Sid Gillman, who is in the Hall of Fame. I want to thank him for giving me an opportunity to play, and for trading me to Miami. I want to thank [my] line coaches Joe Madro in San Diego, Ernie Hefferle in Miami, and Monte Clark.

"Monte Clark, I know you are out here today. You gave not only me but our whole offensive line the kind of pride to be the best in the business, and we were the best offensive line who ever played together because of Monte Clark. I want to thank John Sandusky, who took over later in my career, who kept me believing in myself and helped me to be who I am today. And a very special thanks to you, Coach Shula, for having the foresight to see me at the weight I was, to help me move this weight to be the kind of person I am today and the great football player I was when I retired. And you motivated me to be the best that I could be."[26]

Little also described what the sport of football had meant to him throughout his life. He expressed his love for the game, and how the game shaped his life, from his youth to the present day. He also bestowed his thanks to several of his beloved family members.

"Football prepared me for so many things in life," Little said. "How to deal with the peaks and valleys, the bitter with the sweet, self-motivation and believing in myself, and working with others. When I first went out for football at Booker T. Washington High School in Miami, I was in the ninth grade and only thirteen years old. I know I probably would have been voted the most unlikely to succeed. I was so bad I didn't get equipment until the season started. But I was only a ninth grader. But I had a friend of mine named Joe Walker, who was a blind deejay in Atlanta, Georgia. He made a statement at the end of his show every week, and that statement was 'A winner never quits, and a quitter never wins.' And I took that along with me, because I knew I was going to be a winner. It was always my lifetime ambition to play professional football, and most of all I would like to thank my mom sitting right there, Ida, for always being there for me through thick and thin. She raised me to be the kind of person that I am today. I want to thank my wife Rosie, for being there through the aches and the pains and especially the good times that we shared. I would like to thank my sisters Connie, Linda, Joy, and Betty, for being there for me. And also, my brother David, who could not be here today because he is in Barcelona in Spain with the Pittsburgh Steelers."[27]

It was at this time in Larry Little's speech where he discussed the feelings that he had about his earliest coaches and teachers, his former teammates, and for some more of his honored family members.

"I would like to thank my high school coaches James Everett, Alkin Hepburn, Robert Wilcox, Ralph Burns, Cleveland Paulk, and Cecil Harris, who had so much to do with my development as a young man trying to learn how to play this football game. And for my teammates who would help me after practice and try to make me do better, and for the teachers who helped me realize early the value of an education.

"I would like to give a special thanks to my teammates in Miami," continued Little, "especially the offensive line again, and Bob Griese, Larry Csonka, Jim Langer, Bob Kuechenberg, Wayne Moore, and Norm Evans. And he told me I better mention his name: Eugene 'Mercury' Morris. And there are some people today that are not here physically, but I know they are here spiritually, and they are looking down on me and just smiling. They are my father, George; my older brother George; my roommate for so many years in Miami who was on the offensive line, Wayne Moore; and my grandparents, Ismael and Elizabeth Haynes, who were very close to me; and everybody that has pushed me along the way. If I have forgotten you, I'm sorry. But thank you, and this will be one moment that I will cherish for the rest of my life. Thank you very much."[28]

With his final public decry of thanks to the many family members and friends who gleefully gathered in Canton to see him on this day, and to the many more across the nation who were watching the event on television, Larry Little had fulfilled one of the greatest dreams of his life. He obtained immortality on the front steps of a beautiful penthouse, known as the Pro Football Hall of Fame.

CHAPTER 14

MEMORIES AND FUTURES

The time for reflection for Larry Little is today. . . and it is an ongoing activity. His legendary status is etched in time, and not just because he is a member of the Pro Football Hall of Fame. He was also a vital member of one of the greatest teams in pro football history, and that fact fits well with his own individual accomplishments in the game. Yet Larry Little does not spend his time thinking about whatever fame he achieved on the gridiron. Rather, he prefers to focus on the here and the now, and how he can move forward with his life and with his foundation. Larry Little today is a modest man who is prouder of following the Christian examples of helping others than he is of displaying his football trophies and his Super Bowl rings. In that respect, he has used the game of football to further his hopes of getting to know people better over time and setting a good example for future generations.

Football is a sport about people. It is about those who play it, coach it, and those who make their livelihoods from it. It is also a game about how those men interact with each other. It is a sport of relationships, where friendships are formed that can last a lifetime. As one who has played pro football for more than a decade, Larry Little has naturally gotten to know many different people. Some had something important to do with the sport. Others did not.

Some were fans of his. Many were relatives of his. Quite a few people over the years have sought his opinion on a wide variety of matters. He was building a store case of acquaintances during the past seven-plus decades, some of whom would have a say in the remainder of his life in one way or another.

Larry Little's relationships with other people in his life blossomed over time, and some of them went back even further than his relationship with his wife, Rosie. Several of the young kids who participated in Little's Gold Coast Summer Camp have remained good friends with him to this very day. One such person is Herb Sears, who would join the United States Army, and who would eventually become a successful construction worker. Little's summer camp was an eye-opening opportunity for him, and his memories of the camp are still fresh in his mind over fifty years later.

"I was from the city of Allendale, Florida," said Sears, "and there was a coach there by the name of Coach Lewis. He and Larry got to know each other somehow, somewhere along the line. And Coach Lewis asked me and some of my peers to sign up to go to Larry Little's summer camp, and we had our parents sign the permission slip. I didn't go to the first camp, where they had it on the beach. But I went to the second one. . . the one that they held at the Miami Dolphins training camp at Biscayne College. I was in the seventh or the eighth grade, so I guess I must have been twelve or thirteen years old at that time.

"One thing that I remember was that we were in the college dorms. We had never been in any college dorms before. We were two of us to a room. And then we had three hot meals a day. . . breakfast, lunch, and dinner. But it wasn't just a football camp. It was an all-around camp. We had lots of other activities. We had some swimming. Some of our guys didn't know how to swim, so they learned how to swim at the camp. We had football, of course. But we also had track. We had basketball. We had boxing. And we got to meet Angelo Dundee, who was Muhammad Ali's trainer. We also got to meet a Japanese ping pong champion. And then we met a lot of players from the Miami Dolphins. Guys like Nat Moore, Mercury Morris, and some of the other players would come in and talk to us. And all of us kids could feel the excitement from all of the things that the camp gave us."[1]

Sears's memories of the Gold Coast Sports Camp were furthered by Willie Carpenter, a youngster who also participated in those early camps, and then who stuck around and worked at them as he got older. Today, Carpenter has advanced his experiences in Little's camp to become much more than just a camp worker or a camp counselor. His experiences can probably be best summarized by how much we never know about the seeds that are planted in every moment of our lives.

"I met Larry Little back when I was in the seventh grade," recalled Carpenter. "That was back in 1971. I went to his camp as a kid back in 1971, 1972, and 1973. Then later on I was a camp worker back when I was in eleventh and twelfth grade. Then during my first year in college, I helped out by working as a camp guidance counselor. Now who would have thought that today, I would be the chairman of the Larry Little Foundation?

"All of us who attended Larry's camp were inner city kids. It was a camp for underprivileged kids. It was divided into two parts. The first part was for kids in the southern part of Miami-Dade County. The second part was for kids who came from the northern part of the county. It was a big thrill to meet Larry and a lot of the members of the Dolphins Super Bowl teams. Those guys were instrumental in their perfect season of 1972, and we met them at Larry's summer camp."[2]

Carpenter also got a chance to experience the possibilities of future direction and opportunities while he participated in the camps. He learned—even at an early age—the importance of organization and dedication. His time there during those summers helped to form the foundation of his future.

"Larry gave me my first job as a camper," expressed Carpenter in 2023. "So, I talk about the influence that I got from that camp. I'm now a Senior Vice President of the South State Bank in Miami, and I'll be retiring from there next year after forty-two years in the banking industry. Larry had a direct influence on the kids who went to his camp, including myself. Today, some of those kids are police officers, lawyers, bankers. . . professionals in all walks of life. Larry changed a lot of kids' lives for the better. There were I don't know how many thousands of kids who went through those camps, and whose lives were touched by Larry Little.

"If you look at the things that Larry is doing now, the kids that he is supporting today by giving out thousands of dollars in scholarships with his foundation. . . it truly touches kids' lives. If you asked the average person on the street today that wasn't aware of the Miami Dolphins of the 1970s, they might not know Larry Little as a member of those Dolphins teams. But if you ask people today about what Larry Little has done for the community in Miami, they'll know. I'm sure that Larry is very, very proud to be in the Pro Football Hall of Fame, but he is also very, very proud of what his foundation has done for the kids over the years. He's probably done more now than what he has done as a football player."[3]

Herb Sears would readily concur with Carpenter's viewpoint. Both men shared the experiences that those summer camps provided, and both men applied the lessons that Larry Little and his camp counselors were focused on stressing to the youngsters throughout their lives.

"I will tell you one of the things that I learned as a member of a group in the camp," expressed Sears, "and in the military as well. . . we do everything together. We don't do anything separately. Larry always talked about unity and as a group, and about how we had to pull for one another. And he used to stress that all the time. . . that we all had to stick together. He would tell us that we had an opportunity, and what we do with that is up to us. What you do with that is up to you. And when I think about it, that's what the military was all about too. It was a team-first concept that stuck with us. And I picked that up first from Larry Little. I saw how he gave back to the kids, and that's something that I have tried to do as well. My wife and I lead a Bible Study group, and we try to discuss those lessons of giving back there as well."[4]

Larry Little also gave his football knowledge back to his players for the teams that he coached. A couple of those young men, Michael Floyd and Mark Irvin, suited up for Bethune-Cookman University, and they quickly became the beneficiaries of Little's knowledge and motivation. The stories of Floyd and Irvin are both distinctly individualistic, but they both also point to and latch hold of the fatherly kindness that Little displayed to them all throughout their college careers and beyond. Some of their comments have to do with their time on the football field, but some of their memories also dwell on their personal interactions with Little.

"I played offensive guard and offensive tackle for Coach Little at Bethune-Cookman from 1984 through 1989," recalled Floyd. "I had several offers from different colleges. I had some offers from Division 1 schools, and I had an offer from Florida A&M. I chose Bethune-Cookman because Coach Little showed the most interest in me. Now it was extremely important to me that Coach Little had a championship pedigree, which he obviously did.

"I can tell you that Coach Little was a pretty good motivational coach. He was always encouraging us, and he was absolutely a player's coach. He was very approachable. He was so famous, yet there was not one arrogant bone in his body. What always impressed me the most about him was how much he cared about us as people. We had some guys on our team who were really bad guys. . . guys who had no direction in life and some who had gotten themselves into trouble. Many of them would not have made it in any other program. But because Coach Little, with his sternness, but also with his love for us. . . because of him, a lot of those guys graduated and are very successful today."[5]

Mark Irvin's story of how he eventually played for Larry Little had a few more chapters in it than Michael Floyd's. It speaks of how unexpected connections and chance meetings came to play in one of the most impressive success stories of anyone who ever played for Little, and of anyone who ever got to know Little as a friend. Naturally, it all started with something that both men had in common, the sport of football.

"Coach Little's first year coaching at Bethune-Cookman was also my freshman year there, back in 1983," remembered Irvin, who eventually became a longshoreman. "Prior to that, Coach Little was the athletic director of an inner-city school called Edison, and that was our rival. I played as a linebacker at Northwestern Senior High School in Miami. And so, he had the opportunity to watch me play against them, and to watch me play against other schools in Miami.

"But when my senior year in high school ended, I hadn't gotten any scholarship offers at all, despite the fact that I was named the linebacker of the year. I recognize that I was undersized, but I was also extremely strong. At that time, I had read where Larry Little had taken the head coaching job at Bethune-Cookman, and so I approached him at the roller-skating rink that he and [former Miami Dolphins wide receiver] Nat Moore owned. I approached him and told him that I knew that he 'knew the way of winning,' and I mentioned to him that I hadn't received a scholarship. He asked me, 'Who did you play for?' I told him that I played for Northwestern High School. After telling him that, he asked me, 'Who was that #50. . . that wild guy with the mohawk hair style?' I laughed, and I told him that that person was me. I had that mohawk during the football season, but I cut it off following the season. So, he didn't know who I was. . . without my mohawk."[6]

Going up to a Super Bowl champion in a roller-skating rink was indeed a bold move by the high school senior. But Irvin was looking for any avenue that he could find to somehow continue playing the game of football, and he knew that meant going to college. . . any college that had a viable football program. He threw caution aside and took a chance. Fortunately for him, the person who would inevitably hold at least one of the keys to his future was always looking for good football players to be on his roster, especially if they had a burning desire to play the game, as Irvin did. Moreover, Larry Little actually had a surprise for Irvin that the young grid star did not know about when they first spoke to each other.

"Of course, I knew about Larry Little and his reputation," remarked Irvin. "That's why I approached him in the first place. I mean everybody in Miami is aware—and was aware—of Coach Little, and I being one of them. And so, knowing that, I approached him in the hopes of trying to get him to look at my game films from high school. Little did I know was that he was actually in search of me! Little did I know! He just hadn't put my face with my name until then. And so, when I told him that I was that wild man that he heard about, he just laughed.

"Larry Little kept his word and said that he was going to speak to my high school coach, Calvin Jackson, and he in turn would talk to Mr. Peevy, who was the assistant principal at our school. Both of those guys definitely had my back. So, I said to myself, 'Man, this is guaranteed!' And sure enough, Larry Little was a man of his word. The very next day in school, I was questioned by Calvin Jackson, who asked me, 'Did I want to attend Bethune-Cookman?' I immediately said yes. I recall the time that I signed the letter of intent, and how my mother was so proud. My father. ... was so proud. . . they were proud! I still have a picture of that moment. Mr. Little is a great dude. He's a great human being."[7]

The signed scholarship to Bethune-Cookman University that Mark Irvin received marked the beginning of his long-standing relationship with Larry Little. His gratitude to Little was solidified with the opportunity to attend college and the chance to continue to play football, and the two men would remain close to this very day.

"I'm getting very emotional just thinking about it," expressed Irvin, "because if I hadn't gotten a college scholarship, I probably would have lost my life. Larry Little saved my life by giving me that scholarship. When my parents were gone, and when I got married, Coach Little walked in place of my father at my wedding. And since then, I've always called him 'Pops.' And everybody knew that he was my father. I love him so much, because he was my father."[8]

Their relationship on the football field involved a simple belief that his new head coach held. Little figured that Irvin would deliver that wild, ambitious, and game-breaking hitting that the young man displayed in high school for his defense at Bethune-Cookman. Irvin did not disappoint. He may have played the position of linebacker in high school, but he quickly transitioned to the position of strong safety, and he excelled there for his entire collegiate career.

"I only weighed 168 pounds as an undersized linebacker in high school," said Irvin. "But I was strong enough to bench press over 400 pounds while I was in high school. I always considered it best to do the hitting as opposed to being the man receiving the hitting. Now keep in mind, Coach Little was a genius when it comes to football. He got the best out of me and out of the rest of our players. He surrounded himself with guys who were football savvy. I was never introduced to that in high school because high school is a different level of football in comparison to that of college. And so, I began to learn how to study, to understand downs and distances, to watch film so much that you can pick up tendencies. . . and that was all on account of Coach Little's influence.

"I can recall our homecoming game back in 1985. We were playing North Carolina A&T, and they had a quarterback by the name of Alan Hooker, and he was an awesome quarterback. He was a Randall Cunningham-type of athlete in a sense. We ended up beating them 28-14, but they were on the verge of scoring, and I can recall sacking Hooker on the last play of the game. I had eleven solo tackles in that game, two interceptions, and a fumble recovery. After I sacked Hooker on the last play of that game, I remember that I jumped up and I said to Coach Little, 'This is the reason why you brought me to Bethune-Cookman.' I was just so happy to see him happy."[9]

Little's influence on his team and on players like Mark Irvin was obvious. It was Little's statements about the best approaches to being successful in life, however, that greatly influenced Irvin and his teammates. Little's messages to them were pragmatic and realistic to the vagaries that each of his players would experience throughout their lives. The Super Bowl champion had once been where they were, and because of that, he knew best how to help his players avoid the pitfalls that would show up in their futures. Larry Little regularly explained his own life lessons to his players. . . and those young men took his messages to heart.

"He was always trying to prepare us for life," admitted Irvin, who majored in business administration and had a minor in criminal justice. "And even as I talk to him today, it's always about life. Without a doubt, Coach Little wanted us players to get an education first and foremost. Football was secondary. He would always say that 'Football prepares you for life. You're going to win some things in life, and you're going to lose some things in life.' And so that statement always stuck with me. So, he was always more concerned about building human potential as opposed to building a football player."[10]

Another football player got his chance to encounter Larry Little for several years during the 1990s. He was Greg Williams Evans, and he would eventually become a practicing attorney and an executive at Walmart. He wasn't recruited by Little, however. That was because he was already playing for the next college that Little would serve as head coach.

"I played for Coach Little in 1993 and 1994, in my junior and senior years, at North Carolina Central University," recalled Evans. "When Coach Little came in and took over the head coaching job there, I was already an upperclassman. He looked to me for leadership because I was an upperclassman. Coach Little is a man's man. He was really adamant about raising young men. He really wanted us to be accountable as young men, first and foremost. Clearly none of us from the previous regime were penciled in as starters. Everyone had to prove their worth each and every day in practice.

"Coach Little was the type of coach who would listen to his players. It was very refreshing. He himself was never above reproach. When he was voted into the Pro Football Hall of Fame, a lot of us thought that that may change him, but it didn't. He was always the same Larry Little. He always wanted the best for his players, and he believed in us. He had great expectations for us. He knew that we were the ones who had to go out there day after day and prove our worth, and he was behind us all the way on that. In fact, I ended up being voted co-captain in my junior year, and I was named as the team's captain in my senior year."[11]

Larry Little had experienced the highs and lows that the game provides, and he knew that football could provide his players—regardless of the level—with many moments of inspirational opportunities to prove their worth. Williams Evans remembers one specific moment (see also Chapter 12) where his head coach uniquely inspired his young players.

"It was in my senior year," remembered Williams Evans, "and we were playing Bethune-Cookman. That game made our season. And of course, we knew all about the history there. We knew that's where Coach Little came from. Bethune-Cookman was Coach Little's alma mater. We knew that that game would be very important to him. During the week of preparation for that game, Coach Little was his typical self. . . always calm and level-headed. He never made anything about himself. He would always focus on our next opponent, and then our next opponent. He was always the same. Now at that time, Bethune-Cookman was a Division 1-AA team, and we [North Carolina Central] were a Division II school. Well, we wanted to win that game against Bethune-Cookman really bad."[12]

Williams Evans effectively sets the stage for what happened next. He saw a totally different persona in his head coach just before this game against Little's alma mater. He saw Little use emotion in order to give his team the jolt that it needed, and it worked.

"And so, we went through our warm-ups down there in Florida, and we came back to our locker room," recalled Williams Evans. "Now during his pregame speeches, Coach Little would always have a variety of sayings that he would use, and he would also allow the other coaches to step in and address the team. But on this particular day, right before I ran out as the captain for the coin toss, he came up to address the team. He started off talking to us about our preparation and sticking to the fact that this was just another game on our schedule."[13]

But that game on September 24, 1994, was not just another game for Larry Little. Bethune-Cookman, his beloved alma mater, had found a way to get rid of him by making changes to their athletic department, and by siphoning money out of their football program. Those moves did not sit well with Little, and just like anyone else who has been treated unfairly regarding their work situations, he did not forget the way he departed his former employer. A flood of emotion overtook him amid looking into the faces of his North Carolina Central players.

"He told us that we should go out and play for ourselves and for one another," Williams Evans described, "but not for him. But in this particular speech, as he was talking, he got emotional, and he literally started to cry. He was crying about us playing the game against Bethune-Cookman, and what it would mean. He just broke down emotionally. He was trying to hide it. He tried to express what a win over Bethune-Cookman would do for us. But at that moment, when we saw him begin to cry, he urged us to go on out there and kick their butts. . . and we erupted. We went out and gave by far our most dominant performance that we had ever had.

"I know that defensively, they [Bethune-Cookman] didn't convert a third down until probably the middle of the third quarter. We ended up winning that game, 24-5. At the end of that game, we carried Coach Little off the field, and he was elated after that game. It was an emotional moment for him and for us. Obviously, going back to where it all started for him, and with a lot of his friends in attendance. . . it was such an emotional moment. Again, he was always for us and for our team. He wanted us to play for one another. He was that guy. But he could not mask his emotion during his pregame speech. He lit a fire in all of us, and it was one of my most memorable moments. It moved us, because he was like a dad to all of us. His speech galvanized us in such a way that we went out and played lights out."[14]

It seems that Larry Little was always in the business of moving people. From moving opposing defensive linemen out of his way during his playing days, to moving his summer camp attendees and his football players in college and for the Ohio Glory to go on and do great things, Little was always active in his beliefs to excel. . . and to help those around him to excel. One common denominator in the stories of people who have had a friendship with Larry Little involves the success of their futures. Many of them have all seemed to be able to have improved their lives over time, thanks in part to the lessons that they learned from Little, and to observing and emulating the examples of dedication and desire that he showed all of them. But Little learned some lessons himself over time. His honest remembrances of the wealth of his experiences have proven to be a work in progress. They spoke of learning from his mistakes, and of being honest with himself as he addressed his past.

"I partied a lot when I played," admitted Little. "If I could change anything [in my past], I wouldn't have partied as much as I did back then. I was a party animal. I went out to the lounges, and to the bars, and things like that. Although it did not affect my play [on the field]. But you know I would do something different nowadays, I believe."[15]

An honest assessment of all our lives would probably have to agree with Larry Little on that. Many of us would love to change some of our actions, or perhaps the results of our actions, at least once or twice during our lives. A couple of Little's most bitter and heart-rending moments involved the deaths of his brothers George and David (who went on to play twelve years for the Pittsburgh Steelers). Just as his older brother's death was shocking and unexpected, so too was the death of his younger brother.

"David was forty-six when he died," Little said. "He had an arrhythmia attack while he was lifting weights. A weight fell on his throat. His sons came home from school and found him on the weight bench. He was lifting weights all by himself, without any spotters when it happened."[16]

No one has a perfect life, including Larry Little. He has had to endure some difficult and tragic moments in his life, just as he has had to experience some great moments in his life. He has managed to deal with those tough times, and he has commendably strengthened his mind and his heart throughout all his struggles. All those moments helped in some way to make him the man that he is today.

In the end, one must go back to the beginning if one is to best understand Larry Little. And that beginning involves the sport of football. Outside of his family members, it was his first real love. It was the game that evoked his interest, and it was the game that gave his young life purpose. As he got older, he learned all about the sport of football, and his opinions on it reflected his knowledge of it. Those opinions of his also grew and evolved over the course of time. In a 2023 interview, he discussed the state of the game today and the scenes observable in today's NFL. Little has indeed grown in knowledge in the ways of the world, and his opinions on a variety of sports-related topics take in all his lifelong experiences.

"Well, the NFL is probably the largest corporation in America today," Little declared. "To keep making big money, they are going to continue doing anything that they can in order to keep making big money. That includes the owners, and it also includes

Commissioner Roger Goodell. I think that he is doing all that he can to make the team owners some big money. Regarding players today celebrating on the field. . . it's a sign of the times. I mean, I realize that that's what they do now, but we were doing it back then. We were spiking the football back then, and in the early 1970s, that was a new thing. That's what we used to do. It's a sign of the times, that's all.

"I think that too many teams make the NFL playoffs today, especially when you have mediocre teams making the playoffs. When you have a team with a losing record go into the playoffs. . . that's laughable. I haven't really been watching many of these spring football games these days. I don't know if the sport is being oversaturated. For football leagues to succeed in the spring is tough, especially with NBA basketball playoffs going on, and with hockey playoffs going on. . . there's just too much going on."[17]

Little's opinions on the many different aspects of the game are well thought out. He is also unafraid to address whatever subjects are deemed to be controversial. One such matter was never heard about while Little was an active player in the NFL, and that was Chronic Traumatic Encephalopathy. . . otherwise known as CTE.

"Well, you see so many players. . . we didn't even think about stuff like CTE back then when I was playing," said Little. "And the helmets then can't compare to with the technology with the helmets that are being made today. And unfortunately, a lot of our guys from our era got it [CTE]. I mean with dementia, Alzheimer's, and all of those. . . they are all related. And it was from playing the game. We didn't hear about it back then. . . we didn't even think about it back then."[18]

Another subject. . . the subject of money. . . is never far from the minds of pro football players today. Little had his own issues to deal with when it came to salaries, bonuses, etc. But back in the 1970s, the average salary for most players in the NFL with at least a few years of service in the league hovered around $25,000 a year. Today, most players with similar experience make well into the six figures in annual salary. How does Larry Little feel about the disparity in the monetary amounts from several decades in difference?

"No, I'm not jealous," declared Little, "because I know that we made more money than the guys who played [pro football] before us. Those guys were making $16,000 or $17,000 a year, and some of them without any face masks on their helmets. I know that we made more than they did. I'm for the players today in getting as much as they possibly can. The owners are getting a lot of money. Why not the players? They're the ones who are out there on the field. So no, I'm not jealous of today's players and their current salaries."[19]

While Larry Little was making a small amount of money in his early years in pro football, he would supplement his cash flow with his teaching job.

Little succeeded as a teacher in much the same way that he succeeded as a football player. . . through hard work, sacrifice, and a strong desire to accomplish something positive each day. He helped to make that happen in his classroom amongst his students, and he helped to make that happen in his summer sports camp. Although he might not have realized it at the time, Little was planting seeds of happiness, accomplishments, and future successes within the hearts and minds of many of those kids who sat in his classrooms, and especially in the hearts and minds of many of those kids who participated in those summer camps. That fact has also given Little a great sense of pride over the years.

"It's thrilling for me. . . it gives me a great feeling, because a lot of these kids that went on to be something in their lives," Little remarked in a recent interview. "They came from beginnings where they didn't have anything growing up, and we gave them an opportunity. For the kids in those camps, it was like going to a foreign country. They had never been out of their neighborhood before attending the camp. To see them go through that. . . I don't like to use the word ghetto or the hood, but going to the camp was a whole new ballgame for them. I look at some of those guys right now, and some of them moved out of the city. Some of them went to the south, and some of them went to the north. But whenever they run into each other now, their conversation involves Larry Little's Gold Coast Summer Camp. And I still run into some of those guys, and some of them are in their sixties today, and some of them even look older today than I do. And they would come up to me and tell me, 'I was in your boys' camp years ago!' That is a great feeling for me. That camp and those kids gave me a lot of satisfaction."[20]

Obtaining satisfaction is something that Larry Little has reached and yearned for over the years. Obtaining understanding is also of great importance to him. Little has over the years become more cognizant of national and world affairs, and his opinions on life today have been enlightened by his own experiences, by taking in the opinions of others, and by drawing upon his own education. He pulls no punches when it comes to how the current situations in America have evolved over time, especially in the African American communities that he has seen up close all throughout his life.

"One thing, in politics, we have had a black president," said Little, "but I would like to see more African Americans in powerful positions. As far as football is concerned, we didn't have a lot of African American coaches who were coaching when I was playing pro ball. Not just the head coaches, but the assistant coaches in the league too. So, that's an improvement, because we have more African American coaches in the league today, and we have more African American personnel people in the league today. When I discuss overall progress today, I think that we as Black people have come too far to turn around now."[21]

The progress in football regarding fairness and equity has been visible during the past few decades, thanks mostly to the acceptance of many great African American men in the coaching ranks. And that includes not just in the pro ranks, but in the colleges as well.

"On the current popularity of the HBCU programs, I think that Deion Sanders has a lot to do with that," expressed Little. "Although, when you look back at the history of the AFL, when they were competing against the NFL, a lot of the great players went to the historically black colleges. And there are so many Hall of Famers who went to HBCU schools back in the day. You know, guys like Buck Buchanon, Willie Lanier, Emmitt Thomas, me. . . I think that it was about twenty-four of us who went to HBCU schools and who made the Hall of Fame. There were a lot of great ones."[22]

Speaking of great, Larry Little's family certainly deserves that label. They have been a major factor in his life, and they will continue to be. He mentions them with a voice of obvious pride, knowing that they have all been a treasure to his life.

"I have four kids," Little said, "and they are Lawrence, Ayisha, Damita, and Learon. . . two girls and two boys. I also have four sisters. Betty, who grew up in Savannah, Georgia, is my oldest sister, and Connie is my sister who was two years younger than me. Linda was born after her. And the baby girl of the family—my youngest sister—is Joy. My mother showed her Christian love to our family every day. She passed away in 2019, but I still have dreams about her often at night. I mean she is no longer here, but she's still here. . . with me."[23]

Mrs. Little's Christian examples have taken deep root in her son's heart. Larry Little has made it an unspoken tenant in his life to help people out whenever he can. He has—over the years—spent a wealth of hours in thought and introspection about how best to bring out the lessons of love and sacrifice that he learned from his mother to the forefront of his own life, and to have practical application in his own life.

"I think about that a lot," admitted Little in a statement during the mid-1970s. "I guess most folks think about self. I give a great deal of thought to self. I've worked hard to get the things I want. I know the direction I'm going in. I have a deep feeling and sentiment about where other people around me are going, too. I often think about the days when people helped me out on the way up. I must help others to attain their goals because of what folks did for me when I needed them. I want people to say that I tried to get along. . . that I tried to help people."[24]

The help that Larry Little has given to people has blossomed through his foundation, and through the many examples of the happiness that he has given to so many people—both young and old—over the years. In 2023, a street behind Booker T. Washington High School was named after him for his dedication to helping so many Miami citizens.

"Well, a good friend of mine by the name of Josie Poitier who recently passed away . . . she had tried to get a street named after me for the past twenty years," Little said. "And my sister, Linda, who has always been very resilient, when she believes in something, she goes after it. She organized a lot of people from my old high school, the athletic club from my high school, and the backing of some people from the city commission to get the street named after me. It was something that I felt if it happens, then it happens. But you know it was a great moment in my life when it did happen. And the street is adjacent to my high school."[25]

The street that bears Little's name is on Northwest 11th Terrace, from Northwest Sixth Avenue to Northwest First Avenue, which is near Dixie Park in Overtown. It is indeed a fitting tribute that not many people ever experience in America. It is indeed a fitting tribute to a man who loved the city of Miami for many years.

"I have had lots of honors and recognitions throughout my career," said Little at the street-naming ceremony. "But this is one of the biggest honors I have ever had. This one ranks among the top."[26]

This story of Larry Little's life is never really over, however. Not by a long shot. Not if the voices of those thousands of youngsters whose lives he touched through his summer camps keep getting heard, and not if the memories of hundreds of players whom he coached keep getting retold. The ripples of his effect on their lives may plant further seeds of inspiration for generations yet unborn. In addition, anyone who visits the Pro Football Hall of Fame in Canton, Ohio, will forever see his bust and learn of his accomplishments as one of the greatest offensive guards in NFL history. That honor will never recede from the public eye.

"I still talk to Coach Little on a month-to-month basis," said Greg Williams Evans. "I wouldn't be the man that I am today without him and his guidance. We were all moved by the man and the leader that he was and that he is. So many of us still stay in contact with him today. He means that much to us. He still does. For a lot of us who didn't have fathers, he was that father figure for us."[27]

A father figure, a mentor, an educator, and one heck of a great football player. Indeed, this story of Larry Little, a humble man who traveled a long distance from an outhouse to a penthouse, serves as an inspiration to us all.

BIBLIOGRAPHY

ARTICLES

Anderson, Dave. "The Dolphins' Irresistible Force & Immovable Object." Sport Magazine, January, 1974.

Associated Press. "Dolphins Triumph 21-0, Share Lead." Naples Daily News, November 11, 1974, 30.

Beneckson, Sam. "A Mountain Named Little." Contact Transracial, September, 1975, 28-30.

Braucher, Bill. "Dolphin Little Impartial About Playoff Opponent." *Miami Herald*, December 17, 1971.

-----. "Little, Buoniconti Sign Lucrative Multi-Year Contracts." *Miami Herald*, July 26, 1972.

-----. "Skins No Worry For Larry Little After Tough Dad." *Miami Herald*, January 11, 1973.

-----. "Little Signs Four-Year Contract." *Miami Herald*, May 1, 1974.

Brubaker, Bill. "Little Angered by Broadcaster." *Cox* Newspapers, November 10, 1976.

Davis, Craig. "Hole for Little to enter Hall of Fame plugged." Miami *Sun Sentinel*, July 29, 1988, 1C.

DiCola, Ben. "Larry Little ready for big HOF honor." *Massillon* (OH) *Independent*, July 31, 1993.

Dolphins Profile. "Larry Little." *Pro! Magazine*, August 8, 1976.

Finney, Peter. "Miami's Real No-Names." *The New Orleans States-Item*, January 9, 1974.

Fitzgerald, Ray. "Little pulls, Mercury rises." *The Boston Globe*, December 29,

1973.

Fowler, Scott. "No doubt: Little a Hall of Famer." *Miami Herald*, August 1, 1993, 11C.

Hines, Bea, L. "Larry Little Street Naming." Online Post, March 27, 2023.

Horning, H.R. "Chicken Little is a Wonderful Marshmallow." *Pro! Magazine*, August 23, 1980, 181, 183-184.

Levine, Al. "Big Little isn't a fullback." *The Miami News*, November 19, 1970.

-----. "Anonymous Larry now the new King of Miami." *The Miami News*, May 24, 1972.

-----. "Little's ultimate ambition is to reach Hall of Fame." *The Miami News*, May 31, 1973, Section B.

Little, Larry, as told to Payne, Dave. "The Game I'll Never Forget." *Football Digest*, March, 1979, 80-83.

Long, Gary. "Little Has Big Impact on Community." *Miami Herald*, September 21, 1973.

Markus, Robert. "Dolphins' Little nurses big dream." *The Chicago Tribune*, July 19, 1973.

Mickelson, Arthur. "Intimidation, Dedication, Determination." *Pro! Magazine*, December 23, 1973, 125-126, 137-138.

Mizell, Hubert. "Larry Little: Chicken-Fast on the Sweeps." Pro Quarterback, May, 1972, 58.

Nobles, Charles. "Little's camp is for enjoyment." *The Miami News*, July 21, 1973.

-----. "Critics make sure Little earns pay." *The Miami News*, November 1, 1974.

-----. "The Little Anthology." *The Miami News*, 1981.

Pope, Edwin. "Long Way for Larry Little From That Bed of Sweat." *Miami Herald*, June 1, 1972.

Poupart, Alain. "No letdown this time for Little." *Dolphin Digest*, February, 1993.

Pro! Talk. "A Conversation with Larry Little." *Pro! Magazine*, November 14, 1976, 35.

Ribowsky, Mark. "Larry Little's Lament: Greed Killed The Dolphins." *Black Sports*, November 1977, 42-45.

Ross, Frank. "Joe Greene, Larry Little: A Classic Match-Up." *Football Digest*, October, 1973, 48-54.

Shapiro, Leonard. "Little, Greene Bash." *The Washington Post*, December 27, 1972.

Smith, Don. Pro Football Hall of Fame press release, March 15, 1993.

Strine, Gerald. "Little vs. Greene." *WPSW*, December 28, 1972.

United Press International. "Miami Produces Clutch Victory." *Port Arthur News*, December 3, 1974, 72.

Weskel, Clarice. "Kuechenberg and Little: Keeping the Dolphins on the Run." *Pro! Magazine*, October 1, 1978, 77.

Wieczurek, Dave. "Teammates pause to praise Little." *Miami News*, August 1, 1993.

Willis, George. "Larry Waits For Chance." New York *Newsday*, February 23, 1993.

Zagorski, Joe. "Pushing the Pigskin Envelope." The Coffin Corner, Volume 44, Number 5, 2022.

BOOKS

Clary, Jack. *The Game Makers*. Chicago, Illinois: Follett Publishing Company, 1976.

McLemore, Morris T. *The Miami Dolphins: The Story of Pro Football's Most Exciting Team*.

New York: Doubleday & Company, Inc., 1972.

Shula, Don with Sahadi, Lou. *The Winning Edge*. New York: E.P. Dutton & Company, Inc., 1973.

Zagorski, Joe. *The NFL in the 1970s: Pro Football's Most Important Decade*. McFarland & Company, Inc., Jefferson, North Carolina, 2016.

PUBLIC DOCUMENTS

Jefferson, Thomas. "The Declaration of Independence." July 4, 1776.

Larry Little Pro Football Hall of Fame Induction Speech, July 31, 1993, courtesy of the Pro Football Hall of Fame.

Videos

A Year of Frustration. AFL Films. Written and Directed by Phillip E. Tuckett, 1969. Ed Sabol, Executive Producer.

Author-Conducted Interviews

With Larry Csonka on April 11, 2022.

With Norm Evans on March 13, 2022.

With Michael Floyd on January 14, 2023.

With Joe Greene on August 24, 2022.

With Bob Griese on May 7, 2022.

With Mark Irvin on January 12, 2023.

With Larry Little on January 21, 2022; February 23, 2022; March 30, 2022; May 24, 2022; August 10, 2022; September 21, 2022; October 27, 2022; December 15, 2022; February 22, 2023; February 23, 2023; April 20, 2023; June 15, 2023; September 29, 2023; October 19, 2023.

With Rosie Little on October 27, 2022.

With Mercury Morris on April 10, 2022.

With Herb Sears on February 27, 2023.

With Greg Williams-Evans on January 16, 2023.

NOTES

PREFACE

1   Interview with Larry Little on January 21, 2022

CHAPTER 1

1   Interview with Larry Little on February 23, 2022

2   Mizell, Robert. "Larry Little: Chicken-Fast on the Sweeps." Pro Quarterback, May, 1972, 58.

3   Braucher, Bill. "Skins No Worry For Larry Little After Tough Dad." The Miami Herald, January 11, 1973.

4   Interview with Larry Little on May 24, 2022.

5   Interview with Larry Little on February 23, 2022.

6   Interview with Larry Little on March 30, 2022.

7   Interview with Larry Little on February 23, 2022.

8   Interview with Larry Little on February 23, 2022.

9   Interview with Larry Little on February 23, 2022.

10   Interview with Larry Little on February 23, 2022.

11   Finney, Peter. "Miami's Real No-Names." New Orleans States-Item, January 9, 1974.

12   Beneckson, Sam. "A Mountain Named Little." Contact Transracial, September 1975, 29.

13   Interview with Larry Little on February 23, 2022.

14   Interview with Larry Little on February 23, 2022.

15   Ribowsky, Mark. "Larry Little's Lament: Greed Killed The Dolphins." Black Sports, November 1977, 45.

16   Interview with Larry Little on January 21, 2022.

17   Interview with Larry Little on February 23, 2022.

18   Dolphins Profile, Larry Little. Pro! Magazine, August 8, 1976.

19   Interview with Larry Little on January 21, 2022.

20   Interview with Larry Little on January 21, 2022.

21   Pro! Talk: A Conversation with Larry Little. Pro! Magazine, November 14, 1976, 35.

22   Interview with Larry Little on February 23, 2022.

23   Interview with Larry Little on January 21, 2022.

24   Interview with Larry Little on January 21, 2022.

25   Interview with Larry Little on February 23, 2022.

26   Interview with Larry Little on February 23, 2022.

27   Interview with Larry Little on February 23, 2022.

28   Interview with Larry Little on January 21, 2022.

29   Interview with Larry Little on January 21, 2022.

CHAPTER 2

1   Interview with Larry Little on January 21, 2022.

2   Interview with Larry Little on January 21, 2022.

3   Interview with Larry Little on January 21, 2022.

4   Interview with Larry Little on March 30, 2022.

5   Interview with Larry Little on January 21, 2022.

6   Interview with Larry Little on January 21, 2022.

7   Interview with Larry Little on January 21, 2022.

8   Interview with Larry Little on September 21, 2022.

9   Interview with Larry Little on May 24, 2022.

10   Interview with Larry Little on August 10, 2022.

11   Interview with Larry Little on May 24, 2022.

12   Interview with Larry Little on May 24, 2022.

13   Interview with Larry Little on May 24, 2022.

14   Interview with Larry Little on May 24, 2022.

15   Interview with Larry Little on August 10, 2022.

16   Interview with Larry Little on March 30, 2022.

17   Interview with Larry Little on August 10, 2022.

18   Interview with Larry Little on August 10, 2022.

19   Mizell, Robert. "Larry Little: Chicken-Fast On The Sweeps." Pro Quarterback, May 1972, 63.

20   Interview with Larry Little on August 10, 2022.

21   Interview with Larry Little on September 21, 2022.

22   Interview with Larry Little on January 21, 2022.

23   Interview with Larry Little on March 30, 2022.

24   Interview with Larry Little on October 19, 2023.

25   Interview with Larry Little on May 24, 2022.

26   Interview with Larry Little on August 10, 2022.

27   Interview with Larry Little on September 29, 2023.

28   Interview with Larry Little on September 29, 2023.

29   Mizell, Robert. "Larry Little: Chicken-Fast On The Sweeps." Pro Quarterback, May 1972, 58.

30   Interview with Larry Little on August 10, 2022.

31   Interview with Larry Little on March 30, 2022.

32   Interview with Larry Little on May 24, 2022.

33   Interview with Larry Little on May 24, 2022.

34   Interview with Larry Little on February 23, 2022.

CHAPTER 3

1   Interview with Larry Little on January 21, 2022.

2   Interview with Larry Little on January 21, 2022.

3   Interview with Larry Little on January 21, 2022.

4   Interview with Larry Little on January 21, 2022.

5   Interview with Larry Little on January 21, 2022.

6 Anderson, Dave. "The Dolphins' Irresistible Force & Immovable Object." Sport Magazine, January 1974.

7 Pro! Talk. Pro! Magazine. November 14, 1976, 33.

8 Interview with Larry Little on March 30, 2022.

9 Pro! Talk. Pro! Magazine. November 14, 1976, 33.

10 Pro! Talk. Pro! Magazine. November 14, 1976, 33.

11 Interview with Larry Little on March 30, 2022.

12 Interview with Larry Little on March 30, 2022.

13 Pro! Talk. Pro! Magazine. November 14, 1976, 33.

14 Interview with Larry Little on February 23, 2022.

15 Interview with Larry Little on March 30, 2022.

16 Interview with Larry Little on January 21, 2022.

17 Interview with Larry Little on January 21, 2022.

18 Interview with Larry Little on January 21, 2022.

19 Interview with Larry Little on September 21, 2022.

20 Interview with Larry Little on January 21, 2022.

21 Pro! Talk. Pro! Magazine. November 14, 1976, 35.

22 Braucher, Bill. "A Little Learning Proves A Very Dangerous Thing." The Miami Herald, June 30, 1971.

23 Interview with Larry Little on September 21, 2022.

24 Interview with Larry Little on February 23, 2022.

25 Interview with Larry Little on February 23, 2022.

26 Interview with Larry Little on January 21, 2022.

27 Interview with Larry Little on February 23, 2022.

28 Interview with Larry Little on March 30, 2022.

29 Interview with Larry Little on August 10, 2022.

30 Interview with Larry Little on March 30, 2022.

CHAPTER 4

1 Interview with Larry Little on September 21, 2022.

2 Interview with Larry Csonka on April 11, 2022.

3   Interview with Larry Csonka on April 11, 2022.

4   Interview with Larry Csonka on April 11, 2022.

5   Interview with Larry Csonka on April 11, 2022.

6   Interview with Larry Csonka on April 11, 2022.

7   Interview with Larry Csonka on April 11, 2022.

8   Interview with Larry Csonka on April 11, 2022.

9   Mizell, Robert. "Larry Little: Chicken-Fast on the Sweeps." Pro Quarterback Magazine, May, 1972, 58.

10   Interview with Larry Little on September 21, 2022.

11   Interview with Larry Little on August 10, 2022.

12   Interview with Larry Little on February 23, 2022.

13   Interview with Larry Little on August 10, 2022.

14   Interview with Larry Little on March 30, 2022.

15   Interview with Larry Little on January 21, 2022.

16   Interview with Larry Little on August 10, 2022.

17   Anderson, Dave. "The Dolphins' Irresistible Force & Immovable Object," Sport Magazine, January, 1974.

18   Interview with Larry Little on September 21, 2022.

19   Interview with Larry Little on September 21, 2022.

20   Interview with Larry Little on August 10, 2022.

21   Interview with Larry Little on August 10, 2022.

22   Horning, H.R. "Chicken Little is a Wonderful Marshmallow." Pro! Magazine, August 23, 1980.

23   Horning, H.R. "Chicken Little is a Wonderful Marshmallow." Pro! Magazine, August 23, 1980.

24   Horning, H.R. "Chicken Little is a Wonderful Marshmallow." Pro! Magazine, August 23, 1980.

25   Horning, H.R. "Chicken Little is a Wonderful Marshmallow." Pro! Magazine, August 23, 1980.

CHAPTER 5

1   Interview with Larry Little on January 21, 2022.

2   Interview with Larry Little on January 21, 2022.

3   Interview with Larry Little on January 21, 2022.

4   Interview with Larry Little on January 21, 2022.

5   Interview with Larry Csonka on April 11, 2022.

6   Interview with Larry Little on January 21, 2022.

7   Interview with Larry Little on January 21, 2022.

8   Interview with Larry Little on January 21, 2022.

9   Interview with Larry Little on January 21, 2022.

10   Interview with Larry Little on January 21, 2022.

11   Interview with Larry Little on February 23, 2022.

12   Interview with Larry Little on February 23, 2022.

13   Interview with Larry Little on March 30, 2022.

14   Interview with Larry Little on February 23, 2022.

15   Interview with Larry Little on May 24, 2022.

16   Interview with Larry Little on March 30, 2022.

17   Interview with Larry Little on February 23, 2022.

18   Interview with Larry Little on January 21, 2022.

19   Interview with Larry Little on February 23, 2022.

20   Interview with Larry Little on March 30, 2022.

21   Interview with Larry Little on February 23, 2022.

22   Interview with Larry Little on February 23, 2022.

23   Interview with Larry Little on February 23, 2022.

24   Interview with Larry Little on January 21, 2022.

25   Interview with Larry Little on February 23, 2022.

26   Interview with Larry Little on January 21, 2022.

27   Interview with Larry Little on February 23, 2022.

28   Interview with Larry Little on February 23, 2022.

29   Interview with Larry Little on October 27, 2022.

30 Braucher, Bill. "Dolphin Little Impartial About Playoff Opponent." The Miami Herald, December 17, 1971.

31 Interview with Larry Little on January 21, 2022.

CHAPTER 6

1 Interview with Larry Little on February 23, 2022.

2 Interview with Larry Little on February 23, 2022.

3 Interview with Larry Little on June 15, 2023.

4 Braucher, Bill. "Dolphin Little Impartial About Playoff Opponent." The Miami Herald, December 17, 1971.

5 Interview with Larry Little on August 10, 2022.

6 Levine, Al. "Anonymous Larry now the new King of Miami." The Miami News, May 24, 1972.

7 Levine, Al. "Anonymous Larry now the new King of Miami." The Miami News, May 24, 1972.

8 Interview with Larry Little on February 23, 2022.

9 Interview with Larry Little on February 23, 2022.

10 Interview with Larry Little on February 23, 2022.

11 Interview with Larry Little on February 23, 2022.

12 Interview with Larry Little on February 23, 2022.

13 Interview with Larry Little on March 30, 2022.

14 Interview with Larry Little on October 27, 2022.

15 Mizell, Hubert. "Larry Little: Chicken-Fast On The Sweeps." Pro Quarterback Magazine, May 1972.

16 Mizell, Hubert. "Larry Little: Chicken-Fast On The Sweeps." Pro Quarterback Magazine, May 1972.

17 Interview with Mercury Morris on April 10, 2022.

18 Interview with Larry Csonka on April 11, 2022.

19 Interview with Larry Csonka on April 11, 2022.

20 Interview with Larry Little on March 30, 2022.

21 Interview with Larry Little on October 27, 2022.

22 Interview with Larry Little on February 23, 2022.

23   Interview with Larry Little on March 30, 2022.

24   Interview with Larry Little on October 27, 2022.

25   Interview with Larry Little on February 23, 2022.

26   Interview with Larry Little on October 27, 2022.

27   Interview with Larry Little on October 27, 2022.

28   Interview with Larry Little on February 23, 2022.

29   Interview with Larry Csonka on April 11, 2022.

30   Little, Larry, as told to Payne, Dave. "The Game I'll Never Forget." Football Digest, March 1979, 81.

31   Pope, Edwin. "Long Way for Larry Little From That Bed of Sweat." The Miami Herald, June 1, 1972.

CHAPTER 7

1   Braucher, Bill. "Little, Buoniconti Sign Lucrative Multi-Year Contracts." The Miami Herald, July 26, 1972.

2   Braucher, Bill. "Little, Buoniconti Sign Lucrative Multi-Year Contracts." The Miami Herald, July 26, 1972.

3   Interview with Mercury Morris on April 10, 2022.

4   Interview with Larry Little on March 30, 2022.

5   Interview with Larry Little on March 30, 2022.

6   Interview with Larry Little on December 15, 2022.

7   Don Shula with Lou Sahadi, The Winning Edge. New York: E.P. Dutton & Co., Inc., 1973, 224.

8   Interview with Bob Griese on May 7, 2022.

9   Interview with Larry Little on March 30, 2022.

10   Interview with Larry Csonka on April 11, 2022.

11   Interview with Larry Little on March 30, 2022.

12   Interview with Larry Little on March 30, 2022.

13   Interview with Larry Little on December 15, 2022.

14   Interview with Norm Evans on March 13, 2022.

15   Interview with Larry Little on December 15, 2022.

16   Interview with Norm Evans on March 13, 2022.

17   Interview with Larry Little on December 15, 2022.

18   Interview with Norm Evans on March 13, 2022.

19   Interview with Larry Little on March 30, 2022.

20   Don Shula with Lou Sahadi, The Winning Edge. New York: E.P. Dutton & Co., Inc., 1973, 233.

21   nterview with Larry Little on March 30, 2022.

22   Interview with Larry Little on February 23, 2022.

23   Interview with Joe Greene on August 24, 2022.

24   Ross, Frank. "Joe Greene, Larry Little: A Classic Match-Up." Football Digest, October, 1973, 48-54.

25   Strine, Gerald. "Little vs. Greene." WPSW Interview, December 28, 1972.

26   Ross, Frank. "Joe Greene, Larry Little: A Classic Match-Up." Football Digest, October, 1973, 48-54.

27   Interview with Larry Little on March 30, 2022.

28   Ross, Frank. "Joe Greene, Larry Little: A Classic Match-Up." Football Digest, October, 1973, 48-54.

29   Interview with Joe Greene on August 24, 2022.

30   Interview with Larry Little on May 24, 2022.

31   Interview with Bob Griese on May 7, 2022.

32   Interview with Joe Greene on August 24, 2022.

33   Ross, Frank. "Joe Greene, Larry Little: A Classic Match-Up." Football Digest, October, 1973, 48-54.

34   Interview with Larry Little on February 23, 2022.

35   Interview with Larry Csonka on April 11, 2022.

36   Interview with Larry Csonka on April 11, 2022.

37   Interview with Larry Little on May 24, 2022.

38   Interview with Larry Little on December 15, 2022.

39   Interview with Mercury Morris on April 10, 2022.

40   Interview with Larry Little on December 15, 2022.

41   Interview with Larry Little on October 27, 2022.

42   Interview with Larry Little on December 15, 2022.

43   Interview with Larry Little on May 24, 2022.

44   Interview with Larry Little on May 24, 2022.

45   Don Shula with Lou Sahadi, The Winning Edge. New York: E.P. Dutton & Co., Inc., 1973, 244-245.

46   Interview with Larry Little on December 15, 2022.

CHAPTER 8

1   Interview with Larry Little on February 23, 2023.

2   Interview with Larry Csonka on April 11, 2022.

3   Interview with Larry Little on December 15, 2022.

4   Interview with Larry Little on December 15, 2022.

5   Interview with Larry Little on December 15, 2022.

6   Interview with Mercury Morris on April 10, 2022.

7   Fitzgerald, Ray. "Little pulls, Mercury rises." The Boston Globe, December 29, 1973.

8   Interview with Larry Csonka on April 11, 2022.

9   Interview with Larry Little on December 15, 2022.

10   Shapiro, Leonard. "Little, Greene Bash." The Washington Post, December 27, 1972.

11   Interview with Larry Little on February 23, 2023.

12   Interview with Bob Griese on May 7, 2022.

13   Interview with Larry Little on February 23, 2023.

14   Interview with Larry Little on February 23, 2023.

15   Interview with Larry Little on February 23, 2023.

16   Interview with Larry Little on December 15, 2022.

17   Interview with Larry Little on December 15, 2022.

18   Interview with Larry Little on December 15, 2022.

19   Interview with Larry Csonka on April 11, 2022.

20   Interview with Larry Little on March 30, 2022.

21   Interview with Larry Little on April 20, 2023.

22   Fitzgerald, Ray. "Little pulls, Mercury rises." The Boston Globe, December 29, 1973.

23   Interview with Larry Little on February 23, 2023.

24 Interview with Larry Little on February 23, 2023.

25 Interview with Larry Little on December 15, 2022.

26 Interview with Larry Little on December 15, 2022.

27 Interview with Mercury Morris on April 10, 2022.

28 Interview with Larry Little on December 15, 2022.

29 Interview with Larry Little on February 23, 2023.

CHAPTER 9

1   Interview with Larry Little on February 23, 2023.

2   Long, Gary. "Little Has Big Impact on Community." The Miami Herald, September 21, 1973.

3   Long, Gary. "Little Has Big Impact on Community." The Miami Herald, September 21, 1973.

4   Beneckson, Sam. "A Mountain Named Little." Contact Transracial Magazine, September 1975, 30.

5   Mickelson, Arthur. "Intimidation, Dedication, Determination." Pro! Magazine, December 23, 1973, 126.

6   Interview with Larry Little on December 15, 2022.

7   Zagorski, Joe. "Pushing the Pigskin Envelope." The Coffin Corner, Volume 44, Number 5, 2022, 10.

8   Ribowsky, Mark. "Larry Little's Lament: Greed Killed the Dolphins." Black Sports, November 1977, 43.

9   Interview with Larry Little on February 23, 2023.

10 Interview with Larry Little on February 23, 2023.

11 Shapiro, Leonard. "Little, Greene Bash." The Washington Post, December 27, 1972.

12 Interview with Larry Little on February 23, 2023.

13 Interview with Larry Little on February 23, 2023.

14 Interview with Larry Little on February 23, 2023.

15 Interview with Larry Little on February 23, 2023.

16 Interview with Larry Little on February 23, 2023.

17 Interview with Larry Csonka on April 11, 2022.

18   Associated Press. "Dolphins Triumph 21-0, Share Lead." Naples (FL) Daily News, November 11, 1974, 30.

19   Interview with Larry Little on February 23, 2023.

20   Interview with Larry Little on February 23, 2023.

21   Interview with Larry Little on April 20, 2023.

22   Interview with Larry Little on February 23, 2023.

23   Interview with Larry Little on April 20, 2023.

24   Interview with Larry Little on April 20, 2023.

25   Interview with Larry Little on April 20, 2023.

26   Interview with Larry Little on April 20, 2023.

27   Interview with Larry Little on February 23, 2023.

28   Interview with Larry Little on April 20, 2023.

29   Interview with Larry Little on April 20, 2023.

CHAPTER 10

1   Interview with Larry Little on September 21, 2022.

2   Interview with Larry Little on April 20, 2023.

3   Interview with Larry Little on February 23, 2023.

4   Interview with Mercury Morris on April 10, 2022.

5   Interview with Larry Little on February 23, 2023.

6   Interview with Larry Little on February 23, 2023.

7   Interview with Larry Little on February 23, 2023.

8   Dolphins Profile, Larry Little. Pro! Magazine, August 8, 1976, 92.

9   Interview with Larry Little on October 27, 2022.

10   Interview with Larry Little on April 20, 2023.

11   Interview with Larry Little on April 20, 2023.

12   Interview with Larry Little on April 20, 2023.

13   Interview with Larry Little on April 20, 2023.

14   Interview with Larry Little on February 23, 2022.

15   Interview with Rosie Little on October 27, 2022.

16   Brubaker, Bill. "Little Angered by Broadcaster." Cox Newspapers, November 10, 1976.

17   Ribowsky, Mark. "Larry Little's Lament: Greed Killed the Dolphins." Black Sports, November 1977, 43.

18   Davis, Craig. "Hole for Little to enter Hall of Fame plugged." Miami Sun Sentinel, July 29, 1988, 1C.

19   Interview with Larry Little on April 20, 2023.

20   Interview with Larry Little on February 23, 2023.

21   Interview with Larry Csonka on April 11, 2022.

22   Interview with Larry Little on April 20, 2023.

23   Interview with Larry Little on April 20, 2023.

24   Interview with Larry Little on April 20, 2023.

25   Interview with Larry Little on April 20, 2023.

26   Joe Zagorski, The NFL in the 1970s: Pro Football's Most Important Decade, Jefferson, North Carolina: McFarland and Company, Inc., 2016, 296.

27   Ribowsky, Mark. "Larry Little's Lament: Greed Killed the Dolphins." Black Sports, November 1977, 45.

28   Interview with Larry Little on September 21, 2022.

29   Interview with Larry Little on April 20, 2023.

30   Weskel, Clarice. "Kuechenberg and Little: Keeping the Dolphins on the Run." Pro! Magazine, October 1, 1978, 77.

31   Interview with Larry Little on April 20, 2023.

32   Interview with Larry Little on April 20, 2023.

33   Interview with Larry Csonka on April 11, 2022.

34   Interview with Larry Little on April 20, 2023.

35   Interview with Joe Greene on August 25, 2022.

36   Interview with Larry Little on April 20, 2023.

37   Interview with Larry Little on April 20, 2023.

CHAPTER 11

1   Levine, Al. "Little's ultimate ambition is to reach Hall of Fame." The Miami News, May 31, 1973, Section B.

2   Braucher, Bill. "Little Signs Four-Year Contract." The Miami Herald, May 1, 1974.

3   Ribowsky, Mark. "Larry Little's Lament: Greed Killed The Dolphins." Black Sports, November 1977, 45.

4   Nobles, Charlie. "Critics make sure Little earns pay." The Miami News, November 1, 1974.

5   Interview with Larry Little on June 15, 2023.

6   Ribowsky, Mark. "Larry Little's Lament: Greed Killed The Dolphins." Black Sports, November 1977, 45.

7   Interview with Larry Little on June 15, 2023.

8   Interview with Larry Little on June 15, 2023.

9   Interview with Larry Little on April 20, 2023.

10   Ribowsky, Mark. "Larry Little's Lament: Greed Killed The Dolphins." Black Sports, November 1977, 45.

11   Interview with Larry Little on April 20, 2023.

12   Interview with Larry Little on April 20, 2023.

13   Interview with Larry Little on June 15, 2023.

14   Interview with Larry Little on June 15, 2023.

15   Interview with Larry Little on June 15, 2023.

16   Interview with Larry Little on April 20, 2023.

17   Nobles, Charlie. "The Little Anthology." The Miami News, 1981.

18   Interview with Larry Little on June 15, 2023.

19   Nobles, Charlie. "The Little Anthology." The Miami News, 1981.

20   Interview with Larry Little on June 15, 2023.

CHAPTER 12

1   Interview with Larry Little on April 20, 2023.

2   Interview with Larry Little on April 20, 2023.

3   Interview with Larry Little on April 20, 2023.

4   Interview with Larry Little on April 20, 2023.

5   Interview with Larry Little on June 15, 2023.

6   Interview with Larry Little on April 20, 2023.

7   Interview with Larry Little on April 20, 2023.

8   Interview with Larry Little on April 20, 2023.

9   Interview with Larry Little on June 15, 2023.

10   Interview with Larry Little on May 24, 2022.

11   Interview with Larry Little on April 20, 2023.

12   Interview with Larry Little on April 20, 2023.

13   Interview with Larry Little on June 15, 2023.

14   Interview with Larry Little on May 24, 2022.

15   Interview with Larry Little on June 15, 2023.

16   Interview with Larry Little on April 20, 2023.

17   Interview with Larry Little on April 20, 2023.

18   Interview with Larry Little on April 20, 2023.

19   Interview with Larry Little on April 20, 2023.

20   Interview with Larry Little on June 15, 2023.

21   Interview with Larry Little on April 20, 2023.

22   Interview with Larry Little on April 20, 2023.

23   Willis, George. "Larry Waits For Chance." New York Newsday, February 23, 1993.

24   Interview with Larry Little on August 10, 2022.

25   Interview with Larry Little on April 20, 2023.

26   Interview with Larry Little on June 15, 2023.

27   Interview with Larry Little on April 20, 2023.

28   Interview with Larry Little on April 20, 2023.

29   Interview with Larry Little on June 15, 2023.

CHAPTER 13

1   Levine, Al. "Little's ultimate ambition is to reach Hall of Fame." The Miami News, May 31, 1973, Section B.

2   Davis, Craig. "Hole for Little to enter Hall of Fame plugged." Miami Sun Sentinel, July 29, 1988.

3   Wieczurek, Dave. "Teammates pause to praise Little." Miami News, August 1, 1993.

4   Interview with Larry Little on August 10, 2022.

5   Interview with Larry Little on August 10, 2022.

6   Interview with Larry Little on August 10, 2022.

7   Poupart, Alain. "No letdown this time for Little." Dolphin Digest, February 1993.

8   Smith, Don. "Pro Football Hall of Fame News Release." March 15, 1993.

9   Interview with Bob Griese on May 7, 2022.

10   Interview with Larry Csonka on April 11, 2022.

11   Smith, Don. "Pro Football Hall of Fame News Release." March 15, 1993.

12   Smith, Don. "Pro Football Hall of Fame News Release." March 15, 1993.

13   Smith, Don. "Pro Football Hall of Fame News Release." March 15, 1993.

14   Smith, Don. "Pro Football Hall of Fame News Release." March 15, 1993.

15   Wieczurek, Dave. "Teammates pause to praise Little." Miami News, August 1, 1993.

16   Wieczurek, Dave. "Teammates pause to praise Little." Miami News, August 1, 1993.

17   Wieczurek, Dave. "Teammates pause to praise Little." Miami News, August 1, 1993.

18   Wieczurek, Dave. "Teammates pause to praise Little." Miami News, August 1, 1993.

19   Interview with Larry Little on December 15, 2022.

20   Interview with Larry Little on September 21, 2022.

21   Interview with Larry Little on August 10, 2022.

22   Wieczurek, Dave. "Teammates pause to praise Little." Miami News, August 1, 1993.

23   Interview with Larry Little on August 10, 2022.

24   Fowler, Scott. "No doubt: Little a Hall of Famer." The Miami Herald, August 1, 1993, 11C.

25 DiCola, Ben. "Larry Little ready for big HOF honor." Massillon (OH) Independent, September 31, 1993.

26 Larry Little's Hall of Fame speech, July 31, 1993, courtesy of the Pro Football Hall of Fame.

27 Larry Little's Hall of Fame speech, July 31, 1993, courtesy of the Pro Football Hall of Fame.

28 Larry Little's Hall of Fame speech, July 31, 1993, courtesy of the Pro Football Hall of Fame.

CHAPTER 14

1 Interview with Herb Sears on February 27, 2023.

2 Interview with Willie Carpenter on February 27, 2023.

3 Interview with Willie Carpenter on February 27, 2023.

4 Interview with Herb Sears on February 27, 2023.

5 Interview with Michael Floyd on January 14, 2023.

6 Interview with Mark Irvin on January 12, 2023.

7 Interview with Mark Irvin on January 12, 2023.

8 Interview with Mark Irvin on January 12, 2023.

9 Interview with Mark Irvin on January 12, 2023.

10 Interview with Mark Irvin on January 12, 2023.

11 Interview with Greg Williams Evans on January 16, 2023.

12 Interview with Greg Williams Evans on January 16, 2023.

13 Interview with Greg Williams Evans on January 16, 2023.

14 Interview with Greg Williams Evans on January 16, 2023.

15 Interview with Larry Little on February 23, 2022.

16 Interview with Larry Little on June 15, 2023.

17 Interview with Larry Little on April 20, 2023.

18 Interview with Larry Little on March 30, 2022.

19 Interview with Larry Little on March 30, 2022.

20 Interview with Larry Little on June 15, 2023.

21 Interview with Larry Little on August 10, 2022.

Interview with Larry Little on March 30, 2022.

Interview with Larry Little on June 15, 2023.

Beneckson, Sam. "A Mountain Named Little." Contact Transracial Magazine, September 1975, 30.

Interview with Larry Little on June 15, 2023.

Hines, Bea L. Online Opinion on March 27, 2023.

Interview with Greg Williams-Evans on January 16, 2023.

www.ingramcontent.com/pod-product-compliance
Lightning Source LLC
Chambersburg PA
CBHW070339090426
42733CB00009B/1234